PAPER ROUTE

Also by Philip Meyer

Precision Journalism
Governing the United States (with David Olson)
The Newspaper Survival Book
Ethical Journalism
The Vanishing Newspaper

Paper Route

Finding My Way to Precision Journalism

Philip Meyer

iUniverse, Inc.
Bloomington

Paper Route
Finding My Way to Precision Journalism

iUniverse books may be ordered through booksellers or by contacting:

iUniverse
1663 Liberty Drive
Bloomington, IN 47403
www.iuniverse.com
1-800-Authors (1-800-288-4677)

Because of the dynamic nature of the Internet, any web addresses or links contained in this book may have changed since publication and may no longer be valid. The views expressed in this work are solely those of the author and do not necessarily reflect the views of the publisher, and the publisher hereby disclaims any responsibility for them.

Any people depicted in stock imagery provided by Thinkstock are models, and such images are being used for illustrative purposes only.

Certain stock imagery © Thinkstock.

ISBN: 978-1-4620-8312-1 (sc)
ISBN: 978-1-4620-8310-7 (e)
ISBN: 978-1-4620-8311-4 (dj)

Library of Congress Control Number: 2011962925

Printed in the United States of America

iUniverse rev. date: 2/27/2012

Contents

Illustrations

Introduction

A t interdisciplinary faculty gatherings, the conversation often led to comparisons of research interests. When I mentioned mine, which was also the title of my first book, there was, more than once, a witty response.

"*Precision Journalism*? That's an oxymoron!"

Once, to break the tension, someone asked what else I had written, and I had to purse my lips and say:

"*Ethical Journalism.*"

My last academic book was about fixing the broken business model of daily newspapers, and I was tempted to call it "Profitable Journalism," thus establishing an oxymoron trilogy. But someone wisely talked me out of it.

Such are the risks one takes when trying to be an innovator. I was an early adopter of scientific method applied to reporting the news. Bad idea, I was told at the time. A reporter should ask scientists about their results, not try to use their methods to make conclusions on his or her own. But computers and statistical software were making it easier, and I did not have to step too far outside the box to see the possibilities for journalism.

Thinking outside the box is easier when you have lived there. Digging into family history late in life, I discovered that I come from a long line of outsiders. My Swiss ancestors were members of a tiny and unpopular religious sect called the Antonianers, after their leader Anton Unternaehrer, who died in a Lucerne prison in 1823. They were antinomians, a peculiar subset of Protestants who believed that accepting Christ as one's savior took all the pressure away from any need to follow rules, either God's or man's. In their view, Jesus was a fixer, and they could do whatever they wanted. They liked to cite Saint Paul, who said in his first letter to the Corinthians, "The spiritual man judges all things, but is himself to be judged by no one."

Antinomianism appeared around the time of the Reformation, encouraged by some of Martin Luther's unguarded reflections, and it surfaced in America in the Massachusetts Bay Colony. Anne Hutchinson led a rising merchant class that wanted freedom to pursue its economic interests, unfettered by civil and religious authority. I'm not sure why it gained traction in Switzerland in the early 19th century, but the disruption of the Industrial Revolution surely had something do with it. My people were farmers, and they prized their independence. The industrial system demanded coordination and regimentation to enable production on a large scale.

There is little evidence that observing Unternaehrer's creed led to a great deal of risqué behavior by my Meyer ancestors, although the meticulous records kept by the Swiss show that my great-grandparents, Heinrich and Regula Meyer, were first cousins and that their firstborn arrived two months after their 1843 marriage in Zurich. They named the child after his father, and Henry Meyer Jr., as he became known in this country, was the first of his immediate family to abandon Switzerland for America. He reached Kansas in 1863. Heinrich and Regula followed him to Kansas a year later with their remaining children, including seven-year-old Jacob, who became my grandfather.

In the USA, the Meyers left no sign of their antinomianism. They joined congregations of the Evangelical Association of North America, founded to serve German-speaking Protestants, and followed a pietistic path, free of drinking, dancing, swearing, or violations of the Sabbath. My grandfather would risk crop failure rather than harvest on a Sunday, even if a destructive storm was approaching. He figured the Lord would provide.

The outsider role was apparently more situational than genetic, but accidents of time and geography would, at least in my case, reinforce that sense of otherness. For a journalist, it would prove an advantage.

Jacob and Matilda Meyer, ca 1882

1. The land

W̶e moved often in the Depression years, and the two farms were the constant in our lives that kept us emotionally anchored. My parents were born in adjoining townships in Washington County, Kan., and they spent all but a few wartime months of their married life no more than one county away from their original family farms. The siblings on both sides had grown and scattered, but each family left a bachelor brother who kept the original farm operating both for his own support and as a resource and refuge for the extended family.

The Meyer farm, in Strawberry Township, was the more prosperous. My Swiss-born grandfather Jacob Meyer acquired its first 120 acres from the original homesteader, Christian Wherley, in 1880, and expanded it by buying two adjoining farms, each 160 acres, the standard size set by the Homestead Act of 1862. Roads in the prairie states are neatly laid out in square-mile sections clearly visible on cross-country flights. Four 160-acre homesteads fit in a section. Twenty-five years after his original purchase, Jacob made the final payment on the third farm, and he owned, debt-fee, 440 contiguous acres of gently rolling fields and pasture with a creek running through the eastern portion. It was called Pete's Creek, Peats Creek, or Peach Creek, depending on whose map you used. The original Wherley house had just two rooms, a kitchen and a bedroom, but Jacob kept adding to it as his family grew to its full complement of eight children. Frank Meyer, born in 1886, a decade before my father, remembered the house as it was when he was a small child:

———————————

... a two-room homesteader's frame house; that is, two rooms on the ground floor and two above, which are still unfinished and used only for storage. I can still see the long shelves suspended on wires from the rafters, as a protection from mice. Among other things these shelves contained the year's supply of flour, which was milled from wheat grown on the farm and taken to a mill 17 miles away.

The south room on the ground floor is the kitchen, dining, and living room combined. The bedroom faces the north, with one window on the north wall and one on the east. I am sleeping in a crib facing the north window. I awaken sometime in the night and am aware of being very, very cold and that an icy, gusty wind is beating snow against the window panes and am conscious for the first time of a real Kansas blizzard.[1]

My own childhood memory begins nearly five decades later, and it shows a relatively modern seven-room house with electricity and indoor plumbing. The power came from a bank of six-volt batteries stored in the milk house and charged by a one-cylinder gasoline engine. It was enough to light a single weak bulb in each room and power the radio. The bathroom, built by my father in his late bachelor days, contained a flush toilet and a tub whose water source was a well situated in a draw halfway between the house and barn. A windmill pumped the water to a storage tank in the barn loft, which provided enough elevation to create water pressure for the house. This water supplied the bathtub, the toilet and the kitchen sink. Drinking water came from a well next to the house. We used a hand pump to fill an oaken bucket that we kept on the kitchen counter with a dipper for drinking. Today, we call that kind of living "off the grid," but in rural Kansas of the early 20th century, the power grid had not yet been built.

Two stoves lined the north wall of the Meyer kitchen. The larger one burned wood for winter cooking and heating, and the small kerosene stove was used for preparing summer meals. A pail of dried corncobs was kept handy for kindling. There was a pass-through serving bar to the dining room with china cabinets above. A hand-cranked telephone and a foot-powered sewing machine decorated the far wall of the dining room, which opened to a spacious living room containing a pot-bellied wood stove, a piano, a library table stocked with Dr. Elliot's five-foot shelf of *Harvard Classics*, and a Morris chair whose reclining back adjusted with a rod that fit into grooves at the rear of its wooden arms. A hollow footstool contained playing cards and a cribbage board. The ground-floor bedroom had doors to both the living room and a short hallway leading to the, bathroom, kitchen, and the stairs to the second floor. The fourth and last-built bedroom was above the living room and was large enough to sleep four.

Jacob and Matilda Meyer had eight children in the 22 years from 1884 to 1906, and the house comfortably held them all. That was not the case with my mother's family. William and Zelda Mae Morrison had six children in nine years and raised them in a two-bedroom house a few miles to the east, in Linn Township. I'm not sure how they managed it. The two small bedrooms each had a double bed flush against an interior wall. There was a day bed suitable for one person in the living room, and the enclosed back porch contained a manual cream separator and an iron double bed.

The original owner of the land had built dirt-floored living space in below-ground rooms, accessible on the east side, and perhaps those were still habitable, although by the 1930s they were used only to keep food cool in the summer and to frighten small boys with tales of ghosts. A small bathroom with a tub was located off the kitchen, but water had to be carried to it from an indoor pitcher pump that retrieved captured rainwater from a cistern.

At night, the house was lit with a few kerosene lamps carried from room to room, and the toilet was an outhouse in the far backyard, beyond the chicken house. Life was harder there, especially in the winters when keeping warm and putting food on the table were constant concerns. In 1912, Mae's sixth and last child, my aunt Velma, was born, and my grandmother required an extended stay in the Topeka State Hospital, which provided custodial care for the mentally ill. Her sister, Carrie Lobaugh, moved in and took care of the baby in that period. My maternal grandfather, William Morrison, had a short temper and in 1921, when he tried to enforce discipline with a razor strap, his oldest son, 18-year-old Howard, ran down the road and disappeared. Both families had their mysteries to ponder, and for the Morrisons, it was Howard and his fate.

But I was always glad to visit either farm. My grandfather Morrison died in 1933, but my grandmother would flourish and live to see me graduate from college and marry. When I was small, her two bachelor sons Wilmer and Ernie ran the farm with vigor and good humor. Wilmer was primarily in charge of the home place while Ernie had his own farm to look after a few miles away. They both had musical talent and the Scots-Irish wit. Wilmer liked to perform daring physical feats. The family album includes a photo of him doing a handstand on top of the chimney that topped the Morrison farmhouse. Another shows him doing the same thing on a tractor seat. He evidently thought I was a wimpy kid, because he kept talking me into trying daring things such as climbing the silo, walking across Willow Creek while balanced on a bridge rail, riding an untrained horse. I somehow avoided injury.

Ernie was the storyteller, and he invented elaborate ghost stories based on a specific family of monsters that he called "Skagg-ags." A deserted house, of which there were many in Washington County, was "a Skagg-ag house." The fourth brother, Ellis, was a traveling salesman, and would drop by our house for philosophical discussions. One that sticks in my mind was about Lecomte du Nouy's 1947 book *Human Destiny*, which attempted to reconcile science and religion. Ellis's son and granddaughter would earn the first PhDs in the Morrison family.

On the Meyer place, the bachelor farmer who kept things going was Lester, nicknamed "Pappy." His Swiss-German stolidity masked a competent and caring nature. Both Wilmer and Pappy lived their entire lives on the farms where they were born.

The changing economics of farming worked in the bachelor farmers' favor. Mechanization let them scale up their operations, and, when the siblings departed, the land had fewer people to support. After the war, the Rural Electric Administration brought full electrical power to the prairie. But Washington

County fell steadily in population, from nearly 22,000 at the start of the 20th century to 6,483 at its close. I can remember driving through Strawberry Township with my father while he pointed out the places, two or three in nearly every mile, where there had been a farmhouse when he was a boy and now was only field and pasture.

2. World War I and its effects

One source of Jacob Meyer's early affluence was his skill at judging cattle. He made money by buying promising calves, feeding them and selling them after they had grown enough for their worth to become apparent to less skilled eyes. He knew that the economics of farming would change, and his children would need other means of earning a living, and so he invested far more in their education than was common for early 20th century farm families. The entry-level profession for that generation of country people was teaching, and Jacob and Matilda sent their sons and daughters to what was then called the Kansas State Normal College at Emporia. The name came from the French "école normale," a school to set standards or norms for education, and it was changed to Kansas State Teachers' College in 1923. (Today, it is Emporia State University.) Tuition was free to Kansas residents.

In 1913, five Meyer children went off to Emporia, and Jacob rented a house for them. Its youngest resident was my father, Elmer E. "Bige" Meyer. (The nickname came from one of the first words he ever spoke: an abbreviation of the Old Testament name belonging to a Strawberry Township neighbor, "Abijah.") Bige and his sister Mamie attended the Kansas State Normal High School. Their older siblings Fred, Walt and Ollie attended the college. The 1914 yearbook *Sunflower* lists Bige as high school junior and class treasurer. He was 17, and, with all that family support, his future was promising, but it would not turn out as planned. In Europe, the guns of August were about to speak.

Elmer "Bige" Meyer, Emporia, 1915

Bige played football at Normal High, was graduated in the spring of 1915 and entered the college the following fall. He joined a local fraternity, Kappa Sigma Epsilon. For unknown reasons, he dropped out the second semester, perhaps to help with spring planting, but came back for the fall of 1916 while President Woodrow Wilson was running for re-election on the campaign slogan, "He kept us out of war." The spring of 1917 found Bige enrolled in business law, advanced stenography, penmanship methods, composition and rhetoric, and physical training practice.

The United States had only a small standing army on April 6, the day that Congress finally declared war on Germany, and mobilization in Kansas was primarily through the National Guard. Every one of the Kappa Sigma Epsilon brothers walked down to the Emporia guard headquarters to volunteer, and my father was inducted on April 10. His transcript shows that he received credit for that spring's courses except for physical training and composition and rhetoric. His other education was about to begin.

The Kansas and Missouri National Guard units were reorganized as their own Army division, the 35th, and went to Camp Doniphan, adjacent to Fort Sill near Lawton, Oklahoma, to be trained in artillery and trench warfare. There were 24,068 soldiers, more than 14,000 from Missouri and nearly 10,000 from Kansas. They were good men, but, when they got overseas, their officers made some tragic mistakes. What happened to them has been chronicled by Indiana University historian Robert H. Ferrell. [2] A view from the ground is preserved in my father's letters home.

The first is from "somewhere in England."

June 5, 1918: *After a long time, I have finally gotten overseas. We landed here in England yesterday and came to a real camp, getting here early this morning. I had a very good trip over. I had a good boat, quite speedy for a transport, and the weather was fine all the way. I got thru without getting seasick, but I am not in love with that form of riding. I have not caught up with the company yet, but getting closer all the time. We did not have any thrilling escapes from submarines on the way over but came through without much excitement.*

I have not seen much of England yet, only what I saw from the train as we came up here last night, but as much as I have seen of it has been mighty pretty. It looks pretty crowded up though after coming from a place where we have so much room. The villages are close together and although the houses are all good they are all just alike and jammed up close together and right up against the street so there are no lawns. The farmhouses are all good and all had beautiful little gardens and lawns around them.

I don't think I would want much to farm here though as the little dinky fields would get on my nerves. Young men seem to be pretty scarce around, but I never saw so many kids in my life. It is a lot colder here than it is back in the states, and the days are mighty long. It doesn't get dark until about 10:30, and it gets light before 4 in the morning. I haven't any idea of how long we will be here or where we will go from here, but I suppose that we will go to some training camp before long. ...

When the Missouri-Kansas division reached France, its men spent some time with British troops in the Somme region, in the northwest corner of France, which had been the scene of a major battle two years earlier. That line had stabilized by then, and it was used to teach the American soldiers some of the elements of trench warfare. Then the division traveled to the eastern end of the country where the French were holding down the line in Alsace.

June 19, 1918: *We have been moving pretty steadily ever since we left the States, only stopping a couple of times to rest. We are billeted now in a little French village and I have a mighty small idea as to where it is other than it is somewhere in France. We hiked here yesterday from the railroad. It took us about 8 hours to get here and come through about a dozen little villages every one of them just the same. The houses all look as though they were at least a dozen years old and the barn and house are all together and the streets are lined with manure piles. There are no people left here except a few old men and women and a few kids. The railroads in this country are wonders for slowness especially the troop trains. I was lucky in getting to ride second-class as about ¾ of the men on the train rode in their combination boxcars and cattle cars. The cars are lot smaller than ours and nearly every boxcar has written up by the door 8 horses or 40 men. I am still following that company and sort of doubt whether I will ever catch up with them or not. I do not think that we will stay at this village long but expect that we will move up further. I don't know exactly, but as near as I can find out we are somewhere between 80 and 100 miles back of the trenches so of course we will probably go closer for training.*

It is still much cooler here than it was in the States, and I can hardly see how stuff grows as well as it does. Garden tracts seem to do unusually well, and fruit looks good. A lot of the road that we came over yesterday has cherry trees on either side of the road and the cherries are most all ripe and a lot of them have been picked already. Strawberries are pretty thick here and they are mighty fine. Well, it is nearly time for chow so I better get my mess pan and get up to the kitchen. I will write again as soon as I get time.

When his unit reached Alsace, the assignment was to relieve French forces for duty in the more hard-pressed lines to the west. As Bige saw it:

When we took it over, the French and Germans had sort of mutual understanding that that was to be kept a quiet sector and were free in showing themselves and got along without any fighting. We livened it up a little as we were all raring to get our Germans, and we would crack down on whatever showed up like it might be Jerry and made a few short advances just to straighten out the line a little.

He spent his 22nd birthday there.

July 11, 1918: *We just came back from the front and are resting up now and getting cleaned up a little. We were up there quite a while, and so far I haven't seen a German, but of course this happens to be a pretty quiet front that we are on. It wasn't half bad in the trenches, and it was really a lot better than I thought it would be. But it seems pretty good to get back and to get a bath and some clean clothes and a good long night's sleep. We get enough sleep when we are up on the line, but it is on the two or three hours at a time plan ...*

I had lost all track of dates and didn't realize that this was my birthday until I began trying to find out the date this morning and then I found out that I was a year older than I thought I was. I suppose that the wheat harvest is all over by now back there and it is hotter than a million. That is one thing that hasn't bothered me in the least here. It has been cool and pretty comfortable all the time.

American forces began moving toward their first major assignment of the war in August, 1918. They surrounded a bulge in the line that the Germans had held since 1914 near the town of St. Mihiel. Their mission was to get ready to push the Germans back. General John J. Pershing did not want to risk losing his first battle, and so he assigned his most experienced divisions for the fighting, and the 35th was held in reserve. The attack on the St. Mihiel salient would come on Sept. 12.

Sept. 9, 1918: *We have one hitch in the trenches to our credit so far, but while we were in the front line, it was really but little more than part of our training.*

For the last month, we have done little but drill occasionally and do a little work and stay in reserve. As for what is going on over here in the war, we know but very little what is going on as we do not get to see a newspaper only once in a while and then we can't follow it as we have missed too much. We get a little that is going on in our own sector, but we hear so much that can't believe much of that. But one thing we know, and that is things look mighty good for us and while we figure on being here quite a while yet, we've got our minds made up to see the scenery along the Rhine before many moons.

Speaking of scenery, we have sure seen it. All summer we

have been in places that were before the war some of the places where many of our rich Americans came to spend summer. But viewed from our infantrymen's point of view it lost a great deal of its beauty and made them all wish for the straight and level roads of the states. The roads here are really wonderful, and so far I haven't seen any dirt roads since I have been over here, and I have seen a lot of roads, too.

This company is certainly some hiking company now. We have made believers out of everything in this battalion, and the battalion made believers out of the division in a little 60-mile hike a few months ago. It is remarkable to see how far a bunch can hike on a little pride and guts. We had some men, and quite a few of them, too, who were in the habit of falling out in every hike, short or long, until one night when we had to make about 20 miles in a rain and dark as pitch. Nobody but the guide knew where we were, so it happened that L came through without losing a man, and that made us sort of proud of ourselves as some companies lost as high as 50% of their men. Since then, a man sure catches hell if he goes to crabbing and talking about falling out, and I have seen a lot of them and have had to do it myself a couple of times, come in on pure guts. These rock roads are hard on a man's feet with a good pack. I have the pleasure now of dragging around a Chauchat automatic rifle, and it only weighs 19 lbs. But it is a mighty nice little tool up on the front line.

In fact, the Americans would soon realize that the French-made Chauchat was a really bad tool. Pershing's army had arrived in France without automatic weapons or field artillery, and so it purchased equipment from the French. The Chauchat had a barrel that was too small for its ammunition, causing the gun to overheat and fail after only a few rounds. But that was not a major problem at St. Mihiel, because the Germans were already withdrawing when the Americans attacked, and the main fighting lasted only a day.

Pershing then moved his troops 60 miles west for a much more difficult assignment, capturing the territory between the Argonne Forest on the left and the Meuse River on the right. The troops moved at night to keep the Germans believing that the American attack would come at heavily fortified Metz, southeast of Verdun. The 35th Division was assigned to a sector immediately to the east of the forest, whose density provided plenty of cover for the German defenders.

Oct. 6, 1918: *I suppose that you have been waiting to hear from me for quite (a while), but this is absolutely the first chance I have had to send mail since the last short note I wrote you. Much has happened to me since then, not to me so much as I have been where things were happening nearly ever since then.*

First and of most importance is that I have been "over the top" and have come back unhurt. How I came thru, I do not know as I was in several places where chances seemed pretty small. I will try to tell you about my experiences and hope that it goes thru all right.

One night about 12 o'clock, we left our position back of the lines and went up to the front line where we stood around in the muddy trenches (and) rested as best we could. About 2 o'clock, our artillery opened up and began to bombard the Boche, and they gave him a good one. About daylight, we moved down into a little shallow front-line trench where we laid low for a little while, and the artillery was putting over a terrific barrage.

Then just before the zero hour arrived and as our barrage was lifting, our machine guns began playing over Jerry's trenches just to keep him low. The machine guns stopped, and it was up and over and over we went. I had often wondered what it would feel like to go up and over the top and out across No

Man's Land. I felt just about the same as I always felt going out across the drill ground in any old skirmish line. We crossed No Man's Land without much excitement in my section and across Jerry's front line trenches, across more wire to his second line, and still I never saw a Jerry although we bombed out dugouts and searched everywhere. There was quite a heavy fog, so we could not see what was going on further down the line where the men were having stiffer fighting.

A quail flew up, one of the boys shot it down, and picked it up and went on with it. In fact, we had begun to feel that we were on a small game hunt. For nearly three hours we pushed on in this way, stopping only to clean out a trench or dugout and once to wait for our barrage to lift more.

Then all at once the fog lifted, and I found myself with a little group far ahead of the line and, as it quickly developed, in the middle of a machine gun nest. We got out of that by speed and mostly with some luck and got back to our own lines and got in behind our tanks where we belonged and after that there was no lack of evidence of the Germans.

We carried on for four days and nights and held one night when we were relieved. Of course, we were not in the forward wave all of the time, but were under fire most of the time. You see the advance is played a good deal the same as leapfrog with 6 units.

I will say but little more of the last 3 days but I can say that we came thru as near a hell as any American outfit ever has, and I have had all of war I want at least until I get rested up. We made some mistakes that we will never make again, and next time, if there need be a next, our casualties will be much lighter.

His account shows limited awareness of what military analysts would later declare a major disaster. Communication, through telephone wire laid along the ground, was bad. Planning was poor, and there was a shortage of artillery pieces. According to Ferrell's account, my father's regiment, the 137th Infantry, fell apart almost immediately, but, owing to the fog, this failure was not apparent to the men participating, especially for L Company which advanced far enough ahead of the line to find the enemy and get in serious danger. When the regiment as a whole failed to advance in an organized way, the 139th Infantry passed through it and pushed the Germans back. The whole division was then taken out of the line and sent to a relatively quiet sector closer to Metz.

Despite the failure of the Missouri-Kansas division, the Argonne campaign as a whole was a success, and it motivated the Germans to seek peace.

———————————

Nov. 12, 1918: *Yesterday was a great day around here, especially for the French people who have been kept away from their homes so long by the Huns, and they certainly gave every church bell for miles around one grand ringing. We are billeted in an old chateau now and no telling how old it is. Five (of) us occupy a little square building at the corner of the yard, which has the appearance of being built here for defensive purposes. It is two stories high, and the lower room has loopholes, which look down along the outside of the walls around the yard. It was a pretty cheerless place when we got here, but when it looked as though we would stay here for a few days we got busy and hunted up panels to cover the windows, but we didn't have any stove so we carried in a lot of rocks from a tumbledown rock wall near here and built us a fireplace and used a hole that a shell had knocked in one wall for a chimney and now we are living quite comfortably.*

The fireplace isn't finished off very well, but at that it makes this little old house more homelike. Just below there is quite a large town, or was, but not a civilian lives down there now, but occasionally one can see a group of women and an old man or two coming into the town to look over their one-time homes and make preparations for moving back since Jerry is both out of distance and inclined to be peaceable ....

The railroad that runs thru one of the valleys below the chateau has its switchyards lit up, and the trains are running with lights, and it sure looks good.

While everything looks good for peace, I can't quite realize that we needn't be looking for another hitch in the trenches or in another drive, but I expect I will come to it in time.

———————————

Bige was able to take leave in the French resort city of Aix-les-Bains in the foothills of the Alps near the Italian-speaking part of Switzerland. When he first reached France, he had written home for information about his father's birthplace, Glattfelden, a village between Zurich and the German border. But if he had hoped to see it, he was disappointed. The closest he got was a distant view of Mont Blanc, the highest peak in the Alps on the French-Italian border. While resting there, his thoughts turned to the future, and he disclosed them to his older brother Frank.

———————————

January 17, 1919: *Just what I will do when I get out of the Army, I am not sure of yet. I had my plans pretty well made out two years ago, but things have changed some there, and two years makes quite a difference anyway. I am nearly in the notion of taking a claim as by the time I get out of the Army, I will be able to prove up on one in about six months as the time I put in the Army will count in proving up on a claim. If you get a hold of any good dope about a good place to take a claim ... save it for me until I get back there.*

———————————

That was a reference to the Enlarged Homestead Act of 1909, which gave 320 acres, double the normal homestead, to farmers whose claims were in the more arid lands in the west. All of the good land had been taken. Eventually, this new incentive would create a huge influx of new farmers, overgrazing, massive soil erosion, and the Dust Bowl of the 1930s. And it would make a fortunate few wealthy, because oil was under some of that land.

Bige was still intending to look into the possibility of a claim when he wrote his last Army letter, from Camp Upton, New York. He was discharged with rail fare back to Emporia, and quickly moved west in search of work. The last of his preserved letters from that period is undated, from Alton, Kansas, in Osborne County, and written on a typewriter:

We had pretty good luck all the way out here and got in here about eight that night and stopped to see an old buddy of ours here and as there was a lot of good work here, we just camped. We went to work Tuesday noon and have been at it ever since. We have had a keen place to work and have been pulling down 7 a day and that job will last a couple of days yet, and then we will probably go to threshing. Threshing pays 5 a day and a percent on all over 1,000 bushels, so we can probably get pretty good money right along for a while yet. We had a pretty good rain here last night, but it is so sandy here that it doesn't bother much. Have you gotten any rain there yet? We are going out to see a combination header and thresher this afternoon if it is running today. The wheat here is just about the same as it is there, and a lot of it is down and have to cut a lot of straw even when they are heading it. I suppose you have the oats out and about half of the corn laid by now if you have had any luck at all.

The United States was as unprepared for the absorption of its fighting men back into the population as it had been unready for the war. There were no educational benefits for veterans as there would be after subsequent wars. Medical benefits were available for war-related injuries, but post-traumatic stress disorder was recognized only in its most extreme form, dubbed "shell shock." Judging from films that documented that disorder, the chief symptom was involuntary movement in the form of twitching, trembling or spasms. From his immediate postwar activity, related in the oral history, we know that Bige emerged visibly healthy.

But, "in war, there are no unwounded soldiers."[3] His momentum, if not his spirit, had been broken. Released from the peer pressure of his five older siblings, he put aside his educational goals and kept moving west after the harvest until he found work on a ranch in Wyoming. Then he went east to Gary, Indiana, and worked in a steel mill. The hoped-for land claim never worked out. After two years of wandering and thinking about his future, he decided to return to the farm and make plans to resume his education at Emporia. The record includes a letter of July 19, 1921, from Thomas W. Butcher, president, Kansas State Normal School: "Complying with your request, I am sending a transcript of your record. I trust it will be of service to you."

Bige made a deal with his father. He would help on the farm for the next crop cycle, and a specified wheat field would be dedicated to paying his college expenses. It could be planted, harvested, and marketed in time for the fall semester in 1922. But on Sept. 21, 1921, everything changed. Jacob Meyer was bringing in a team and a wagon after hauling a load of wood, and the horses bolted across a dry gully. An axle support broke, and the bed of the wagon fell to the ground. The impact ruptured Jacob's bladder, and he died before medical help could arrive. He was 65.

That left Bige as the senior male in residence at the farm. The younger siblings, Lester and Gladys, were still teenagers. The older ones had moved on. Fred, Walt, and Mamie had begun their teaching careers – Fred in Jewell, Kan., Walt in

Tombstone, Ariz., and Mamie in Washington County. Ollie had moved in with Walt to help raise his twins after his wife died in childbirth. Frank had located his family in Colorado. The day-to-day work of managing the farm fell to Bige.

The record suggests that he was a good manager, particularly in a crisis. In 1923, lightning struck the barn, and it burned to the ground. With hired help, Bige built a bigger and better barn, equipped it and the house with lightning rods, and installed the indoor plumbing in the house.

It was in this period that he met Hilda Grace Morrison. She had attended summer school at Emporia and gained enough credit for a temporary teaching certificate that could be renewed with more credits in subsequent terms. This was a quick and practical way for the less affluent to enter the teaching profession. Her first post was Brown School, a one-room structure between the small towns of Barnes and Greenleaf, in the 1924-1925 school year. She was 19. The following year, she moved to the one-room school at Reiter, a community barely large enough to be recognized with a dot on the old maps. (All that survives today is its cemetery.) It was on a branch of Peats Creek, a mile and a half south and a mile and a half east of the Meyer farmstead and an equal distance from her birthplace, the Morrison farm to the east.[4]

Professional entertainment was scarce in those years, but the population density on the prairie was enough to support amateur theater groups, and that is how my parents met. They participated in a play called, "Looks Like Rain." Assuming they met in 1926, she was 21, and he was 30.

Bige was apparently content to be a farmer, but, as with any family business, the large number of heirs complicated matters. Jacob left no will, and Kansas law gave half the estate to the widow and half to the children. So the farm had nine owners. The first attempt at organizing the management of the place set Bige up as a partner with his mother. That would give him 5/16 ownership, but not much liquidity.

Whether the problem stemmed from his dissatisfaction or that of his older siblings is unknown, but Fred Meyer was appointed to represent the nonresident owners in a renegotiation. Fred was the oldest brother, born in 1884, and he had earned a master's degree at Emporia and become superintendent of the schools in Jewell. The family was accustomed to his leadership. In 1905-1906, he had been the sole teacher of the one-room Diamond School, not far from the Meyer farmhouse, and siblings Bige, Walter, Ollie, and Mamie were among his pupils.

Hilda Grace Morrison, ca 1926

Fred met on November 28, 1924, with Bige and their mother Matilda, and they worked out a new arrangement. The partnership would be dissolved as of January 1 and replaced by a landlord-tenant relationship. Bige would purchase the farming equipment at a price to be set by an appraiser. He would then sharecrop the land. The rent would include two-fifths of the corn raised, one-third of the small grain harvested, plus per-acre fees for various tracts of land, the amount depending on their use and productivity. And he could pasture his horses in exchange for keeping up the fences.

The final paragraph: "Landlord agrees to board the tenant and farm hand, and tenant in turn will take care of the cows, furnish them feed during the winter months, and do the milking." The farm hand would have been the youngest brother Lester.

The deal appears to have worked well for all concerned. Fred came back in July 1928 to audit the books and reported that Matilda had used her earnings from the farm to buy back the shares of all of the children except Gladys. And Bige had earned enough to own most of the farm equipment.

It was a good time for Bige and Hilda to marry, and he had a plan for their living arrangement. The last of the three adjoining farms that Jacob had acquired, known as the Heck place, included a house that was still standing. Older brother Frank had lived there for a time with his wife and children. It could be a convenient place to take a bride.

But closer inspection showed that the house was no longer habitable without extensive rebuilding. Bige's farm equipment might have served as collateral for a home-improvement loan. Perhaps that was their plan when they decided on an unannounced wedding in the country church at Throop, with the parson's wife and mother-in-law as witnesses. They took a honeymoon trip to Colorado Springs and then moved into the Meyer farmhouse with Matilda and Lester. But before they could resolve the issue of permanent housing, a business opportunity appeared.

Hilda's younger sister, Velma Morrison, had learned the beautician's trade and was looking for a place to open her own shop. She found a viable market in nearby Deshler, Neb., a town of about 1,100 souls in Thayer County whose southeast corner touches the northwest corner of Washington County, Kan. It contained a hardware store that was in bankruptcy and could be purchased at what seemed like a bargain. Bige and a Washington County friend, Hardy Robbins, checked it out, pooled their funds, and bought it in February 1929. Velma opened her beauty shop at about the same time. Younger brother Lester was left to run the Meyer farm.

3.   My arrival and the long disruption

The newlyweds rented a two-story duplex at what is today 306 First St. in Deshler. The house faced west, and the upstairs had two bedrooms with a southern exposure and a bathroom with a claw-footed tub. I was born in that house on October 27, 1930, one day short of the first anniversary of Black Monday on Wall Street.

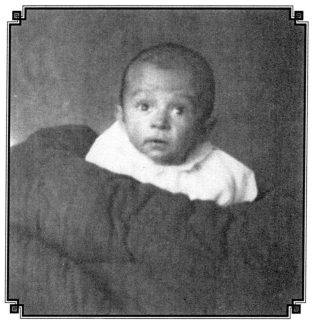

Philip Meyer, Deshler, 1931

Family legend attributed the failure of the Meyer and Robbins hardware store to the Great Depression. But in 1993, I used a lecture date at the University of Nebraska as an opportunity to drive west into the Sand Hills and learn a little more about my past. Naturally, I went first to the editor and publisher of the *Deshler Rustler*, Harold Struve. My senior by 10 years, he remembered my parents and the hardware store, but he had a more vivid memory of my Aunt Velma. She was attractive, and he had enjoyed meeting her in his first newspaper job, delivering the *Omaha World Herald*. And the failure of the hardware store, he suggested, could be blamed more on the social dynamics of small towns than on the Great Depression.

Longevity is everything in a tight community. Local retailers stick together, organize service clubs to send each other business, and generally look out for one another. The bankrupt seller of the hardware store was a member of a pioneer family that had earned respect and many friends. To the old families in town, it looked as though the young upstarts from Kansas were taking advantage of his misfortune. And so, when they could, they purchased their hardware elsewhere, even going to the trouble and expense of traveling to Hebron, the county seat, for their needs. Meyer and Robbins were outsiders, and, in Struve's view, their enterprise was doomed from the start. Nevertheless, they managed to hold on for two-and-a-half years, finally declaring bankruptcy in fall 1931.

My mother did not measure value by material things, but she had to have been disappointed. She had thought she was marrying up. Bige was good looking, came from a relatively affluent family, and had been a success as a farm manager. People in his home county looked up to him. But those advantages, in the social climate of the rural and small-town Midwest, were community-specific and did not travel well. We went back to Kansas.

Aunt Mamie and her husband Earl Cozine took us in. Mamie taught in a one-room school, and Earl had acquired a country store in Enosdale, a hamlet just north of the Meyer farm. A house came with it, but Mamie preferred to spend weeknights at the farm because it cut her trip to school by three miles. So we lived in their Enosdale house, while Bige helped in the store and looked for a job that spring.

He found one in Washington, the county seat located just four miles north of the farm where his grandfather, the Swiss immigrant Henry Meyer Sr., broke the virgin prairie and started his homestead in 1869. Here, the Meyers were a pioneer family, and the social dynamics were on our side. George Higginbotham, the Chrysler-Plymouth dealer, hired Bige to sell cars on commission. We moved to Washington, and by summer it seemed we were settling down.

July 4, 1932, fell on a Monday. A celebration followed by a ball game was held in the city park, and Bige worked the showroom at the dealership in case any visiting farmers wanted to come by and kick the tires on a new Plymouth. It was almost closing time when the tornado struck from the southwest. The storm ruined the courthouse, two schools, the National Guard armory, the town opera house, the standpipe, the Episcopal Church, and several businesses. Years later, my mother said she stood outside and watched the clouds boiling like water and at one moment she believed she was looking straight up into the funnel cloud. Our house was spared, although wind drove a board through a bedroom wall.

When Bige was asked whether he had been indoors or out, he said, "Indoors at first. And then I was outdoors because the storm blew the building away." Unhurt, he ran home to find his wife and child safe. Four persons died of injuries from the storm. And work at the car dealership was disrupted for a while.

So we moved again. Bige's next job took us to Linn, the first town to the south, where he drove a truck selling and delivering eggs and dairy products for the Washington County Cooperative Creamery Company. It produced its own brand of butter, with George Washington's picture on the one-pound package. His route covered a wide territory, requiring some overnight stays.

The house we lived in was near the railroad tracks, and when I was frightened by the noise of a train, I would crawl into the tunnel formed by the sofa's slanted back and the wall. There was always joy when Bige came in from the road.

After the tornado, July 4, 1932

After a year, Higginbotham's Garage reopened, we went back to Washington in time for my third birthday, and Bige was selling cars again. We moved twice more before I started school, finally, in 1935, settling in a dusty former farmhouse around which the town had grown. It was a rambling white frame structure at 205 E. Fifth St. owned by Anna Meitler, a widow who lived on the second floor. We paid ten dollars a month to rent the ground floor with its two bedrooms, living and dining room, and a very basic kitchen. The house had been wired for electricity in a rudimentary way with exposed wires running along the baseboards. Lighting was primarily from bare bulbs hanging from the middle of the ceiling of each room plus a bridge lamp for reading. In what might be considered my first scientific experiment, I stuck an index finger into the empty socket in my bedroom. The result was an odd tingling sensation, uncomfortable enough to convince me not to do it again.

Bige with Phil, ca 1932

Heat was supplied from a gas stove in the dining room. In the winter we would close the sliding door to the living room after moving the sofa, the radio, and a reading lamp into the dining room. Baths were taken in a round washtub that we rolled in from the back porch on Saturday nights. Plumbing consisted of cold-water faucets in ours and Mrs. Meitler's kitchens and a toilet in my bedroom, which Mrs. Meitler could reach by a door at the bottom of her enclosed stairway. If I happened to be in bed when she needed to use the toilet, I would pretend to be asleep. She had a habit of talking to herself while sitting on the toilet at the foot of the bed, reminiscing and worrying about absent family members. She was aided by a Depression-era welfare program that entitled her to surplus farm commodities, and one of the services that I provided was hauling her bags of flour, corn meal, or whatever was being given away that month from the downtown distribution center, in my little red wagon.

By now, the dust storms were bad enough to give the Dust

Bowl its name, but for all I knew, it was normal for Kansas. We were east of the worst storms, but still found dust filtering into the house on dark days. In March 1935, Uncle Fred, writing from Jewell, just 68 miles to the west, reported one storm "so bad that in many houses, the dirt was carried out in scoop shovels."

The best thing about Mrs. Meitler's house was its location. The huge lot included a barn, a crumbling outhouse, and a storage shed that we called "the cob house" after its original purpose. (After corn grown in that period was shelled, the cobs were dried and kept as fuel for heating and cooking.) And there was room for a garden so large that Bige hired a man with a horse and plow to prepare it for planting each spring. We grew leaf lettuce, carrots, potatoes, beans, peas, radishes, and tomatoes. Hilda canned the beans, peas, and tomatoes, and we stored the potatoes in the cellar. A cherry tree stood near the back door, just the right size to be climbed by a small boy, and, next to the garden, we had a mulberry tree whose tasty fruit stained our fingers. On the hottest summer nights, we slept on blankets spread on the ground between the house and garden.

A vacant lot across the street provided a spot where children could play in pickup softball games. When we chose up sides, I was always the last to be chosen, but we seldom had enough players to form two teams. So we played work-up, which functions with as few as nine players and lets everyone rotate through each position. Sensing some social discomfort on my part, my mother persuaded me not to worry: my superior brainpower would give me the advantage eventually. I trusted her.

We were only two blocks from Ellra Patrie's grocery store, which extended credit, a handy feature in the Depression. It also delivered. We had no telephone to order groceries, and no car of our own to bring groceries home, but I was easily dispatched to the store with a list.

At irregular intervals, Bige would come home and announce,

"I sold a car." That brought cheers and hugs because it meant we could pay the grocery bill, and Mr. Patrie would express his gratitude by including a bag of candy with the next delivery.

Not owning a car was not much of a problem because one of the benefits of working for a dealer was that Bige had access to one for personal use as well as sales calls. I enjoyed the variety and had an odd preference for really old, rattling cars with holes in the floorboards and cracks in the windows. Perhaps it was because I could imagine the interesting lives they had led.

There was one problem that we had not anticipated. In that simpler time, new cars came from the factory in only two configurations, standard and deluxe. Because of the Depression, the standard models were much easier to sell. But small town dealers had little clout with the manufacturer, and the standard models were snapped up by metropolitan dealerships while buyers in the hinterlands had to pony up for the less marketable deluxe models. Still, Bige found buyers, and we got by.

The ball-playing across the street yielded for a week every summer to a traveling theater company called the Chick Boyes Players. It was based in Hebron, Nebr., and had two modes of operating, "tent rep" in the summer and "circle stock" the rest of the year. Circle stock was so named because the company operated from a central location and made day trips to surrounding towns. The cast would present the same play in each of five or six towns on successive evenings and rehearse the next week's play in the afternoons.

In the summer, when heat inside the halls made circle stock unappealing, the company switched to tent repertory: it would widen its circle, but stay in one place for a week and present a different play every night for five nights – plus a Saturday matinee in some cases. The shows were all performed by the same players, working on a portable stage inside a large tent. Admission was typically 10 cents for children, 20 for teenagers, and 30 for adults. A cash-short patron could barter for payment with produce or baked goods. In our case, we bartered with water. The cast lived in tents and trailers parked on the lot, and its members needed to fill their buckets for drinking and washing. We gave them access to our outdoor hydrant in exchange for tickets, and that was my first exposure to professional theater. The content was always family friendly. Some of the material came from Broadway shows old enough to be available for reduced royalties, but most was the work of Midwestern playwrights.

Vaudeville acts filled the time between curtains. The actors were happy to find work, and at least one had Broadway experience. Another Chick Boyes player, Lloyd "Slim" Andrews, advanced to Hollywood and played sidekick roles in B westerns.[5]

The lot that the tent rep theater used had a well-worn path that led northwest from our house on Fifth Street, and, when school started, it was the first leg of my twice-daily walk. The distance was only five blocks, but it took me through the business district and past the courthouse square. My mother briefed me very carefully on the procedure for crossing streets. "Look both ways to be sure no cars are coming," she said. "Then run as fast as you can to the other side." At noon, I walked home for lunch. There was no kindergarten. I was five years old when I entered the first grade.

That was the year we found our church home. My mother's people were Methodist, and my father's belonged to the Evangelical Church. But our faith was flexible, and we were likely to attend whatever church happened to be close by.

I was in the first grade when my teacher decided to produce a dramatic reading based on a Christmas play, "Why the Chimes Rang," by Elizabeth Apthorp McFadden. She had adapted it from a story of the same name for Harvard/Radcliffe Professor George P. Baker, who had been Thomas Wolfe's mentor. It came with detailed costume and stage direction. The climax of the story takes place in a church, and my teacher found an ideal venue in Grace Episcopal Church, whose new limestone building had replaced the one destroyed in the 1932 tornado. I did not have a speaking part, but was chosen to play the acolyte, the boy who carries the cross at the head of the procession. The minister, H. S. Giere, liked my performance, and asked my parents if they would bring me back on Sunday to lead the procession in a real church service. They consented, found they enjoyed the Anglican way of worship, and I was baptized in that church.

That worked out well, but it planted an awareness of one of the Meyer-side mysteries. What was the religious history of the Meyers, and why did no one ever talk about their faith as practiced in Switzerland – or, for that matter, their reason for leaving? It would take me decades to find out about the Antonianers.

We did not think of ourselves as poor, although there was a point where I realized we were a little different. There came a day when my second-grade teacher forgot to wind her watch, and she interrupted class to ask me to go to the telephone out in the hall and ask the operator for the time. I dutifully trudged down the hall and found the phone mounted on a wall. I looked up at it and scratched my head. I didn't know how to work the thing.

I went back to class and signaled my frustration with a puzzled shrug.

"What?" said the teacher, turning to address my classmates. "Class, can you imagine anyone who doesn't know to use the phone?"

She paused and looked at me.

"Do you have a telephone at home?"

"No," I said.

Eventually, I learned that when you picked up the phone, a central operator's voice would say, "Number, please." And she would plug in a cord to connect you to the party you wanted to call. If you wanted to know the time, you would say, "Time, please." And she would tell you.

Although I did not realize it then, our lack of a telephone was not so deviant. Telephone penetration reached its pre-depression peak at 42 percent of U.S. households in 1929 and then declined. In 1937, the year I started second grade, only 34 percent of households nationally had phones.[6]

And I was not completely clueless. Both of the family farms had telephones, but rural phones used a different system with party lines. To call my cousins from the Morrison farm, I knew to stand on a chair to reach the crank on the wall phone and turn it to make two long rings and a short. That was heard all along the line, and it signified that only the Meyer farmhouse should pick up the receiver. But there was nothing to stop eavesdroppers at other points along the line from picking up, too, if they wanted.

Once in the middle of an animated conversation with my cousin Ralph, the line suddenly went dead. I complained to my grandmother.

"Maybe the operator thought you boys were having too much fun," she said.

Every Christmas, my Aunt Velma, still single and having left Deshler for a larger market in York, Nebr., wrote and invited me to request an extravagant gift. One year, I suggested a sled, and she sent me a Skippy Racer, a top-of-the line model with a tubular frame and fantastic maneuverability. It was one of the two best sleds in town, made evident when we children all took our sleds to school on the first snowy day. My other big material gain of that period was a new Schwinn bicycle, awarded by a car manufacturer as a prize in a sales promotion. There was a catalog of prizes to choose from, and we had some family discussions over whether to go for an electric mixer or let the points build up to assure the bicycle. It was shipped from the factory in Chicago, had balloon tires, a fixed gear suitable for flat terrain, two horizontal tubes, and a pedal-powered coaster brake. This configuration was designed for simplicity and economy in the Depression-damaged market. It was known as a "cruiser" or "paperboy bike."

When there was a school event whose attendance required a fee, my father would sometimes give me an extra dime in case there was a child who could not pay. Our local pioneer ancestry brought us respect, and Bige was elected commander of the American Legion post and was active in the Masonic Lodge. The teachers expected much of me, and I delivered except in singing and on the sports field. I couldn't carry a tune, and I couldn't reliably catch a ball. My parents restricted my access to comic books (too violent) and radio drama (too disturbing), so I took refuge in books from the Carnegie Library, which was on the route home from school. I began with age-appropriate material and worked my way up through the Bobbsey Twins to the Rover Boys and then the Tom Swift series. When I ran out of male adventure stories, I switched to girls' literature, the Nancy Drew and the Judy Bolton series. And, best of all, the library had what appeared to be the complete Oz series, starting with *The Wizard of Oz* and branching into stranger and stranger material. In the summer, I would visit the library in the morning, check out two books, the maximum, take them home and read them, and then return to the library to exchange them for two more in the afternoon.

Every winter, it seemed, I got sick from one disease or another, some serious like whooping cough or hepatitis, and the usual childhood diseases like chicken pox, measles and mumps. I avoided getting scarlet fever, a serious disease before antibiotics, and I remember the red-and-white quarantine signs posted on various front doors around town. My parents were terrified of polio, not unreasonable as one of my classmates used crutches, an outcome of one of the seasonal epidemics, and they kept me out of the municipal swimming pool most of the time. As a result, I would not learn to swim until college, and then only well enough to struggle one length of the indoor pool with an awkward sidestroke. My disease-mandated rests did not hold back my academic development. Returning to school from one mid-winter confinement, I casually placed on my teacher's desk, the math workbook with all of the problems solved for the rest of the year.

In 1938, our family got larger. When my mother's labor pains began, we climbed into a borrowed car, I was dropped off at Aunt Mamie's house in Linn, and my brother John was born in Clay Center Hospital 32 miles to the south. My immediate concern was how long we would have to wait before teaching him to talk. Boredom came easily in the small-town Midwest, and I needed a peer with whom to chat.

It was also in that year that Bige changed jobs again, taking a post as manger of a brand new Sinclair service station where U.S. Route 36 passed through the city. It had a restaurant attached. The company's logo was a dinosaur, symbolizing the origin of fossil fuels, and it gave out dinosaur stamps that could be pasted into an album that would help children learn the difference between a brachiosaurs and a polacanthus. I peered into my father's cash drawer where he kept the stamps that were awaiting release. The drawer also contained an impressive supply of bills and coins.

"That's a lot of money," I said wonderingly.

"Not really," Bige said. "Most of this has to be used to buy gas." It was my first lesson in economics.

And then he was offered a better job, one with a fixed salary plus commission, selling cars for the local Chevrolet dealer. One of his customers was my uncle Wilmer Morrison, who bought a 1939 business coupe with a vacuum-assisted shift mounted on the steering column. Wilmer liked to show how easy it was to drive, holding the gearshift lever between his thumb and forefinger, the other fingers extended to show that their lifting power was not needed.

My other main memory of 1939 is one of worrying, walking to school, thinking about the news of Germany invading Poland and my parents' conversation about the possibility of another world war. In 1940, I first became aware of presidential politics. There were hardly any Democrats in Washington, Kan., and we fifth-graders proudly wore buttons that proclaimed "No Third Term." I asked my father why nobody liked President Roosevelt. "He's crazy," he said.

We were home-delivery customers of the *Kansas City Times* when it was the morning edition of the *Kansas City Star*. It reached us in the afternoon. I was a faithful reader of the comic strips, including Thimble Theater with Popeye, a sailor who drew super strength from eating spinach. I liked his statement of self-validation, "I yam what I yam what I yam."

But my favorite was Superman, which began in Action Comics in 1938, and then became a newspaper strip. The fact that the baby Superman was adopted by a Kansas farm couple made it seem real, and I rejoiced with the child Clark Kent when he discovered his superpowers. As one who was skinny and clumsy, I felt as though the fantasy was created just for me.

So I read avidly as Clark Kent, determined to use his powers to aid humanity, grew up and moved to Metropolis to assume the role of Superman. He found his first case by reading about it in a newspaper, but by the time he could reach the scene to right the wrong, it was too late. The evildoers had done their damage and fled. Superman needed to get his news sooner.

He figured out a way, and I loved it. Clark Kent decided to become a newspaper reporter. Professional news gatherers were always among the first to know what happened. So, as Clark Kent, he applied for a job at the *Daily Planet*. This story had a profound effect on my own daydreams. With my physical limitations, I could never be anything like a superhero. But I could certainly be a mild-mannered reporter. And, in the world where I lived, words, properly applied, could have powers of their own. That is when the thought of a newspaper career first entered my mind.

In 1940, Congress passed the Selective Service and Training Act – the first peacetime military draft in our history. My uncle Wilmer, legally blind in one eye, was ineligible, but Ernie started to make his plans.

On the Meyer side, my uncle Earl Cozine fell ill and died, leaving Aunt Mamie a single mother with two children. Ralph was my age, and Eileen was two years younger. The Meyer farm became their anchor point, as Mamie found teaching jobs in Washington County. They worked out a pattern of spending summers living and working on the farm and then living wherever Mamie was teaching, first around Washington and then in Greenleaf. Uncle Pappy became the substitute father figure. The extended family closed ranks and continued to function.

4.   The World War II Years

In the summer of 1941, we made another move, our first intercity relocation in eight years. It took us to Concordia, the seat of Cloud County, which shares a border with Washington County at the latter's southwest corner. When I said goodbye to the librarian at the city library, she promised that if I ever came back to visit, I could check out books there as long as she was in charge. Then we took our leave of Mrs. Meitler, and friends drove us the 49 miles to Concordia.

It must have been the attraction of a better job, found through the network of Chrysler dealers, because our living standard went up. Our new rented home at 618 West Fifth Street had good plumbing and electric facilities, a nice yard in an attractive neighborhood, and, at the end of the block, we could look down from a hill and see the Republican River winding its way east. Ward Marshall was the new employer, and my father was happy to be selling Chryslers and Plymouths again. I started sixth grade in Concordia and delighted in surprising the teacher and fellow students whenever a grammar rule or math procedure that I had already learned was introduced. We joined the local Episcopal Church and adjusted nicely, as far as I can remember.

Unlike most people alive at that time, we did not get word of the bombing of Pearl Harbor immediately. Maybe our radio was broken again. Our daily paper was the *Concordia Blade*, and it arrived in the afternoon. And so I did not know that America had been attacked until I heard my fellow students talking about it at school on Monday morning, December 8.

Retooling for war production meant halting the auto assembly lines that had been producing the 1942 models. As business slowed, Ward Marshall needed a smaller sales force, and so he found another job for my father, with his brother Porter Marshall who owned the Chrysler-Plymouth dealership in Clay Center, one county to the east. We celebrated Christmas in Concordia and then moved. Clay Center's three grade schools were named for the martyred presidents, and I finished the sixth grade at McKinley School.

It was spring 1942 when my Arizona cousin Walt received his engineering degree from Kansas State College of Agriculture and Applied Science in Manhattan (Now Kansas State University) and joined the Army's combat engineers. He left his cornet with me so that I could take music lessons from Wayne Snodgrass, the director of the high school band.

We lived at Ninth and Court streets, where the city route of US 24 turned a corner. Motorized units from Ft. Riley used it on training maneuvers. When the Army convoys rolled by, my brother and I stood in the front yard and saluted. The house had a storage shed in the back yard, and I was encouraged, when weather permitted, to take my cornet practice sessions there. I joined the grade-school band.

All the young men were going off to war. My father was 46, too old for this one, but my mother's younger brother Ernie was already in the Army, having left the farm in Wilmer's care in February 1941. After he completed basic training at Camp Roberts, Calif., he was sent to Fort Brady in Sault Ste. Marie, Mich., to guard the canal that links Lake Superior to the St. Lawrence River. When he came home on furlough in the spring of 1942, he spent a day with us, and my parents let me skip school so that I could visit with him and take him on a bicycle tour of our new community.

Writing home later, Ernie remembered, "that last night

bicycling with Phil. I don't know, I felt sort of gloomy, and then we sort of cut loose by going on that ride, and the gloom never caught up again."

Ernie and Wilmer Morrison, Ft. Benning, 1943

The following year, Ernie was sent to Ft. Benning, Ga., for infantry training. At 32, he was older than most of his peers, and, when the training was finished, he was given the choice of staying as an instructor or assignment to a combat unit. He chose the latter and was posted to the 77th Division, bound for the Pacific theater. Wilmer traveled down to Georgia for a last visit with Ernie before he shipped out. I have photographs of the two of them sitting on a park bench there, soberly contemplating the horizon.

I don't remember feeling anxiety when my dad lost his job again. Perhaps I was used to moving by now. But for my parents it was devastating. War production left the dealers with no new cars to sell and not much trading in used cars. It was time to find another line of work. Bige got on the train and headed first to Topeka and then to Kansas City hoping to find war-related work, perhaps at the Sunflower Ordnance Plant in Johnson

County, Kan. He knew accounting, had carpentry skills, and, having being a versatile farm boy, he could repair almost anything, including cars. There were enough relatives in the Kansas City area so that he did not have to worry about a place to stay. His brother Frank lived then in Hickman Mills, a suburb of Kansas City, Mo. Bige posted a letter to my mother from Frank's address, on the eve of their 14th wedding anniversary:

August 31, 1942: *My darling little wife: Tonight rounds out another year of our life together, and I hope that you have enjoyed these years as much as I have. In a material way, they have not been the richest, but they have been rich in love, and I am so thankful to have you right by all the time. I wish that we might spend the day together and honeymoon again. You will never know how much I have appreciated your deep understanding and patience this last month. It has looked at times as though we were wasting a lot of time and money, but the pieces are beginning to fall into a pattern now, and I believe that within a couple more days we will see the right way through it and then we can plan right. If I hadn't felt so sure of your faith and understanding, I would have gotten panicky and jumped wrong several times. I will explain all of that when we are together again.*

... Remember this, sweetheart, that I am deeply in love with you and pray that we may have at least 46 more years rich with love and happiness. I know in my heart that we will see such happiness as we have only dreamed of yet ...

The outcome of that trip was an invitation from a cousin, John Henry Myers, to relocate our family to his farm at the edge of Edgerton, Kan., not far from Kansas City. Myers (who clung to a variant spelling of the family name that his third-grade teacher had insisted on using) had moved to Johnson County in 1918 to work as a buyer in the famous Kansas City stockyards.

He went into farming there, raising cattle and hogs, and by 1926 was prominent enough to be tapped to fill a last-minute vacancy on the Republican ticket for the Kansas legislature. There were not many Democrats in Johnson County, and he won by a large majority. His high energy level and domineering personality got him noticed, and he was elected speaker of the House for the 1929 session. By 1942, he was approaching retirement, and his sons were involved in the war effort. The plan was for Bige to ease into the position of fulltime operator of the farm so that John Henry would not have to wait for the war's end to retire. We were going back to the land.

Our furniture went into storage in Clay Center. Our last meal there was a truly unappetizing breakfast of oatmeal and graham crackers. Then we boarded the train for Kansas City, Mo. Once in Union Station, we had a painfully long wait for the train that would take us back into Kansas, 36 miles southwest to Edgerton. We sat on the hard benches and looked at the big clock high in the concourse, watching the hands move with awful slowness. Only two trains a day stopped at Edgerton. Sometimes they merely slowed down. The station had a rack on a pole next to the track to hold the outgoing mail sack where a crewman in the postal car could pluck it off with a large hook and pull it into the car without the need for the train to make a full stop. The farm practically abutted the town, and John Henry took us there in his 1941 Dodge club coupe.

His farm was highly diversified. It included a small dairy operation. We milked the cows and bottled the milk by hand, put Grade A labels on it, and delivered it to local grocery outlets, although it did not seem that we met the Grade A requirements of sterilized utensils and a clean barn. The house was close enough to town to get its electricity, but it lacked plumbing facilities. We lived in two upstairs bedrooms and shared living and kitchen facilities with John and his wife MayBelle. The family ate well. I remember an excellent Thanksgiving dinner and my first-ever taste of oyster dressing. It was here that I witnessed my first hog butchering. The meat was preserved in a smokehouse.

Like most family farms, this one had a horse that could be saddled for riding the fence lines to look for spots that needed repair. A neighbor boy sometimes did this chore for John, and he invited me along. Once out in the field, he asked if I would like to try riding solo. It seemed easy enough. But when I was in the saddle and before I could secure my feet in the stirrups, the horse took off, headed for the barn at a full gallop while I held on to the saddle horn as best I could. We came to a gully and instead of stepping through it carefully as it had on the way out, the horse decided to jump.

Somewhere in midair, the horse and I separated, and I came down clinging to the animal's side with my right leg over the saddle and the other in empty space. We passed through a narrow gap between a huge rock quarry and a fence corner where it seemed as though I might tumble into the void, but I held on. The horse stopped of its own accord when we reached the barn, and I slid thankfully to the ground.

My school was in Edgerton and its seventh and eighth grades were combined. Teacher Nedra Erskine had a hard time keeping order. She was distracted by worry over her husband who was one of General George S. Patton's soldiers landing at Casablanca on Nov. 8, 1942. One of the pupils in that school, Richard Hickock, would later become Edgerton's most famous son by dying on the gallows as described by Truman Capote in his nonfiction novel *In Cold Blood*. Although Hickock was about the right age to have been in Mrs. Erskine's class, I have no specific memory of him.

The playground consisted of a large field and its equipment was a soccer ball. At recess, we would cluster around the ball to kick it vigorously this way and that, everybody trying to get a foot on it. We played with zero planning, direction, or coordination – much less strategy. Many years later, watching real soccer teams compete, I would marvel at the difference that planning and coordination can make.

We had still not fully adjusted to the Myers farm when, with winter approaching, my father came in from chores and found a telephone message from Porter Marshall in Clay Center. To return the call in privacy, he walked in the dark to the telephone office in town. The news was good. Although there were no cars to sell, the parts business was booming. The government was encouraging the production of both vehicle and farm machinery parts so that existing equipment could be maintained for the wartime economy. Marshall needed Bige's organizing skills to enlarge and supervise the parts department.

John Henry did not seem disquieted by this loss, and he adapted to the reduction in manpower by investing in a milking machine. We helped him set it up and gave it a shakedown run on the night before we left. Then we thanked John and MayBelle for their hospitality and lit out for Clay Center by train, once again sitting out the long wait for a transfer while watching the clock in Kansas City Union Station. I never saw the Myers farm again except once, in 1955, from a low-flying plane. I recognized it from the rock quarry and the spot by the fence corner where the runaway horse had almost dumped me. Decades later, the farmstead was consumed by the quarry, which was enlarged to provide road-building materials for the Interstate Highway System.

Back in Clay Center, Bige looked for a place for us to live while my mother, brother, and I stayed at the Morrison farm. Long-distance calls were expensive, and we communicated by mail, delivered twice daily.

December 18, 1942: *I have been out walking down houses again. I heard of one empty way out NE that sounded about what we wanted and walked out there and, after inquiring around, the neighbors said that the owner was just away working and had his furniture stored in there and did not want to rent it. I called another real estate man tonight and made an appointment with him in the morning to look at some houses he has to rent. Most everything I have run onto has been a long way out, although I haven't scouted around the SE part of town any yet. I thought if possible we would try to give Phil a break by getting him back in the same school.*

... I have been sticking with the inventory pretty close, and I think in about 4 to 5 days more, we will have it all done but the part that will have to be left until the first, which won't be much. It would be about perfect to be back here if we had our own home going. But we will get that done in a few days now.

I am looking for a letter from you tomorrow. Lots of love to the three finest people in the world.

The house that Bige soon found for our family was the best we had lived in, a one-story bungalow with a front porch big enough for a swing, hot and cold running water, full unfinished basement, a garage and small garden. It had central heat from an old coal furnace that had been converted to gas. The owner was a foresighted farmer who had purchased the place for his own eventual retirement, judging that postwar prices would be higher. We were in a mixed neighborhood of blue-collar and white-collar people facing K-15, the state highway that ran north to Washington County. We were once again within a short drive of the two family farms. And we had the use of an automobile for those trips.

It was a few days before Christmas when we moved in, and the town had sold out of trees, so we resigned ourselves to a treeless holiday and went to the midnight service at St. Paul's Episcopal Church. The next morning, my brother and I awakened to an amazing surprise. A beautifully decorated tree, rising all the way to the ceiling, graced our new living room. It was the tree from the Parish Hall of the church, which the new minister, Sherman S. Newton, had kindly donated. We decided we were going to like it here.

Back at McKinley School, my first class was band. The music teacher in Edgerton had told my mother, "The boy has talent." He was lying. But Wayne Snodgrass, the Clay Center band teacher, had more credible encouragement: "He has made up his mind that he is going to learn to play this horn, he works hard at it, and that's worth more than all the talent in the world."

Little by little, that message would change, so that eventually it would be, "He has the music in him; he just can't get it out."

But I was good enough to get by in both the grade school and high school bands. And as soon as I turned 12 in the fall of 1942, I joined the Scouts. I was the only member of Boy Scout Troop 54 who could play any kind of brass instrument at all, which qualified me to be bugler. A bugle is easier to play than a trumpet or cornet because it has fewer notes, and they are keyed in a lower range. I liked Taps the best.

A desire to raise money for Boy Scout camp drew me to my first summer job, hoeing weeds in Ned Engler's watermelon field. I already had an occasional after-school job, substitute newspaper carrier for my classmate Pat McDaniel, delivering the *Clay Center Dispatch* on my still serviceable Schwinn. Pat, like me, was relatively new to town, which might have had something to with his getting the indisputably worst route. It followed a winding seven-mile tour of the poorest part of town, south of the railroad tracks, all the way down to the county fairgrounds. The low density of paid subscribers and the slow collections in that neighborhood made for hard work.

But the *Dispatch* was easy to carry, four to eight broadsheet pages that folded into a package with just enough weight to throw. I enjoyed the camaraderie outside the press room where we carrier boys stuffed our bags before throwing them over our shoulders and riding to our appointed rounds. Eventually, I advanced to substituting on Tom Hanna's better route, just two short parallel streets where the lots were small and the houses were close together, but with enough affluence so that just about everybody took the paper and paid on time. We had as many customers in two miles as the other route contained in seven.

Between delivering the paper and cultivating watermelons, I had no trouble paying my way to Boy Scout camp. With the war still on, scouting was more of a paramilitary activity than it might otherwise have been. We learned close-order drill, shot at targets with .22 rifles and bows and arrows, and played a war-like nighttime game, "Capture the Flag." We also took swimming lessons in a lake. Much of the time was spent waiting in our tents for the rain to stop. There was some good-natured hazing. One of the leaders told me his cot was too short and asked me to go find the cook and ask for a cot stretcher. The cook sent me to another source. It was only after about the fourth iteration, that it dawned on me that there was no such thing as a cot stretcher.

In my second year, the camp leader looked at my record, and said, "Shame on you." I was still a tenderfoot. So I became more energetic and started earning merit badges. But I never advanced beyond second-class Scout because I couldn't meet the swimming requirement for promotion to first-class. Or maybe the underlying problem was that I didn't have the drive to keep working my way up in a hierarchical system.

Was this a character defect? It would be several decades before I would read the magnificent C. S. Lewis essay "The Inner Ring," but I was already collecting experiences that would enable me to understand its message. The purpose of the Inner Ring is the pleasure of keeping other people out. But getting in doesn't do you any good. Every Inner Ring has another ring inside it, he warned in a lecture at King's College, University of London, in 1944. Inside the formal structure of any hierarchy, you can find a more important informal structure where the real decisions are made. And inside that is yet another structure. Striving for it is like trying to penetrate the skin of an onion, and "the quest of the Inner Ring will break your hearts unless you break it."[7]

I would encounter that very thing over and over again. Back in high school, music would lead to my next painful failure to penetrate an Inner Ring. Wayne Snodgrass chose the best high school musicians to play popular music in an elite group, "The Stardusters," whose theme song was the Hoagy Carmichael standard. I never qualified. But at least I made the marching band and could perform at halftime in football games when we multitasked by making music while marching in odd formations that spelled things. In both band and Scouts, I learned the essentials of military drill, and liked the precision of coordinated activity.

There was another benefit. Sitting back in the third-cornet section, playing mostly harmony instead of the melody, I learned to appreciate music. Maybe it was the location, being surrounded by the music. Or maybe it was the participation, being so much more than a passive listener, hearing my sounds and the sounds of others creating something greater than the sum of the parts. I learned that you don't have to be good at music to enjoy it – especially if you play loudly. I have always been grateful to Wayne Snodgrass for never discouraging me.

My teachers evidently never expected me to attend college because they routed me into the general curriculum rather than collegiate. Or it might have been my fault because I indicated a strong interest in taking wood shop and mechanical drawing. I wanted to deal with things as well as ideas. The only foreign language offered was Latin, perhaps on the theory that it would prepare us to learn a variety of languages later on. Translating Caesar was like solving a puzzle, and I enjoyed it for a while. Ruth Raynolds, the English teacher, taught us to diagram sentences, and I loved the logic and symmetry of assuring a home for every dependent clause. I thought of Miss Raynolds decades later, when I read in the *Miami Herald*, "Armless and headless, searchers found the body in the swamp." It was for her class that I read *The Autobiography of William Allen White*, learning about Emporia, my parents' college town, and the newspaper business at the same time.

But my favorite was Blanche Perkins, who was in charge of speech, drama, and journalism. I tried out for every one of her plays, tried to participate in every publication, and she gave me some challenging parts, for example the Russian dance instructor in *You Can't Take It with You*. And I loved hamming it up in her speech class. Not naturally outgoing, I found that the role-playing in speech class let me step out of my quiet persona. It also improved my mood.

By 1944, the year I turned 14, we were following the war news closely. Ernie's letters were coming by V-mail – photo copied and reduced to 4 by 5 inches to minimize the weight. On August 12, he wrote to my mother:

I know there is little use in telling you and Bige I'm in Guam because Bige is so up on the news he probably knows more about where we landed and what we have been doing than us guys right here.

The situation is well in hand, and I've been neither scratched nor sick, so I feel pretty lucky. ...

And on October 9: *By the way, you asked me if I drive a jeep yet. No, never did after I left my old outfit. My job has been lugging that damn automatic rifle ever since I hit this outfit. Bige can probably tell you all about it. It's a nice thing to have when things get bad, but heavier than hell to lug over hills all day long.*

Guam marks the boundary between the North Pacific Ocean and the Philippine Sea, so my father could probably guess what lay ahead. General Douglas MacArthur was about to keep his promise to return to the Philippines. We saw the pictures in Life Magazine of the general wading ashore on the island of Leyte on October 20, 1944. Ernie was encouraged by that news, and his thoughts turned to home.

October 24: *Well, another birthday came and left me since I've been in. I had them in rather strange places, don't you think? I spent this one on KP. No it wasn't quite as nice as the one I had while on my furlough. Do you remember it?*

To be honest, though, I never get homesick like I used to. ... Every place I've been, there has been one picture stand out more beautiful than the rest. Ask Bige if he can remember one evening when I went home with you two in the fall while you were still on the farm. We were walking back just at sunset, all those white-faced calves on that green piece south of the house. I really enjoyed that winter more than any I can remember. ...

Bige, don't you think you should be sending another letter? Yours are the real letters. (I think Hilda knows what I mean). ... There's something about a letter from one of the old school that gives a guy a lift. I know you're not hardly old enough to be my dad, but there are times when I think you're wise enough.

And a week later, in a letter to Vern Sizemore, a family friend who had left the ministry to enter the poultry business, Ernie recalled his own efforts at raising chickens.

October 31: *How about the New Hampshire Reds, are there any flocks in the county at all? I had my best luck with them as winter broilers. Dreaming about those days makes a guy really wish this was all over with. Also makes one wonder why and how he always took so much for granted.*

It takes a few nights on guard in a foxhole, with the night black as tar and raining so hard you must bail out with your

helmet, to make a man really appreciate the beautiful sunrise.
Believe it or not, we spent one of those nights in a little clearing
where there were a few native shacks. An old hen had some
baby chicks somewhere near. As I took my turn at sleeping, I
could hear them. I dreamed I was home and was having trouble
with my brooder stove, and the chicks were too cold. It worried
me, so I woke up. It was a nice dream anyway.

Things unfolded swiftly after that. Ernie's division, the 77th, was assigned to the west coast of Leyte, opposite the original MacArthur landing. Its initial objective was capturing the city of Ormoc, and it landed south of there on December 7, 1944. I'm sure my parents were following those details, which were well reported in the newspapers, but I can remember no special concern then. The riflemen of the 77th Division went ashore unopposed and moved north along the coast while Ernie's regiment, the 305th, guarded the rear. Then they encountered strong opposition at Camp Downes, a prewar constabulary post on a hilltop overlooking Ormoc. Ernie's letters stopped.

On Friday, January 12, 1945, I was walking home from school and just passing the Sixth Street Grocery when I saw my younger brother John coming to meet me. "Ernie was killed," he said. I was disbelieving. "Don't you mean wounded?" I asked foolishly. "No," he said. "Killed."

The telegram had been delivered to the Morrison farm that morning:

The Secretary of War desires me to express his deep regret that
Private First Class Ernest R. Morrison was killed in action on
10 December on Leyte. Confirming letter follows.

That was all we would know for a while.

We would later learn that the 77th Division's casualties were light as it approached the city. Ernie used his automatic rifle, a much better one than the French-made piece that my father carried in the previous war, to cover the extreme right flank of a front that encountered heavy machine gun fire.

The citation for his Bronze Star Medal tells the rest of the story:

With outstanding courage and zeal, he advanced to within 25 yards of an enemy gun, knocking it out. While executing this heroic act, Private Morrison was mortally wounded. Inspired by his heroism, his squad swept forward.

Ormoc fell on the same day.

The medal was given to my grandmother on Memorial Day 1945 at the nearest federal military installation, which happened to be the German prisoner-of-war camp at Concordia. We looked at the directional signs in German as we were escorted to the commander's office. I would read about that camp, decades later, when a German graduate student of mine based his thesis on the Concordia camp's German-language newspaper. It was written and edited by the prisoners, and they were given broad discretion over its content to prepare them for the freedom of speech they would enjoy in their eventual postwar democracy back home.[8]

Mae Morrison was asked to make a decision. Her son's body could be brought home to Linn for burial in the family plot, it could go to a national cemetery in the USA, or it could be left in the Philippines for interment in the American cemetery to be constructed there. She chose to leave him in the land where he fell, and I quietly promised Ernie's spirit that some day I would visit his grave.

John and Philip Meyer, 1944

Mae Morrison, 1945

Historic events were piling up rapidly that spring of my high school freshman year. Hap Rose's neighborhood grocery store was at the halfway point on my new *Dispatch* route, and I was stopping there for my usual snack on April 12, 1945. The radio was on, and I heard a news bulletin. President Roosevelt was dead. I looked down at my half-empty bag of papers, acutely aware of the power of a news delivery technology that was faster than a boy on a bike.

The war in Germany ended on May 8. One of the high school boys celebrated by producing a firecracker that he had been hoarding for the occasion and setting it off on top of a locker in the hall. By then, I had a steadier after-school job, general help-out person at a new food store that specialized in locally produced fruits and vegetables. Summer came, and I was visiting my Cozine cousins on the Meyer farm on August 6 when the *Topeka Daily Capital* brought news of the bombing of Hiroshima. In an odd piece of interpretive reporting, a wire service writer noted that atomic energy was the same power source that fueled the sun, and, since the sun had a sacred connotation in Japanese culture, it would give us a propaganda advantage. Interesting, but the writer had missed the point of nuclear war.

A Japanese surrender was anticipated, and we were back home in Clay Center, waiting expectantly by the radio, when the announcement came. Now we could look forward to the end of wartime shortages, food and gas rationing, and the retooling of America's productive capacity – especially in Detroit. We wondered what the postwar cars would look like.

5.   High school journalism

Material circumstances improved for everyone after the war. We acquired our first refrigerator. We got our first telephone, a candlestick model that sat on a small table in the dining room. My father switched from roll-your-own cigarettes to tailor-mades. And there was an unexpected blessing. Howard, my mother's long-lost brother, came home. He had been gone for 24 years, and she leaped into the air when he came walking down the road to the old farm.

Howard had drifted west to Oregon, worked as a nurse's aide in a military hospital during the war, married and divorced. He had heard of his father's death by heart attack, worried that he might somehow have been responsible, and was reluctant to face the family on that account. But the end of the war seemed like a good time for starting over, and he quickly found work at a military hospital in Leavenworth, Kan.

Meanwhile, I was discovering that journalism, on the school paper, *The Promoter*, and the yearbook, *Tiger Roar*, was my favorite part of high school. It gave me a way of participating that was one degree removed from actually participating. The role of observer made me a legitimate critic of any Inner Ring and freed me from the pain of striving for it. As a way of moving more fully into the observer role, I decided to teach myself photography.

I started with a how-to book from the library and a cheap, small-format roll-film camera. A local radio repair shop, branching out, started serving photo hobbyists by stocking a few supplies, and I quickly learned how to develop roll film by dipping it up and down in a tray under a safelight in the basement after dark. I made contact prints with a printing frame. I purchased a very cheap enlarger from Johnson Smith and Co., a Detroit mail order house that specialized in selling novelties to kids in my demographic, and quickly found that its single-element lens did indeed make pictures bigger, but at the cost of losing detail.

I needed better equipment. First, I built a contact printer, using scrap lumber and taking tinfoil from one of my father's cigarette packs for the electrical contacts. This was not quite as dangerous as sticking my finger in the electric socket, but it was close. And I upgraded to a flash camera with a larger format.

My parents noticed that while I was making pictures, I was not hanging around the pool hall, and they encouraged me in the new hobby. Soon, with a little help, I was able to acquire an adjustable 35-mm. camera and buy a real enlarger with a good lens. My father bought some drywall and two-by-fours and built a darkroom in the southeast corner of the basement so that I would not have to wait for sundown to be creative.

High school is a place where very long-term habits are formed, and how my parents protected me from the dangerous ones is still a mystery. But postponing my driver education was one strategy. The country kids could get restricted licenses at 14 for the purpose of driving to and from school. An unrestricted license was possible at 16. My driver training was delayed for a painfully long period, and I was a senior by the time I got my first license. The lack of a family car was one inhibition. But, looking back, I can appreciate that it also meant postponing risk – not such a bad idea.

Perhaps the constant moving made me immune to social pressure. Or perhaps I was gifted with the imagination to factor the possible long-term consequences into some of the important decisions. Eventually, I would smoke, drink, and chase women, but not in high school. The benefits were transitory, the costs unknowable.

There was also the pietistic aspect of our religious history. The Episcopalians were liberal, but my family's habits remained more like those of the Evangelicals. My father smoked, but there was never alcohol in our house. The health consequences of tobacco were suspected, but not proven. And there were plenty of visible examples of the pain that alcohol abuse could bring. Kansas was dry at that time, but we had our town drunks. Some were old guys who would buy vanilla extract at the grocery store for the alcohol content. Bootlegging was fairly open, and 3.2 beer was legal. I didn't like the idea of loss of control or depending on a substance. If I got along without it, why even open the door to the possibility of trouble?

To gain social standing in high school, I realized, you had to do only one thing well. My photography skills were soon obvious enough to gain me the privilege of skipping some study halls to help P. V. Allen, the chorus director, make group photos for the yearbook. At one point, I shot some color slides of the Stardusters in concert on a beautifully decorated stage. I set up a tripod in the balcony of the auditorium, used a slow shutter speed and captured the lighting effects in a fairly dramatic way.

That led to a summer job offer. My work attracted the attention of Don Wilson, who ran Clay Center Engraving Co., with his father and his uncle, and they taught me how half-tone images were reduced to little dots and etched into zinc printing plates with nitric acid. I also ran the hand-fed printing press and used the shop's pre-anniversary Speed Graphic press camera, my first experience with larger negatives. And it turned out that Wilson was an early adopter of new technology, having acquired a small, rotary offset press.

"It's based on the principle that oil and water won't mix," he said.

The offset plate was flexible, and we transferred the image

to it by a photographic process as we did for zinc etchings. This image was oily. The plate was wrapped around a drum, and the press rotated it first through a water bath and then across an ink roller. Water stuck to the plate everywhere there was no oily image, and the ink would not stick to the water so it remained only on the image. It was thus transferred from the plate to a rubber blanket wrapped around a cylinder, and then to sheets of paper.

Offset printing was faster, cheaper, and higher quality than letterpress. The principle had been discovered in the 18th Century, but newspapers would not begin to adopt it on a large scale until well into the 1960s when its synergy with computer typesetting made it irresistible. (The *Miami Herald's* first offset edition was published in June 1976.) But, as far back as 1947, I could see that postwar publishing technology was not going to be a steady-state enterprise.

This exposure to more technology led me to talk about a possible career in photography, which alarmed my parents. To them, it seemed too much like a blue-collar trade, almost a regression back to the farm.

My cousin Ralph Cozine in Greenleaf contracted the enthusiasm from me, for which Aunt Mamie was grateful, because she was as anxious as my parents to keep her son out of the pool hall. Our shared interest in photography would be relevant to both our college majors, his in art, mine in journalism.

Gasoline rationing ended with the war, and the Rev. Mr. Newton, who had come to Clay Center as a deacon and been ordained to the priesthood there on November 11, 1943, took advantage of it. He found a way to provide the teenagers in the congregation with some summer travel experience. Arranging to borrow a cabin in Allen's Park, Colo., not far from Estes Park, he led a caravan of cars in his 1939 Nash on the 400-mile journey across the prairie to a mountain adventure. We drove after dark to avoid the Kansas daytime heat, and, by switching drivers frequently, we made the westward crossing in one night and early morning.

Those summer trips became regularized, and Mr. Newton's performance was later topped by his successor, Sidney A. Hoadley, who took us to his home state of Wyoming. He drove a small group of us, Lee Sheppeard and I plus six girls, in his Ford station wagon towing a trailer packed with our luggage and a surplus Army tent. The load was too much for the Ford's tires, and we suffered frequent blowouts, which only added to the excitement, and we ended by camping in Jackson Hole in the shadow of the Grand Tetons.

The problem of paying for my college education remained unsolved for a long time. Financial aid was scarce in those days, and I was, on the whole, no more than a weak B student. My mother had a recurring fantasy in which some affluent professional in town would notice my obvious talent and offer to sponsor my education. But my talent was not that obvious. Finally, after the war, when new cars were being sold again, John Mouse, the owner of the local Ford agency, offered my father a job as service manager – with a salary equal to what he was getting at Marshall's plus a commission. "This could take care of a lot of things," Bige said, meaning, primarily, my college expenses.

But it didn't work out. After my father had left Marshall's and established himself as the Ford service manager, a job he could do well because he knew how to repair cars himself, Mouse changed the rules. "Sorry," he said. "No more commissions."

That setback turned out to be a blessing, because Bige became desperate enough to take some risks. He decided to go into business for himself. The starting date is revealed in his old ledger, which my brother has preserved: Sept. 2, 1947. All of us, father, mother, brother, and I, went to the Morrison farm, where Uncle Wilmer wrote a check for a loan of $3,000 (equal to more than $29,000 in constant 2010 dollars). Then we made our way north to Fairbury, Nebr., where a dealer was offering some war surplus vehicles. My father purchased three: two 1941 Dodge command cars and a 1940 three-quarter ton Dodge truck. He paid $920 each for the cars and $822.84 for the truck. I don't remember exactly how we shuttled them all back to Clay Center, but I do remember driving one of the cars.

It was a brilliant move. Detroit production was still far behind postwar demand, and the shortage pushed the value of a good, clean 1941 or 1942 used car to an amount higher than the list price of a new one. Once he realized that, Bige put together two things that he had learned from his past. One was the example of his father making money by trading cattle on the basis of his superior skill at judging them. My dad was a superior judge of cars. The second was the realization that Detroit's bias in favor of the big-city dealers, which had frustrated him when he sold cars in the Depression years, was back in play. This time it meant that the main flow of postwar production was going to the cities, leaving pent-up demand in remote places like Clay Center, Kan.

The people who bought new cars in Kansas City were trading in the vehicles that they had treated with great care during the war years because they had no way of knowing when they could get new ones. So Kansas City had a surplus of good used cars, and Clay Center had a shortage. Bige added value to those used cars by screening them in Kansas City, finding relative bargains, and taking them to willing buyers back in Clay Center.

To sell used cars, you need a lot for parking and displaying them. Bige found one on South Sixth Street. It was next to an independent repair shop started by two mechanics who had formerly worked at Marshall's. The arrangement gave him working space for sprucing up the merchandise and a desk for closing deals. And – this to me was the really good part – it gave us permanent access to an automobile. The downside was that as soon as I would fall in love with a particular car, somebody would buy it. My all-time favorite was a 1939

Plymouth convertible with a rumble seat. It was faded and dented when Bige took it as a trade-in, but he had the body restored and replaced the top, making it look like new. It sold all too quickly.

And I honed my driving skills by traveling with my father on his buying trips. He developed good long-term relationships with the city dealers, and they were glad to have their used-car inventories thinned. We began to feel relatively prosperous.

6.   Off to college

When the time came to choose a college, I knew that my first choice wasn't feasible. On July 19, 1947, *Colliers'* magazine had published an article on the University of Missouri School of Journalism, which was unique because it produced, not just a campus paper, but also the daily *Missourian* for the entire town of Columbia in competition with a privately owned daily. That gave students a concentrated dose of reality to go with the theoretical aspects of mass communication. And from the magazine article, it was clear that the students were having fun. The title of the article was, "City with No Secrets," and it depicted a crowd of enthusiastic student reporters enjoying themselves by poking into everybody's business.

But my family could handle neither the out-of-state tuition nor the transportation costs. Moreover, there were two pretty good journalism schools in Kansas. The University of Kansas at Lawrence might have had the better program, but my best friend in high school, Lee Sheppeard, was going there, and he planned to major in journalism and try out for the school paper. I didn't like the idea of competing with him. We were both talented, he got better grades, and the place surely wasn't big enough to hold us both. Moreover there was the start of a family tradition at Kansas State. My aunt Gladys Meyer had gone there as had my Army engineer cousin Walt Meyer. And it was only 39 miles from Clay Center. If I got hungry, I could hitchhike home for a meal.

Kansas policy at the time gave every graduate of a Kansas

high school automatic admission to the state's colleges and universities. That meant large freshman classes that were held to high performance standards in order to thin out the entering class's population by the second year.

My cousin Ralph chose K-State for much the same reasons, and we headed to Manhattan together to find housing and jobs. Our first stop was Gene Guerrant's photo studio in the basement of the Palace Drug Store across the street from the campus. I was hired on the spot because Guerrant had decided to go into the photoengraving business as a sideline and set up a shop in the basement of his home. He had acquired relatively inexpensive Tasope equipment, including a very basic eight-by-10 view camera mounted on a rail for close-up copying to film through a half-tone screen. "Tasope" was an acronym for The Aurora School of Photo-Engraving in Aurora, Mo. With my experience at the Clay Center Engraving Co., I could be of immediate help. Ralph had to wait a few days longer, but he got hired, too, as a darkroom technician, for which his hobby work well qualified him. His job would also include taking pictures at fraternity and sorority parties, submitting proofs, taking orders, and doing the final processing. Guerrant was a Manhattan minister's son, K-State alumnus, and ebullient free spirit who had served in the war as a naval aviator.

My cousin and I took a room together, the closed-in sun porch over the garage of a bungalow on Pierre Street. It was on a bus route, and the walking distance was reasonable. We paid $10 each in rent, but had to share a bathroom with the landlord, who was a linotype operator for the *Manhattan Mercury-Chronicle,* and his wife. We also got the use of their telephone, a candlestick model on a table at the foot of the stairs.

More students lived in the basement, all of them veterans. We were near the peak of GI enrollment, three years after the war. They weren't called "the greatest generation" then, but maturity of those veterans still in school greatly enhanced the social and intellectual climate. But that came at a cost. The veterans drove the gender ratio, already normally skewed male, to an appalling six to one. This meant that enjoying the company of women was going to take some strategic planning. Not only did the vets drive up the competition quantitatively, they had a qualitative advantage as well. The G. I. Bill made them relatively affluent, and every time you saw a nifty convertible cruising down Poyntz Avenue, you could be pretty sure that it was driven by a still-single veteran. Ralph and I sat on a park bench watching the variety of makes and models one evening and tried to evaluate their relative merits. My favorite: a flashy yellow Dodge roadster.

We knew there were fraternities, and that they had something to do with social life. Otherwise, we were puzzled about their purpose and how one became a member. A clue to the former question came from Robert M. Hutchins who took some time off from his post at the University of Chicago to give a lecture at K-State that first semester. The auditorium could not handle the attendance, so his voice was piped out to those of us sprawling on the lawn.

"Football and fraternities," Hutchins said, "are designed to make college palatable for those who shouldn't be there."[9]

That made sense to me, but I eventually figured out another function, not quite so harsh as the Hutchins concept. The purpose of fraternities was to preserve the social stratification of the small Kansas towns that fed most of the college's enrollment. Everyone was aware of the hierarchy: Beta Theta Pi and Pi Beta Phi were the top fraternity and sorority respectively. Those lacking their own houses and/or national affiliation were at the bottom, and there was a fairly obvious ordering between. The temptation of the Inner Ring was appearing again.

Guerrant made an observation about fraternities that I would later compare to C. S. Lewis's warning. "If you can't belong to the best one," he said, "there's no point in belonging to any of them." This was a moot issue for me in my freshman year, but later, as my contributions to student publications became

67

visible, I started to get dinner invitations from low-to-midlevel fraternities, which led to offers of membership. The problem with joining, I reasoned, was that it would immediately mark me at a fixed level in the basic social structure. If one were at the top of that structure, that would be no problem. But Guerrant was right. Rather than be pigeonholed at a defined place lower in the hierarchy, I would rather remain undefined, an enigma. One could even imagine that situation appealing to a certain interesting subset of women for whom the mystery would give me an advantage in the dating marketplace.

Phil Meyer as college freshman, 1948

And it was a very serious marketplace. Women in the late 1940s had been liberated to some extent by the need to fill in for men in the workplace during the war, as the famous "Rosie the Riveter" poster illustrated. My own mother went to work part-time in our neighborhood grocery store, taking phone orders and serving customers, with no objection from my father. Without the war, he would have considered it shameful to have a working wife. But by 1948, the old notion of keeping women in their place was regaining its traction. Some women, not all, came to college for the primary purpose of finding a man and had no qualms about saying so.

This situation made it even harder for a freshman, non-veteran to get a date. The vets were more mature, would be more employable upon graduation, and were therefore more desirable marriage prospects.

The notion of important matters like gender relationships as market-based came from my reading of libertarian literature left lying around Dugan's Barbershop in Clay Center. It was there, from Henry Hazlitt's *Economics in One Lesson,* that I learned about Frederich Hayek's *Road To Serfdom* and the logic of Adam Smith's hidden hand. And, while I didn't have the word for it at the time, I was "positioning" myself in the dating market for brand distinctiveness, something that the makers of laundry detergents and other marketing-intensive products would do two decades later.

But first, I needed a way to meet people outside the classroom. Eventually, student publications would fill that need, but for starters I found something quicker. The Canterbury Club, the college Episcopalians, met for dinner and "fellowship in the kitchen" every Sunday night at St. Paul's Church in downtown Manhattan. It was a happy, eclectic mix from cool kids to the totally dorky. Ann Cleavinger, who would later become the first wife of North Carolina Coach Dean Smith, was a Pi Phi and one of the cool kids. Thinking about that wonderful group is painful today because of the way I would later let it down.

K-State was a land-grant college, meaning that it benefitted from the Morrill Act of 1852, which gave federal lands to the states in return for building colleges that offered programs in engineering, agriculture, and home economics. In that spirit, the journalism major was called "industrial journalism," later changed to "technical journalism." Another side effect of the Morrill Act was a military training program that was made compulsory for male students for the first two years. To my surprise, I was excused from ROTC and the physical education requirement in my first semester because the qualifying physical examination turned up a suspicious sound in my heart that was backed up by a deviant pattern in the electrocardiogram. I felt fine, but Student Health decided to keep me out of both ROTC and physical education for the first semester. In the second semester, having demonstrated that I could function normally, I enrolled in both classes and sent a report home:

February 7, 1949: *One side of my heart is little weak, but it isn't serious. As for ROTC and phys ed, I'm to go to both for a week or 10 days, then if I think it's too strenuous, I can drop one or both. It seems that it isn't bad enough for me to keep out if I don't want to, but still, if I'd rather not take gym and ROTC, I don't have to.*

The doctor said that the evidence on the cardiograph alone wasn't enough to make me stay out of these activities. He says that we'll have to go on how I feel and how it affects me. In other words, the ultimate decision of whether I shall take gym and/or ROTC is mine to make.

I continued to feel okay, so, not wanting to miss anything, I continued in both classes.

Milton S. Eisenhower, brother of the general, was president of the college, and he addressed the assembled freshmen. For those who had not yet made a career choice, he suggested a major in journalism because its curriculum included a broad general education. He was an admirer of James Bryant Conant, president of Harvard, who stressed patriotism, informed citizenship, and the liberal arts. At K-State, Eisenhower sought to borrow an idea from Harvard with a new curriculum feature, a collection of four "comprehensive courses" that, combined, covered "the entire field of human knowledge." The four courses were Man and the Social World, Man and the Biological World, Man and the Physical World, and Man and the Cultural World. Each included large lectures and small discussion sections. Students were expected to take all those in fields not covered by their majors. Journalism students, however, were required to take all four of them. I was impressed.

This postwar period was also a time when ability and aptitude testing were becoming fashionable. We took a battery of tests, from the Strong Vocational Interest Inventory to the Minnesota Multi-Phasic Personality Inventory. The Strong test had separate versions for men and women because its creators did not expect males and females to be interested in the same careers. The college gave me a report that combined all the tests into ratings of my fitness for various endeavors. It said I would be average in business or engineering, good in artistic, medical, or technical fields, and excellent in social services, law, or writing.

Those last three things, I said in a letter to my mother on September 22, 1948, "add up perfectly to one thing: journalism. Good deal."

The test that I liked most was the English Placement Exam, which required writing an autobiographical essay right there in the auditorium. I was careful not to start mine with a cliché, e.g. "I was born in ..." And that might be what made it stand out enough to place me out of freshman English and into advanced composition. The central project for that course was a 2,000-word research paper on a topic of one's choice. To save myself trouble, I wrote on the comparative advantages of capitalism over other economic forms, drawing on my readings in Dugan's Barbershop. I was also influenced by my habit of listening to the news filtered through the right-wing lens of Fulton Lewis Jr., a Washington-based broadcaster. The teacher, a graduate assistant named Isabel Powers, loved it, and awarded my first collegiate "A." Unfortunately, to discourage plagiarism, the department required us to hand all the papers back after reading the instructors' comments. And then it destroyed them. Mrs. Powers expressed regret that she had not warned me so that I could have made a carbon. I might have used Guerrant's equipment to make a photocopy, but it seemed not worth the trouble.

The other memorable first-semester freshman course was introductory logic, taught by a farmer-philosopher named Cecil Miller. Its textbook was the only one that I saved from that period: Edwin Leavitt Clarke's *The Art of Straight Thinking: A Primer of Scientific Method for Social Inquiry*. It did not bother me that the book was published in 1929, before I was born. This sort of knowledge was eternal. It appealed to my sense that life was a puzzle to be solved. Indeed, my father would later say, "Life is just a series of problems. If you enjoy solving problems, you will enjoy life." He obviously did, and, without being fully aware of it, I was already making that my code.

The Clarke text was supplemented with Miller's own collection of problems in deductive reasoning. He taught while sitting at a desk in a large, sunny classroom in the south wing of Anderson Hall, the venerable limestone building that houses the administration and is still the symbolic icon of the university.

But the comprehensive courses were something else. They might have worked at Harvard with its spellbinding lecturers, but K-State just didn't have the horses. Man and the Physical World and Man and the Biological World were bearable, but Man and the Social World, the one in which I should have been the most interested, was a disaster. The course was broad and shallow, the lecturers intent on giving us facts without much conceptual framework to tie them together. If it had been based on empirical social science such as Clarke advocated, it might have been interesting. Maybe the lecturers needed a better understanding of the great books they were discussing. Or perhaps it was just the need to cover such vast territory in so little time. And the discussion section! Because of the swollen enrollment caused by the return of the veterans, K-State had to offer both 7 a.m. and night classes. For the recitation section of Man and the Social World, I drew a really dull teaching assistant in a class that met at 7 a.m. in the basement of East Agricultural Hall, at what was then the north boundary of the campus.

By this time, I had the use of a car most of the time, borrowed from my father's lot, and I worked out a survival strategy. I would wake up to the alarm at 6:40 a.m., pull on a sweat suit over my pajamas, don sneakers and drive to East Ag and park illegally next to a side door, trusting that the parking enforcers would not be up that early. I would sit glassy-eyed in the back row. And as soon as the class was over, I drove home and fell back into bed.

"Gosh," said journalism classmate Everett Browning when I explained my strategy, "it's not much worse than getting up to go to the bathroom!"

Man and the Social World provided one priceless benefit, however. I wrote a sophomoric but satirical piece about it and submitted it to the Collegian. Marvin Hammer, the war veteran who was editor that semester, liked it and gave it good display. It caused a nice buzz on campus, even the Social World instructors said they were amused, and I got an early start at being a visible campus journalist.

Reporting and writing came easily. I was nervous on my first reporting assignment, which required seeking out and interviewing the head of the Department of Speech. I felt more at ease when I reminded myself of the might, power, majesty and glory of the newspaper that sent me. I was in what Stanley Milgram, the great innovator in experimental psychology, would later call "a state of agency." In other words, it wasn't really little, timid, insignificant me asking questions of the high and mighty, it was the newspaper! That took some of the pressure away.

So I volunteered for both the newspaper and the yearbook. By the first semester of my junior year, I would be on the masthead of the *Collegian* as photo editor and on the *Royal Purple* staff as a chapter editor.

It was also in my sophomore year that I started to date college women. As part of our land-grant practical education, we had to learn to set type by hand. There was an attractive blonde, a junior transfer, in that class, and she belonged to one of the high-tier sororities, way out of my league. But one day, after class, I was getting into one of my father's used cars, a 1939 Hudson with questionable brakes, and she saw me and stuck out her thumb. So I gave her a ride home, and that led to my first date.

If you are selling something in a buyer's market, it helps to plan ahead. And I found out that I could get dates, despite the unfavorable gender ratio, if I asked far enough in advance. So I developed a routine. It was to seek dates at least six or more weeks ahead of time. That was one third of a semester! Too self conscious to use the landlord's telephone, I would walk or drive to the Palace Drug Store, and use one of its pay phones. I chose what I knew would be quiet time in the sorority house, after dinner and before lights out. K-State still considered itself *in loco parentis*, particularly regarding women, and life in their dormitories and houses was well regulated, which made them easy to find. The downside was the strict closing hours, 10 on week nights and 1 a.m. for Friday and Saturday dates. Such regimentation led to some crowding on sorority house lawns. If you took a woman home before the last minute, her sisters would assume it had been a bad date, so everyone took pains to show up in the last quarter hour.

My strategy worked pretty well, even getting me dates for major college functions like the Royal Purple Ball or the Homecoming Dance. Our conduct on all of these dates was painfully decorous, and I could not afford more than two or three per semester.

Now here's the sad part. There were lots of smart, attractive women who, for one reason or another, did not belong to sororities. I was too insecure to ever ask one of them for a date. I thought I was thumbing my nose at the system by dating across the social boundary, showing those fraternity boys that I could go out with their women. Only years later did it dawn on me that I had compromised myself and validated their system by paying any attention at all to that arbitrary social dividing line. In an odd, perverted way, I had been a snob. I should have been smart enough to give sorority membership a weight of zero in my market-influenced calculations. And as a believer in the power of the free market, I should have known not to risk market failure by limiting my choices.

I outsmarted myself in other ways. Another of the land-grant considerations was a requirement that every journalism major complete a technical option, a set of courses in a practical field such as agronomy or civil engineering. That plan played to K-State's strengths. But as I scoured the fine print in the catalog, I found a loophole. Radio broadcasting could count as a technical option.

It worked because radio was part of the speech department, outside the journalism department. So I signed up for Survey of Broadcasting early on. The professors who supervised registration were dismayed. You'll end up with too many journalism-related courses, they said. You need to learn something besides journalism, something to report and write about. I quieted them by claiming that I aspired to be the Washington correspondent for *Broadcast Magazine*, the radio industry's trade journal.

The sound of Prof. George Arms, opening his first lecture in his broadcaster's voice, is still clear in my mind: "I can remember (suspenseful pause) when there was no radio."

Wow! This guy was old. But, decades later, I would pull that trick on my own students: "I can remember (pause) when there was no television." And I enjoyed the same reaction.

I became a disc jockey for the student station. It used the campus electrical wiring for its antenna. "Wired wireless," it was called. And reception was good on campus and up to four or five blocks away, not so good beyond that. I loved sitting at the control board, cuing records, ad-libbing introductions, taking requests over the phone. Broadcasting could be a good career, and I thought about my hero, Fulton Lewis Jr., and his 15 minutes a day of right-wing commentary. Maybe I could do that.

In the middle of my sophomore year, in February 1950, I wrote a triumphant letter home. My budget of $800 for the academic year was working out exactly right: $75 a month for food and lodging, $62.50 per semester for fees (there was no tuition for in-state students). Only years later did I appreciate what a strain that was for my parents. They were still postponing their dream of home ownership. But college was a bargain compared to today's cost. The inflation adjustment for that sum of $800 in 1950 would take the total to $7,242 in 2010 dollars, close to what K-State charged for tuition and fees alone in 2010-2011.

The money I earned working for Guerrant covered my books and supplies, some meals, walking-around money, and fuel for the car that I had on loan from my father's lot.

Once into journalism courses and the chance to write for the Collegian, I quickly identified my favorite professors. They were both young, both starting their careers: Merrill Samuelson, tall, quiet Army veteran, deliberate in his manner, and John W. McReynolds, a moody, sometimes flamboyant intellectual who was 4-F in the war due to episodic bouts with a form of multiple sclerosis. Neither had the PhD, both had newspaper experience.

McReynolds had joined the faculty, just out of Chapel Hill with a master's degree in political science that he spent four years earning. His thesis was on the political thought of the Italian jurist, Giambattista Vico (1668-1744). McReynolds had an eclectic list of publications in academic journals, mostly thoughtful essays on the role of information in whatever field the journal covered. One contained an intriguing reference to the then-exotic concept of game theory, introduced by John von Neumann and Oskar Morgenstern in 1944. McReynolds' publication history so impressed the faculty that he was hired as an associate professor. His office was lined with books, many of them quite old, and, in the course of any argument, he could spot the relevant volume and pull it down to make a point in an instant. This resource would be useful when I needed philosophical backing for my approaching conflict with the college administration.

7. Becoming a newspaperman

In that spring of 1950, my sophomore year, Milton Eisenhower was offered the presidency of Penn State, and he decided to leave his alma mater. A national search led to the appointment of James Allen McCain, who had served as a Lieutenant Commander in the Navy in World War II and went directly from there to be president of the University of Montana (then called Montana State University). While holding that demanding post, he found time to prepare a 435-page dissertation and receive his doctorate in education from Stanford University in 1948. The title was "The Enlisted Selection Program of the United States Navy During World War II." I learned later that this timing had led to a rumor in Montana that the dissertation was based on plagiarism, but I eventually looked into it and found that, while he had a lot of help, there was a benign explanation.

McCain's wartime duty was officer in charge of "enlisted selection" in the Naval Training Division's Standards and Curriculum Section. His commanding officer had been a professor at Stanford. This blending of wartime service and higher education was explained by Stanford School of Education Dean A. John Bartky in a foreword to McCain's dissertation.

McCain, the dean said, ... *created and directed what is presented herein. He was the chief administrative officer of the Navy selection organization all through its activity. In this capacity he planned the development of the enlisted selection program and directed its overall operation. He either prepared or supervised preparation of all the operational manuals referred to. He initiated most of the research.*

This dissertation should be read not as a catalogue of research projects accomplished by many, but as one huge mass of individual research, controlled and functionalized by President McCain.

Like Eisenhower, McCain believed that college should provide a laboratory for citizenship with student participation in student-related decisions. But he arrived at K-State with a strong authoritarian streak, a preference for a rigid command-and-control structure, perhaps a consequence of his military experience. The postwar period was a fertile environment for authoritarianism. The war had induced a climate of conformity as Americans pulled together in the war effort. Students were not inclined to assert themselves, much less test their capacity for wielding political power. *Time* magazine dubbed us "the Silent Generation."

"Educators across the U.S. complain that young people seem to have no militant beliefs," said a Time essay in 1951. "They do not speak out for anything. Professors who used to enjoy baiting students by outrageously praising child labor or damning Shelley now find that they cannot get a rise out of the docile note-takers in their classes."[10]

One member of our generation, writing in *Time* three decades later, said, "Above all, we were the last generation to accept without question—or to pretend to accept—the traditional American values of work, order and patriotism."[11]

For a budding journalist, this situation was ideal. All one had to do to stand out from the crowd was to show the slightest trace of nonconformity or rebellion against authority. Soon enough, I would discover that McCain's authoritarian streak and my ambition were made for each other. We could generate sparks.

But first I had to find a 1950 summer job. I took a position on a work crew for the Chicago, Rock Island and Pacific Railroad. To keep my mind busy, I resolved to spend evenings and weekends trying to write and sell short fiction. I tried a short story with a surprise ending about a railroad worker. Nobody bought it. My favorite rejection slip: "We have read your manuscript, and it's not for *Esquire*."

Out on the real railroad, the task was to replace worn-out ties on the track, using pick and shovel to dig out the old tie, unfastening its spikes with a crowbar, and pulling the heavy timber out with iron tongs. We needed straw hats and long-sleeved shirts for protection from the sun. "If you can stand this work for a week," said one old-timer on the crew, "you can stand it for a hundred years."

I stood it for two weeks, and then I got a better idea.

A new requirement for journalism majors at K-State was a summer internship. In order to graduate, we needed to complete a certain number of hours actually working in journalism. I called on Harry Valentine, editor of the *Clay Center Dispatch*, explained the requirement, and he hired me. For minimum wage, then 40 cents an hour, I would report, edit, wrap papers for mailing, and do whatever else needed doing in the front office of the paper that I used to throw from a bicycle. The railroad paid better, but this would be a learning experience, and get me out of heavy lifting in the hot sun.

Mid-20th century was a good time to enter the newspaper business. In 1950, weekday household penetration for newspapers in the United States was 124 percent. The number of newspapers sold was greater than the number of households! I was convinced that I had made a great career choice.

As promised, I did a little of everything: covered the town's Class C professional baseball team, made an unsuccessful stab at selling ads, wrapped single copies for mailing, and swept out the office.

One of my daily tasks was rewriting the Associated Press

pony service. The *Dispatch* lacked the space for a full national and international report, so the AP would send a daily telegram with the half-dozen top stories of the day written in cablese, a kind of shorthand designed to maximize the information in messages that are paid for by the word. My job was to walk around the corner to the Western Union office, run by Loren and Pauline Law, pick up the daily telegram from the AP, bring it back, and turn its cryptic messages into coherent news stories under deadline. The telegram for Friday, June 30, contained life-changing news.

On the previous Sunday, Jack James, a World War II naval aviator and 1947 K-State journalism graduate, had scored a two-hour beat for United Press with a report that the North Korean People's Army had crossed the 38th parallel to attack South Korea. President Truman took pride in his ability to make quick decisions, and the American response came just five days later. It was announced in time for afternoon newspapers. As I decoded the pony-service telegram, I realized that the President had committed the United States to waging air, sea, and ground war in Asia. We had enjoyed only five years of peace since the Japanese surrender.

My draft registration card was already in my billfold. The pressure of the cold war had led Congress to set up a system for peacetime military conscription in 1948, and I registered when I turned 18 in October of that year. Now the dormant Selective Service System would be reactivated. I checked the list at the local draft board and found that the name at the top was that of Frank Obenland, who had been a few years ahead of me in high school and now worked in a local bank. Draftees were to be taken in order of age, oldest first, so I had some time. I might even finish college. Congress, recognizing the importance of having trained manpower, provided that any man called while in school would be allowed to finish his current academic year. And, at the option of the local board, college students at any level could have their inductions postponed until graduation.

America had enjoyed four productive and carefree years from 1945 to 1949. We had won the war and had a monopoly on nuclear weapons. Then in August 1949, the Soviet Union tested its first nuclear bomb, and we were no longer invincible. A master narrative took hold that communism was a centrally controlled monolith and that the North Korean action was Soviet directed. The Korean "police action," as President Truman called it, was the first application of the domino theory, that if we let the communists take one nation, they would take another and another and eventually own the world.

For my personal planning, it seemed prudent to assume that conflict on the scale of World War II or worse was inevitable, but it might take some time to build. Now there was a sense of urgency in getting the books I had always wanted to read, pursuing the college women I had admired, doubling down on my goal to become editor of the *Kansas State Collegian*. Maybe I could make it in my junior year, before the draft board noticed me. While I would not choose military service voluntarily, the prospect had its good side. When my turn came, I thought, I would wear the uniform proudly and command the respect and admiration enjoyed by the brave servicemen of the first and second world wars. I could follow the duty, honor, country code of my father and my uncle.

Registration in the fall of 1950 was in Nichols Gym. We sat at tables across from faculty advisors and wrote our course choices on IBM cards, taking care to write around the little rectangular holes that had already been punched in them. Floyd Sageser was a graduate assistant, and he sat on the other side of the table and gave me some advice. "Sign up for advanced ROTC," he said. "It's the royal road to a commission."

I wasn't sure that I would be eligible, having taken only three semesters of basic ROTC. And I was tired of wearing the uniform to class two days a week. I did not want my military and civilian lives blended, so I passed up the ROTC option.

Not long into the semester, I received a call from Sid Hoadley, the pastor in Clay Center who had enabled us to experience the wilderness in Wyoming. He was visiting Manhattan, and he invited me to lunch. We met at the cafe in the Hotel Wareham in downtown Manhattan, and he, too, had some advice:

"Get in the National Guard."

He had learned that policy makers planned to keep the Guard on the home front and that its members would get automatic exemption from the draft. But it seemed to me that if I had only a year or two left for college, it would be a distraction and a dilution of the experience to put on a uniform and attend weekly drills. I rejected that plan for the same reason that I had passed up advanced ROTC. I needed to focus on becoming editor of the *Collegian*.

For my junior year, I had good wheels. At a vigorously negotiated price of $100, saved from my *Dispatch* earnings, I bought a gorgeous 1932 Pontiac coupe with 75,000 miles on the odometer, a rumble seat, box trunk, and side-mount spare tire. It was fire-engine red, and the back window rolled down so that rumble-seat passengers could talk to the people inside. One reason that it came so cheaply was that the engine was about worn out. You could hear the pistons slapping loosely in their cylinders. To gain maximum longevity for it, I established a self-imposed speed limit of 40 miles an hour, which was a problem only on intercity trips. Women loved my little car.

Photography was the wedge that got me an early start on the *Collegian* staff. Since the paper used Guerrant's engraving service for its photos, I got to do both the creative and the production parts of the process. If a picture looked bad in the paper, I had no one but myself to blame. And I continued to write.

Editors served for a term of one semester, and as the Board of Student Publications, three students and two faculty, looked ahead to the spring 1951 semester, there were no obvious choices. So a bunch of us applied for the job. Both McReynolds and Samuelson gave me their private rankings of the candidates.

I was at the top of both their lists. And the both had the same name in second place, Dick Nichols.

Meyer with Pontiac, a K-State junior in 1951

Nichols was a senior and a latecomer to journalism, having matriculated in agriculture, and then taken journalism as a second major. He was president of the best fraternity, Beta Theta Pi, and we liked the same women. I had gained this last bit of intelligence by looking at the Greek party pictures in their processing trays in Guerrant's darkroom to see who was pairing off with whom. Nichols was also a member of Blue Key, the men's honor society, and a power broker in student politics, which were, of course, dominated by the voting discipline of the Greek organizations. And he was a veteran, having been a Naval officer in the last months of World War II.

On the day that the selection was to be made, I drove out to Pillsbury Crossing, southeast of town, for some time to reflect. It is a shallow ford on Deep Creek, made easy to cross by a natural slab of limestone that forms its bed. Downstream from the crossing is a popular swimming hole. We students liked to wash our cars by parking in the ford, walking around barefoot, and dipping our sponges in the clear water from the stream. There were a lot of alternate futures to think about. If I could make editor as a junior, being drafted wouldn't be such a big deal. At least I would have achieved my main goal.

Back in Kedzie Hall, I quickly learned the news. Dick Nichols would be the next editor. There were tears in his eyes as we shook hands. "You were my candidate, Phil," he said. And he graciously offered me a choice of staff jobs. I chose issue editor, meaning that, one day a week, I would be in charge of both layout and the daily editorial. And I got another consolation prize. Every January, the *Topeka Daily Capital* celebrated Kansas Day by allowing a team of K-State journalists to edit the paper for a day. I was chosen to lead the 32-student staff as its editor. I got to sit in the city editor's chair, assign stories, and help lay out the paper. Afterwards, I was congratulated for not getting flustered and confused when deadline approached. I never let on that I wasn't sure when the deadline was.

The *Collegian* did well under Nichols, although it did not lead him to choose journalism as a permanent career. After spending some time in broadcasting, he went into banking in his hometown and became prominent enough to be elected to Congress for the 1991-1993 term. He would have been re-elected except for an accident of timing. Reapportionment based on the 1990 census deprived Kansas of one of its five members of the House of Representatives. The Republicans who controlled the state legislature chose to sacrifice their most junior member and awarded pieces of his district to the surrounding ones. Nichols ran in one of the revised districts anyway, and lost in the Republican primary.

As issue editor for Nichols in 1951, I looked for ways to demonstrate the power of the press. My editorials were mostly rants against the notion that ours was destined to be the "silent generation." I wanted students to be activists, find a cause, have a voice in university and public affairs. My exhortations were not very well written, but the fact that I was trying to stir things up was in itself notable. For example, this from March 29, 1951:

Within the next few weeks, student politics will stage its annual drama on the campus. As usual, the drama will be highly pretentious with speeches and parades while the campus is littered with campaign signs. And, as usual, it will have little or no meaning. It is simply politics for the sake of politics.

When less than 50 students showed up for the Independent caucus, party leaders expressed concern because the student body didn't seem very excited about the elections. It may have been because the campus political system doesn't offer very much to get excited about.

Study the platform of any party on the campus during the last academic generation of four years. You will find three kinds of planks: generalities of the "against sin" variety, specific measures which had already been put into effect or were about to be put into effect regardless of the outcome of any election, and specific measures which were promptly forgotten after the election. . . .

A lot of people, myself included, have complained because the student government never seems to get anything done. But the time to start getting things done is before the election. Find a party – or start one – that will stand for something; something more *tangible than "good government," something more important that smoking in the fieldhouse or repairing Claflin Road.*

If just one party will take a side on a controversial issue, other parties will be forced to take other sides to justify their existence. Then a student will know that his vote means something. And maybe the voice of the student body will begin to gain the strength and prestige it deserves.

The problem was that I was an activist without having

much specific to be active about beyond the perennial college overemphasis on athletics. The *Collegian* took a small role in that by refusing to adopt a popular but unofficial name for the football field in Memorial Stadium. Some sports writers and broadcasters had taken to calling it "Ahearn Field" after Mike Ahearn the late, popular director of athletics. We were pretty sure that the idea for this originated with fans of Jack Gardner or maybe even Gardner himself. He was our winning basketball coach. The hidden agenda was to name the new field house, then under construction, for Gardner instead of Ahearn. But giving separate names to the field and the stadium made no sense, and it seemed to us that Gardner and his fans were overreaching.

We should have done more about college sports. K-State's football team had a popular, talented defensive lineman named Harold Robinson, an African-American from Manhattan High School. We were in the Big Seven league, which included the then segregated University of Oklahoma, and when we played there in 1950, Robinson had to stay home. We should have written angry editorials about that, but we stood silent, even though his absence helped Oklahoma humiliate us 58-0. Somebody profiled Robinson for the paper and wrote about his "watermelon smile," and nobody flinched. When he married a white student, a professor's daughter, the *Collegian* played it straight – too straight. There was no acknowledgment of the interracial nature of the marriage and their courage. There were no photographs.

But there were other opportunities that I would not miss. Inspiration for my blooming activism was reinforced from several sources. Charles Laughton, Sir Cedric Hardwick and Agnes Moorhead appeared at K-State in a reading of George Bernard Shaw's *Don Juan in Hell*, which drove me to the library to find the larger play from which it was excerpted, *Man and Superman*. I found that Shaw had included an addendum, "The Revolutionist's Handbook." It included a set of aphorisms, and my favorite was this: "Any person under the age of thirty who, having any knowledge of the existing social order, is not a revolutionary, is an inferior."

Another inspiration was Philip Wylie who in 1949 published an iconoclastic novel, *Opus 21*, that set a vigorous example of social criticism. His more famous work was the pre-war, book-length essay *Generation of Vipers*. Wylie was a wildly successful rebel that I could emulate. He attacked authority figures and social conventions in language that was clear and strong. Today, he is pretty much forgotten.

A third source of my social and political attitudes was Ayn Rand. I saw the film version of *The Fountainhead* and was charmed by the stubborn integrity of the architect who insisted on doing things his way even when only a few understood or cared. That drove me to the book and a fuller exposition of Rand's ideas. (The book in turn contributed to my appreciation of music. A Rand character expresses admiration for the third movement of Rachmaninoff's 2d Piano Concerto, so I bought the record. It is still a favorite, although I like the second movement better.) I took a similar film-to-print path with *Cyrano*, reading both the Brian Hooker translation with blank verse and another that preserved the rhyming couplets of the original French. Here again was a character with a quality that I later learned in a psychology course is called "ego strength." It was also called "functionally autonomous motivation." It signified immunity from social pressure and the ability to know oneself sufficiently well to chose a goal and follow it despite obstacles. Having started from pretty far back, but feeling some momentum from my education and career choice, I was developing a sense of personal efficacy and a tougher skin.

8. The Topeka Daily Capital

L ate in the spring 1951 semester, I applied for the editor's job again, but it was a pro forma move. The obvious choice was Lyle Schwilling, a hard-working Air Force veteran who was scheduled to graduate in December. The board felt that we both deserved to be editor, and this was Schwilling's last shot. Lyle created a new post for me, associate editor, which would give me freedom to report and comment on topics of choice. He also had a major tip for me. The editor of the *Topeka Daily Capital* was looking for a temporary hire to serve as summer replacement for its various vacationing staff members. It had tried to recruit Professor Samuelson, but he was already signed up with the *Kansas City Star*.

"Go to Topeka and talk to Jim Reed," Lyle said. "You can get that job."

So I did. Reed knew me from the Kansas Day operation, had observed my spurious calm under deadline pressure, and awarded me a summer job for $50 a week. I found a third-story room to rent in a Victorian house near Washburn University. Life was good. And then in May, in the interval between final exams and commencement, an unexpected thing happened. I got my draft notice. It said to proceed to Kansas City for a physical exam and then prepare to report for duty on September 24. If there were to be no senior year for me, at least I would still have the summer clear to be a newspaperman. And there were avenues of appeal to try.

Topeka's population was 79,000, making it by far the

largest city in which I had ever lived. The *Daily Capital* had about 60,000 paid circulation, much of it outside Topeka with a state edition that followed the Union Pacific line west to the Colorado border. Its format was broadsheet with eight columns, each two-inches wide, which, along with the 8-point type (on a 9-point slug), allowed much more information per page than our early 21st century newspapers can contain. The typical comic strip was given a space eight by two-and-a-half inches, more than twice the area allotted to a typical newspaper strip today. That space made it possible to provide detailed artwork and story-building dialog equal to that seen these days only in graphic novels. The paper was owned by former Senator Arthur Capper, who also published magazines: *Capper's Farmer* and *Household*. He had served five terms in the Senate, 1918 to 1949 and, at 84, was in poor health but still managing to make a weekly radio broadcast of news commentary that was also published on the editorial page.

The paper was among the first in the nation to enter into a joint operating agreement (JOA). The afternoon *Topeka State Journal* shared the building, the production facilities, and the business office but ownership and the news-editorial staffs were separate. That was enough competition to keep us sharp.

The newsroom had a wonderful cast of characters. City editor Newton Townsend, and his brother Robert (Bear) Townsend, a reporter, were postwar graduates of the University of Missouri School of Journalism. Bear proudly showed me his copy of "The Journalist's Creed" by the school's founder, Walter Williams. Clif Stratton, a World War I veteran, had been the Capital's Washington correspondent since 1926, but now limited himself to a column, "Clif Stratton Writes," which consisted mostly of "guest columns" lifted from *Human Events* and other conservative publications. Jim Reed, the executive editor, kept his desk out in the city room, where he could see, and be seen by, his reporters and editors. Anna Mary Murphy wrote good features and covered the schools. "And "Scoop"

Conklin covered the police beat, mostly from his phone in the newsroom, and wrote obituaries. Constance Van Natta worked on the society page, knew everybody in town, and got around energetically despite a leg brace, the consequence of childhood polio. James L. Robinson, who had a seat on the rim of the copy desk as state editor, was the hardest working of the lot. After the last deadline, he would move to an unoccupied desk in a far corner of the newsroom and work on a weekly column that he self-syndicated to small papers in central and western Kansas. Supervising this diverse crew on Jim Reed's behalf was Ward Moore, tall and bald, who reminded me of the kindly puppet maker in *Pinocchio*. He had the title of news editor and sat in the slot of the copy desk assigning stories and headlines to the copy editors. He had been lured away from the *St. Louis Post Dispatch* where he had been the telegraph editor. "Come back here, when it is time to spread your wings," he advised me. The easy mixing of ages and genders made me feel very comfortable in that fellowship. And Topeka was enough of a small town that people would wander in just to chat. Alf Landon, the former governor and 1936 presidential candidate, was a frequent visitor.

It rained a lot that summer, but I got out of the office to cover some memorable stories. One was a courthouse interview with the plaintiff's attorneys in Brown v. Board of Education, which was then being tried by a special three-judge federal court so that it could be appealed directly to the Supreme Court. That was the first time I heard the legal theory in the desegregation case. Black and white Topeka schools were equal in resources, but, Brown's attorneys were arguing, segregation, in and of itself, created inequality, a different view from that established in the leading case from 1896, Plessey v. Ferguson.

Meanwhile, a storm was brewing. We had experienced a wet spring and early summer. The rain kept falling, and the rivers were rising.

Historically, Topeka was two cities, Topeka and North

Topeka, connected by bridges across the Kaw River. (It's the Kansas River on all maps, but Kansans call it the Kaw). The river flows west to east and hugs the southern boundary of its flood plain. North Topeka, built in that flood plain, suffered a disastrous flood in 1903, and dikes were installed on the north side of the river to prevent a recurrence. No one knew if they would prove to be high enough or strong enough for what was coming in this rainy summer.

On Saturday night, June 30, I worked a late shift and then drove to my rooming house. The rain had stopped, and there was a clear midnight sky. Dozing in the room, listening to the radio, I was jolted awake by an interruption to the music. It was an appeal for volunteers to relieve the men who had worked a nine-hour shift reinforcing the North Topeka dike with sandbags. The river was still threatening to break through.

I drove to the fairgrounds, the meeting point for the small group of volunteers. Not many had been listening at that hour. We were loaded into trucks and taken to the dike where it was starting to leak near the Brickyard Bridge. Instead of relieving the sandbaggers, we joined them. A line of men nearly half a mile long stretched along the dike. It had a few gaps, and we newcomers filled them in.

Sandbags weighing 25 to 75 pounds each were unloaded from trucks at the north end of the line and passed along whenever someone spotted a leak. Passing them hand to hand was too awkward. The man at my left would drop a sandbag at my feet, and I would pick it up and drop it at the feet of the man on my right. When a leak was patched, we rested and looked at the stars until another weak spot was found.

The man on my left had gone 24 hours without sleep. He had answered the call for volunteers after driving all day from Colorado. The one on my right lived nearby. He was working to save his own neighborhood.

By dawn, the leaks were coming at more widely spaced intervals, and the line broke up. The more recent arrivals carried sandbags on our backs to the places where they were needed. At 5:30, airmen from Forbes Air Force Base relieved us.

I went home, opened my portable typewriter and pounded out a first-person story, slept a bit, then took it to the office. It earned my first page-one byline under the headline "Weary men win fight with flood." How I loved the newspaper business!

By the next weekend, the incessant rain acquired a grimmer pattern. A high-pressure ridge over the eastern Pacific ocean was blocking the normal west-to-east movement of weather. A low-pressure trough was sucking cold air from Canada to meet another movement of air, this one warm and moist from the Gulf of Mexico. They met over Kansas in what meteorologists call a warm-air advection. The moisture rose, cooled, and was condensed into more rain, which began to fall on July 9. It kept falling for four days and four nights.

But the ground in the river's basin was already saturated from the abnormally wet spring, and its creeks and rivers were swollen. On July 11, the weather bureau warned:

At Topeka, the Kansas River will crest at about 12 feet above bank-full by tomorrow evening, which will be slightly higher than the all-time record set in 1903 . . .

The present very serious situation is almost sure to become worse due to further heavy rains that are forecast to fall over Kansas, Missouri, and southern Nebraska during the next 48 hours. The floods . . . are really catastrophic.

We needed reporters everywhere. I was assigned to stand by at police headquarters, the one place where all of the information came together. The police let me sit in the radio room, notebook in hand, where I could listen to the reports coming in from the area.

Ken David was doing rewrite, consolidating reports from several sources. When the dike broke at 1:15 a.m. Thursday, water surged into the North Topeka business district. I called David, and he put a new lead on his story, and the desk gave it an eight-column headline, "Flood Breaks North Topeka Dike."

An hour later, I called in a story that forced the production department to stop the press for a page-one replate. The new front page was rearranged just enough to make room for my paragraph in boldface type atop the lead story:

BULLETIN

A second major break split the North Topeka dike shortly after 2 a.m. Thursday. A 75-yard stretch of the levee burst about 200 yards west of North Lincoln. Water poured into North Topeka from both east and west of Kansas Avenue.

When the rain finally stopped and the flood waters receded, the story shifted from a weather disaster story to a political story. The Army Corps of Engineers had three planned dams that had been authorized by Congress but were waiting in vain for the follow-up appropriations to build them. Two were on upstream tributaries of the Kaw, the Republican River at Milford, Kan., and the Blue River at Tuttle Creek north of Manhattan. The third was planned for a spot downstream from Topeka on the Delaware River at Perry, Kan. General Lewis A. Pick, chief of the Corps of Engineers, in an "I-told-you-so" announcement, declared that if those three dams had been in place, Manhattan, Topeka and Kansas City would have been spared any flood damage.

Jim Robinson, the state editor, checked that claim with some paper-and-pencil calculations that left me forever convinced of the need for journalists to collect their own evidence instead of relying solely on official spokespersons.

He collected the stream flow reports of the U.S. Geological Survey and derived the average stream flow in excess of channel capacity at Topeka. It was 213,000 cubic feet per second. Then he multiplied that number by the number of seconds during which that flow existed. It came to 147 hours. That calculation yielded the total volume of water that the dams would have needed to hold in order to avoid topping the dikes. It was 2.8 million acre feet. (An acre foot is the equivalent of an acre of water one foot deep.)

That made a page-one story because the three dams together had been designed for flood storage capacity of only 2.5 million acre feet. Moreover the total capacity of those three dams would not have been available because of runoff accumulating in the wet spring. And much of the critical rainfall had occurred below the sites of the three hypothetical dams. General Pick had gotten it wrong, and the Corps of Engineers was forced to come up with a new plan. It finally realized that three new dams would not be nearly enough and eventually made a new proposal. This one called for 22 additional dams instead of three.

Upstream from the site of every proposed dam were landowners and towns that would have to be moved to make way for the water storage space. I did not realize it at the time, but I would be following this story for years to come. And I would make a textbook example of Robinson's data-driven reporting.

Meanwhile, I still had the draft to worry about. I reported as ordered to Kansas City for the Army physical and passed. The examining physician heard my suspicious heart murmur and dismissed it as "functional," which I took to mean that my heart still worked despite the noise. I was good to go on September 24 as ordered.

So I appealed my local draft board's decision to the state board.

Under the law, if I had been called during the school year, I would qualify for an automatic postponement until the end of the academic year. But year's end was defined by commencement, and that was only three days away, giving me no more than a useless three-day postponement. The draft board could, under the law, grant a deferment until graduation, but college men in my small-town environment were already considered a privileged few, and the Clay Center board had a firm policy of granting no more than the obligatory completion of the current year.

There was an appeal process, to the state board, and I tried several ways to make a case. One opening was provided by the national Selective Service System. It created an aptitude-testing program to help local draft boards allocate the longer, good-until-graduation deferments. Test scores could be used to rule out registrants who might be hiding out on campus but weren't really college material. It was also intended to identify students with science and engineering aptitude that might be applied to national defense. By this time, I was really good at taking tests, and I aced this one, but my draft board didn't see the point of the testing program.

It was August when I exhausted my last appeal. More aggressive now, I walked from the *Daily Capital* office to Kansas Selective Service headquarters to find out why. I found a secretary who tried to comfort me by explaining that the appeal board was refusing all student appeals, and that the local board in Topeka had a policy like that of mine in Clay Center – refusal of them all. At that point, I revealed that I was a *Daily Capital* reporter. (The journalism ethics of that day were rather undeveloped.) She properly stopped talking and referred me to her boss who was equally uncommunicative. So I went to the next floor to the local board's office to try to verify directly what the secretary had told me.

I was given a book full of records and a table on which to examine them, and I worked out a tabulation system to calculate the proportion of registrants who were students, the number of student deferments, and the frequency and outcome of appeals. It looked like the job would take about two hours.

But I was only 30 minutes into the task when three men

in work clothes came in. They were followed by the Kansas deputy selective service director. The workmen picked up the table, record book, and all right out from under me, and carried it out of the building.

But I had partial data, and I took it back to the office and told City Editor Townsend what had happened. He took me off the story and gave it to George Mack, an experienced reporter on the statehouse beat.

Eventually Mack got a story, using the little bit of information that I had as a wedge and consulting multiple sources. He got the chairman of the state appeals board to confirm that it had received approximately 100 student appeals from local boards and turned them all down. And he confirmed that local boards in urban areas were more likely to give student deferments than those in rural areas – and that the aptitude tests were having little effect. The paper gave the story good play, top of page one on a Sunday. But it did not cause much of a stir.

Back home in Clay Center, my *Daily Capital* experience over, I sought the counsel of my local board's secretary, Thelma Mailen, and found her sympathetic. She made a suggestion that sent me racing to Manhattan to see Eric Tebow, the registrar at Kansas State. He then wrote a letter in support of yet another appeal that applied the board secretary's logic to my case:

1. The Selective Service rules mandated that an enrolled student be allowed to finish the academic year in which he was called.
2. I had been called the previous May, after taking my last final, which meant that I had completed the 1950-1951 academic year.
3. Upon that completion, I was, under existing college policy, automatically enrolled for the 1951-1952 academic year. And that was the year to which the mandatory draft postponement should apply.

The decision, made by the state board and routed through Local Board No. 11, came with no time to spare. "By authority of Selective Service Regulation 1632.4 (college student) your induction into the armed forces heretofore fixed for 24 September 1951 ... is hereby POSTPONED (caps in original) until May 26, 1952, at which time you will present yourself to this board for delivery for induction."

It was signed by Harry Bauer, the local chairman. Later, through unofficial sources, I learned that the deputy director of the state board, the man with whom I had the encounter over the records in Topeka, had made an inquiry to the Clay Center office. Was this the same Phil Meyer who had been a reporter for the Topeka *Daily Capital* that summer? I hoped it was just curiosity, not fear of the press, that led to his question. And I rationalized any guilt I felt at being a draft dodger with the assumption that our armed forces in Korea were settling in for a long haul, and that when I graduated in 1952, the war would be waiting for me. With a college degree, I could get a commission and be more useful.

Reasoning from analogy, I had a picture of World War II in my head and assumed that this, too, would be a long one. Korea in 1950 was like Poland in 1939. The war would spread from there, and I would have plenty of chances to wear my country's uniform.

9.   The Silent Generation speaks

B ack at K-State, I took a single room with private bath
and entrance in a new development just west of Memorial
Stadium. A work-intensive year was ahead, my hours would be
irregular, and there wouldn't be time to wait in line for either
telephone or bathroom. My journalistic skills and motivation
had been enhanced by the Topeka experience, and I immersed
myself in the *Collegian*. I took interesting courses, including
an elderly professor's interpretation of abnormal psychology,
where I learned about dementia praecox and involutional
melancholia.

Editor Schwilling gave me a free hand, and I used it liberally.
When he and the director of student publications, C. J. "Chief"
Medlin, were out of town at a student journalism conference, I
experimented with page-one design and tried a front page that
made a mini-tabloid out of our regular tabloid. I told the back
shop to turn the page form sideways and divide it into two half-
size pages. When folded, the paper looked like a magazine, the
effect enhanced by devoting most of the space to photographs.
Lyle later told me that Chief exploded in anger when he saw
it on their return to campus. Order and predictability were
important values in this postwar period, and there was little
room for experimentation or whimsy. This trait was tested
again when a student named James Divilbiss showed up for his
yearbook photograph with his hair parted in the center, pince
nez glasses, and a Herbert Hoover celluloid collar. He protested
the rejection of his picture, and I wrote a sympathetic story,

but when the yearbook was published at year's end, his picture was absent.

Trying to liven things up that fall 1951 semester, I entered into a conspiracy with my high school buddy Lee Sheppeard, who was at the University of Kansas and on track to be editor of the *University Daily Kansan.* Before the war, the two schools had a football-season feud going that involved statue painting, mascot stealing and other shenanigans. The Silent Generation wasn't interested in that sort of thing.

Hoping to change that, I organized some statue painting on both campuses. At K-State, I rubber-cemented a wig to the head of Alexander Harris, whose bust was in front of Fairchild Hall. Then I painted his nose red and the letters "KU" on the front of his pedestal. And in Lawrence the next night, with a little help, I poured water-based purple paint on a statue called "The Pioneer." It got some publicity but wasn't the catalyst for student activism that we were seeking. On the way home from Lawrence, I stopped in Topeka to visit the *Daily Capital* newsroom. The state edition was just out, and it contained the story that I had filed on the K-State statue painting. The headline was, "KU Paints Statue at K-State."

"Uh, Bob," I said to the news editor, Robert Riley, "this headline isn't backed up by the story. It doesn't say KU painted the statue."

"Yeah?" he said. "Who do you think painted it? K-State?"

Back in Manhattan, I was sitting at the news desk in late afternoon and was visited by a delegation from the Canterbury Club, which I had ignored the previous year. Its members congratulated me on my *Collegian* work and invited me back. I allowed that I missed those Sunday evenings of Episcopal fellowship and promised to get back on occasions when the Monday paper didn't need me. To my everlasting regret, I never made it. Every Monday paper seemed to have a Sunday evening problem of one sort or another, and I let them down. The club had given me a bit of social life when I was a new kid in town, and now it could benefit from my blooming into a big man on campus. Years later, I would try to atone for that sin of omission by volunteering as a faculty sponsor for the college fellowship at the Chapel of the Cross in Chapel Hill. I served for two years, but I would have been far more valuable if I had made the time in Kansas.

Lyle Schwilling ran a good paper. I still wanted to poke the Silent Generation and get my peers interested and active in public and university affairs, but I lacked an issue that would interest students. And then, in November, as if in answer to my prayers, one appeared.

Richard Neutra was a member of that group of architects whom we now call "midcentury modern." In those years, they were revolutionary. He and his colleague Rudolf Schindler were both from Vienna and both had worked briefly for Frank Lloyd Wright before moving to California to promote modern sensibility in the receptive social climate of the coast. Ayn Rand, the author of *The Fountainhead*, lived in a Neutra-designed house in the San Fernando Valley.

So when Neutra came to lecture at K-State, students in the Department of Architecture were naturally excited. Neutra made his then-standard plea for abandoning traditional design to take advantage of the many possibilities created by new construction materials and techniques. And then he put an idea into their heads. He suggested that postwar construction on the K-State campus was far too traditional and missing the opportunities provided by more modern design. In doing so, he created a spark that ignited the latent activism of a small but select group of students.

K-State in that immediate postwar period was architecturally interesting, primarily because of the artful use of open space, a plentiful commodity in Kansas. Its native limestone buildings had quaint Victorian and Gothic touches. They were sound and functional for their time with load-bearing exterior walls sometimes sculpted in interesting detail to form fake battlements or medieval parapets, but all quite different from what Neutra was proposing.

The newest building, Ahearn Field House, used steel for its structure, but covered it with a limestone facade to make the building look like the others. A recently completed dormitory also used structural steel, and it, too, was covered with a limestone facade to mimic the traditional appearance of its older neighbor whose limestone *was* the structure. The state architect was ignoring the possible advantages and design flexibility afforded by new materials and methods. In other words, K-State was not practicing architecture with the level of creativity and innovation that it was trying to teach. The students knew this and wanted to do something about it. For them, no more "silent generation."

The college was planning a new student union, and that gave the architecture students an opening. The existing union was a temporary one-story barracks building with meeting rooms, a coffee shop, and not much else. In 1941, the student body had voted to assess itself a fee, added to each semester's tuition, with the money to accumulate and be eventually applied to the construction of a union. By 1951, there was nearly enough to proceed, and the state architect had submitted a design. On this project, some organized student intervention would clearly be legitimate, and student activism was born.

But it came in an awkward form – an anonymous circular widely distributed on campus and mailed to the state architect and the Board of Regents. Its colorful language, decrying "pseudo-striped windowed engineering additions" and "eclectic, castellated dormitories" sent me scurrying to the library to learn a little bit about architecture. As soon as I found out what a castellated dormitory was, I didn't like it either.

And so I wrote an editorial. Its headline: "If we must raise hell, let's do it right."

A healthy sign in this period of student apathy on almost everything that concerns them appeared this week when a group of students, presumably architecture majors, decided to raise hell about the new student union plans.

Trouble was that K-State students raise hell so seldom, it has become a lost art, and the job was botched horribly.

Mimeographed pamphlets were distributed to organized houses and in classrooms. A partial transcript from the recent talk by Richard Neutra, architect, and some other remarks, purportedly by "we the students" were included.

The gist of the thing is that you don't need to use outmoded architectural styles to keep harmony in a group of buildings, such as on a college campus.

Some of the remarks:

"We the students are revolted by our existing architectural environment. Please, no more pseudo-Gothic Field Houses.

"Please, no more pseudo-modern striped-windowed engineering additions!

"Please, no more eclectic, castellated dormitories!

"We demand to see the drawings (of the student union) now and have explained fully the thoughts and ideas, if any, employed up to this point. If those drawings prove inadequate following complete investigation, we demand that we employ first-rate people who will tune in with contemporary work."

The spirit of the thing would be fine, except that no person or group felt strongly enough about those views to sign the statement. And the campaign has the general air of something hurriedly thrown together at the last minute. It's kind of ridiculous for students to "demand to see the drawings now and have explained fully the thoughts and ideas ... employed.". The drawings have never been hidden from students.

The work of the union planning committee is explained in minute detail in an inch-thick report available in the class reserves section of the College library. You can have the ideas in the plan explained to you by any member of the committee –

in fact, the committee is so eager to explain it that any one of its members will talk your arm off. And if you want to see the plans, just drop into Dean Craig's office where they are on file.

This shouldn't be construed to mean the plan should be allowed to go through without protest, even at this late date. For the record, the Collegian's taste does not lean toward Field Houses with thick limestone walls that don't hold anything up, nor toward dormitories with imitation battlements, nor toward any kind of pseudo-modern.

The Collegian also believes that if the students don't like the architecture, and if they want to do something where there is still a chance – as there still may be in the proposed student union – then the thing to do is to first get all of the facts straight, then come out in the open with those facts instead of circulating them in anonymous pamphlets. Then raise untold hell.

Five students quickly wrote to the Collegian to identify themselves as the authors of the circular. And the administration just as quickly denounced their work as a non-legitimate form of expression. The students should have worked through their existing student government structure, officials argued.

That response aroused the ire of one of my journalism professors, John W. McReynolds. He invited me to his office and started pulling books from his well-stocked shelves. The first included a copy of the Constitution of the United States. He opened it to the Bill of Rights and pointed to the First Amendment. It guarantees, in addition to freedom of speech, press, religion, and assembly, the right of the people "to petition the government for a redress of grievances."

Then he pulled down books of English philosophy and jurisprudence to show where the founders got that idea. And then works of the older Greek and Roman philosophers to show even earlier origins. And the university administration was saying that directly petitioning authorities was illegitimate!

It was time for some reporting.

Walking the short distance to the School of Engineering and Architecture, I started tracking down members of the architecture faculty. It took more than one trip. I interviewed them one, two, or three at a time. I found ten of the 14. Nine were quite critical of the design practices in the new buildings on campus. The tenth declined to comment.

For once, I wrote a pretty good lead:

Kansas State teaches one kind of architecture but practices another, a series of interviews with 10 of the 14 faculty members in the architecture department revealed this week.

Nine of the 10 agreed that architecture as practiced in the current building program is less advanced than that taught in the classroom. They differed only in the matter of the degree of discrepancy. One refused to comment.

All agreed, however, that contemporary buildings could be added to the campus without disrupting harmony . . .

As far as I could tell, my story did not much affect the general apathy of the student body. It was still the Silent Generation. But there was excited reaction among the architecture students and the college administration. I had good student sources, primarily because a ringleader of the protestors was dating the former business manager of our yearbook, The *Royal Purple*. The word they brought to the *Collegian* was that a meeting of the architecture faculty had been called to discuss the controversy. It was to be addressed by M. A. Durland, dean of the School of Architecture and Engineering. It would be closed to students and the public.

Editor Schwilling and I pondered the ways that we might cover that meeting. One would be to stand outside and interview the faculty members as they exited. A more imaginative method would be to borrow a recording device from the student radio station and plant it in the room, plugged in and running. We really liked this idea, but rejected it as impractical. The only tape recorder we knew about used vacuum tubes and was bigger than a case of beer, impossible to conceal. We chose a third option: undercover reporting, an honorable journalistic tradition since Nelly Bly emulated a madwoman to investigate an insane asylum for the *New York World* in 1887.

I donned a white shirt and black knit tie, tried to look older than my 21 years, and mingled with the faculty during the milling-around stage before the meeting. Then I filed in with the professors and took a seat in the center of the back row, folded copy paper in hand for note taking. The professors knew me, but the dean did not. No one challenged me. Apparently, my entry was so casual that those who knew me assumed that I had been invited.

Dean Durland was blunt. He issued a hush order. He told the professors not to say anything critical of the state architect or any other state official. There was some argumentative discourse about academic freedom. When the meeting was over, the dean bent his head down toward the lectern, the veins on his bald head forming a prominent "V." This had been hard for him. I hurried back to Kedzie Hall and rolled a sheet into the typewriter.

And then I wrote a really bad lead. The situation called for straight-ahead, let-the-facts-speak-for-themselves reporting. But I, being young and foolish, had to put some spin on it.

Members of the architectural faculty are in the uncomfortable position of having to publicly defend views they do not believe in.

That wasn't strictly true. Their orders were to keep quiet, not to lie. But to me it amounted to the same thing. With that off my chest, I moved closer toward a just-the-facts mode.

Although it has always existed to some degree, the situation became official Tuesday afternoon when Dean Durland told a meeting of the architecture faculty, "It is improper for any staff member to publicly criticize College or state officials."

He referred to Friday's Collegian story quoting faculty members who criticized campus buildings and to the original "hell-raisers" pamphlet which presumably was produced with knowledge of an unnamed faculty member.

No one on the state payroll should criticize the state architect, Durland said.

"There is no substitute for loyalty," he said.

Asked by an instructor if this meant he should give a dishonest opinion when a student asks him about treatment of limestone in campus buildings, Durland modified his statement to exclude private conversations and classroom instruction.

But such critical comment should not be given to newspapers, he pointed out.

The rights of free speech do not include anonymous criticism in pubic, he said.

The discussion pointed up some of the causes for the air of general frustration that exists in the department.

State Architect Charles Marshall has final legal authority on all buildings erected on campus. Members of the architecture department may, through the Campus Planning Committee, submit their own drawings to the state architect. He may either use them, modify them, or use a different plan drawn by his own staff.

Faculty members who do not like Marshall's buildings are torn between "loyalty" on one hand and their own professional convictions on the other.

Future policy as explained by Dean Durland will be to express their own convictions only in private or, with reservation, in the classroom.

Publicly they must remain silent.

On the morning of Wednesday, Dec. 12, we dummied a three-column front-page headline on my story. Then Dean Durland called.

He told me to kill the story. I politely declined. About an hour later, President McCain called Lyle Schwilling, the editor, and said he would like to see the story before it was published. Lyle politely declined.

This resistance was rather bold of us because the college owned the newspaper and the press on which it was printed in the basement of Kedzie Hall. That made McCain, in effect, the publisher and final authority on its content. But the role of the college as a place for students to learn the democratic process through participation had been part of the institution's rhetoric since the Milton Eisenhower administration. Freedom, we knew from our study of history, had to be asserted to exist at all. And there had never, so far as we knew, been a faculty or administrative review of the content of the *Collegian*.

McCain wasn't giving up. His next move was to call Ralph Lashbrook, chair of the Department of Technical Journalism, and ask him to review the story before it was published. It was now getting close to press time, and word was sent to the pressroom to put the paper on hold while Lashbrook thought about it. Shortly, he called back and told McCain that if he wanted the press held and the story censored, he would have to do it himself. Now it was McCain's turn to think things over.

The president's office had a smart staff member named Max Milbourn, whose title was director of public service. I never found out for sure that Milbourn's advice was even sought, but, if it was, I'm confident that his wise public relations counsel would have been to let the story run. Holding the press and pulling the type would only bring greater public attention to the underlying issue.

After about a 30-minute delay, the papers came rolling off the press with my story on the front.

The state's major newspapers quickly picked up the story. Floyd Sageser was the *Kansas City Star's* campus correspondent, and I was making him easy money as he rewrote every twist and turn from my stories and sent them to the *Star*. I performed the same service for the *Daily Capital*. The administration issued a statement saying the story was in error, that the faculty meeting had been a routine discussion of professional ethics. Hardy Berry, editor of the *Manhattan Tribune*, came to my office to question me and look at my notes. He left satisfied, and the *Tribune*'s story was based on mine.

Things got easier the next day. Two members of the architecture faculty, Tasso Katselas and Maurice K. Smith, went public with a letter to McCain in which they confirmed my account by asserting their right to offer their opinions "whatever, wherever, and to whomever it may be."

"Silence, indifference, or agreement with a faulty situation would merely contribute to existing chaos, and would continue to inflict upon people a way of life that is contrary to our sincerest interests," they said.

"It takes a considerable period to build lives around beliefs and ideals – these are cherished possessions, and nothing any state can offer will make their sacrifice worthy."

The next word from President McCain was an affirmation of academic freedom. It was in the form of a well-stated and persuasive press release. "Nobody knows the words and music like McCain," said a cynical faculty member.

Some of my peers figured that I had cooked my own goose, that my expectation of replacing Lyle as *Collegian* editor had been dashed by my behavior. But a funny thing happened. I submitted an application to the Board of Student Publications, and it was the only one. Nobody challenged me. Now I understood the concept of solidarity. Prof. Byron Ellis, who had left a job as department head at a college in Texas to protest censorship of the student paper there, invited me into his office. Were my grades going to be high enough to guarantee eligibility for the *Collegian*? I allowed that I thought so but confessed to a bit of uncertainty. He raised the C that I had barely earned in his advertising course to an undeserved B, thereby removing the uncertainty.

Now I was really interested in architecture. After taking three of the four required comprehensive courses at K-State, I had dug in my heels at the prospect of eight semester hours of Man and the Cultural World. I negotiated with the authorities for the right to substitute three specialized courses: I had three hours each of Western Civilization and Appreciation of Music to my credit, and for spring 1952, I chose Appreciation of Architecture. The course was taught by Earl Layman, and drew a large attendance stimulated by the controversy. Layman's slideshow made me long to live in the kind of house that people like Richard Neutra and Rudolf Schindler were designing. But he also had a respect for designs of the past. Honesty was the key, he said. For example, he declared that Farm Machinery Hall, the oldest building on the campus, built in 1873, was the most honest of all of K-State's buildings. The details of its stone-upon-stone construction were perfectly visible.

The spring semester went smoothly, mostly because of my choice of Marillyn Weisbender, the smartest member of the staff, as associate editor. She kept things well buttoned down, enough to make the paper one of only seven nationally to win an All-American award from the National Scholastic Press Association. President McCain, evidently wanting to bring the *Collegian* editor into his inner circle, invited me to join a meeting of deans to discuss how to handle cases like the architecture rebellion in the future. But, to my disappointment, the discussion never went to the merits of the architects' case. It was all about keeping order. And the president harbored a suspicion that dissident faculty members had manipulated the students. "Are they hiding behind students?" he asked. If there was an answer, I don't remember it.

And it turned out to be a quiet semester, except for two

things. Five untenured members of the architecture faculty were notified that they were not being rehired. My professor Earl Layman was one of them.

Someone on the faculty, probably Tasso Katselas, had the connections to get Frank Lloyd Wright to come to K-State for an all-campus lecture, and to dine with the five fired faculty members, a wonderful gesture. I got to interview Wright standing on the porch of Thompson Cafeteria, an example of the building style that he decried as "General Grant Gothic." I also assigned myself to cover his lecture. Wright was 84 and still feisty. "Kansas is in a backwater," he said. "It doesn't know what goes on around the world." He warned students that, "Habituation is the death of imagination. That's what's ugly about this town – the habit started, and you can't get rid of it."

The purge of the dissident young faculty members robbed the department of a source of postwar energy and was especially unfair in the case of Layman. He had finished his probationary period and had been due to get tenure the following fall. Layman moved west and eventually became the director of historic preservation for the city of Seattle. Tasso Katselas started his own firm and, years later, designed the new airport terminal for the city of Pittsburgh, Pa. Professor McReynolds left, too. He owned a small farm east of town and needed some time, he said, for writing and thinking.

McReynolds shared with me a letter he had written to President McCain after resigning. His departure, he said, should not be interpreted as criticism of Chairman Lashbrook. The department had been given too many collateral responsibilities: the college news bureau, the college press, sports publicity, alumni publications, student publications. That left too little time for teaching.

It seems to me that the most important thing we can teach the young (people) who come here is that they are morally obligated to do their best to inform the public, honestly, completely and effectively. I do not see how we can teach this if we, as a department, are expected to devote our major attention to providing "good press" for the administration of the college.

The most important thing we have to sell, it appears to me, is integrity and devotion to high purpose. A student press which on the one hand does not receive the faculty's full attention, and on the other is made to provide "good press," where it may or may not be the honest thing to do, can hardly be expected to acquire much integrity or devotion to high purpose.

That system, mixing journalism education with institutional public relations, was eventually cleaned up. Effects of the disruption in the architecture department were not as easy to evaluate. It turned out that I had something of a personal stake in the outcome because my brother would eventually earn a degree in architecture at K-State. I hoped that the *Collegian's* intervention had not diluted the department's creative spark.

But John Meyer did well, practicing in Frank Lloyd Wright's home state of Wisconsin and, after retiring, mentoring students at Wright's Spring Green estate, Taliesin. His daughter Kimberli Meyer is an architect, too, and became director of the MAK Center, the Austrian-owned memorial to Rudolf Schindler in West Hollywood, Calif.

Decades afterward, James C. Carey, writing a history of what by then was Kansas State University, offered a perspective informed by time. For K-State, he said, "The experience may have been a necessary part of growing up."

"A few may have suffered injustices, but the institution benefitted from the incident by learning that it was impossible to encourage thinking and stifle ideas at the same time."

In Carey's view, the experience left McCain better prepared to deal with the next generation of students, the baby boomers who would spark the uprisings of the 1960s. The architecture students, with a little help from the *Collegian*, had contributed to his education.[12] And McCain very quickly became a vocal defender of academic freedom. In 1954, a quiet, affable professor in the English department, James D. Koerner, published an article in Harper's describing his experience in teaching a class of 28 primary and secondary Kansas school teachers. "In the broad sense of the word," he said, "these men and women were downright, hopelessly illiterate" and probably representative of a national problem.

The article hit the stands while an assembly of Kansas teachers was in session in Topeka, and their reaction was swift. In a wire to President McCain, they called Koerner's remarks "destructive, vindictive, and unethical" and demanded "appropriate action." McCain's response was equally swift.

"We at Kansas State College respect freedom of speech," he said, and added that Professor Koerner was "properly exercising" that freedom. He suggested that the teachers might think about ways to correct the situation that the professor described.

McCain's attitudes toward architecture did not change as visibly, however, and in 1963, Professor Layman's favorite building, Farm Machinery Hall, was torn down.

Back at K-State in the spring of 1952, it turned out that the draft was not the only potential barrier standing between me and the completion of my senior year. My father had given up his successful used car business to seize what seemed like a greater opportunity: the chance to be general manager of a new-car dealership. The overture came from Walter Merten, young member of an affluent family headed by his mother Abbie Merten, who lived in a brick tudor house in the northwest section of Clay Center. Abbie was well-liked, and she did not consume conspicuously. Years after the war ended, she still drove her 1938 Chrysler. "It fits me," she would explain. And she meant this literally as well as metaphorically. Cars of the

1930s were parsimonious with their interior space, and Abbie was small of stature.

Walter had dropped out of the University of Nebraska to enlist in the Army and went back to his education after the war. He seemed equally modest. The only other Merten I had met was a younger woman who bought her groceries at Boogart's grocery store when I was in high school and working there as a bagger on Saturdays. "I have some other errands," she said on one such Saturday. "Please put these groceries in the Cadillac outside."

"Is it a late model?" I asked, concerned that I might encounter more than one Cadillac.

"It's the very latest there is," she said. "It has 'Cadillac' written right there on the front bumper."

Walter had the capital to qualify for start-up Dodge and Packard franchises, but not the maturity or experience. His promise to put my dad in charge satisfied both companies, and the deal was made.

The immediate consequence to me of this new business relationship was that I could borrow a higher class of car when I had a heavy date. But the lending had to be short-term. The most important all-school social event of the 1950-1951 academic year, was a farewell party for Milton Eisenhower, featuring a dance and concert with Gene Krupa's orchestra. I drove my old Pontiac home, picked up a gorgeous fast-back Packard trade-in, and used it that afternoon and evening. After taking my date back to her sorority house a little bit ahead of the usual 15-minute interval before closing time, I drove back to Clay Center, switched cars, and returned to Manhattan in time to enjoy a sleepy breakfast at the bus station, which had the only restaurant open at that hour.

But it was too good a deal to last. By November 1951, it was evident that the owner-manager relationship wasn't working. Maybe the difference in age and experience was too great. Looking back, I suspect the presence of another factor. The supply of cars had caught up with postwar demand, leaving less room for an additional dealership in Clay Center. There was also long-term population decline. Clay County lost 12 percent of its population in the decade of the 1940s, and the downward trend was continuing.

Whatever the source of the trouble, Bige's position was untenable. He found work with a farm implement retailer and advised me to seek a loan for financing the rest of my education. He could connect me with a bank in Clay Center, if necessary, he said.

It wasn't. I went straight to the alumni office, whose director, Kenny Ford, supervised the Alumni Loan Fund. He fixed me up with a loan that, along with my salary as *Collegian* editor, could keep me going through commencement. I should have done that much earlier and spared my parents the worry.

10. Another war

The days were getting longer, and it was time to get serious about military service. But I didn't have to take a chance with the discomfort and danger of the infantry as my father and uncle had done in their respective wars. Now I could go for the branch of my choice. I wanted a commission in the United States Navy. And the academic year deferment had given me plenty of time to check out the available options. First, I applied for Navy Officer Candidate School at Newport, R. I. That led to another trip to Kansas City and another physical examination.

I flunked, but not because of the heart murmur.

"Too much overbite," said the medical corpsman peering morosely at my jaw. "You'll never get a commission in the United States Navy."

That news was disappointing, but the decision validated my faith in markets. Lots of young men wanted to be naval officers because the navy was a relatively safe and comfortable spot in a ground war. Amphibious ships had been shot at when they landed troops at Inchon in September 1950, but the episodes of danger were brief, and sailors could usually eat and sleep well. It made sense for the Navy to take a first cut at reducing the applicant pool by setting the highest possible physical requirements.

But I wasn't through with the Navy. It had another officer school that recruited directly from civilian life, one that was not so safe, the Naval Aviation Cadet program. It took 18 months to get a commission, but it would be an interesting 18 months, and learning to fly had been a dream of mine since boyhood. I applied for that one, and this time the law of supply and demand worked in my favor. Flying was dangerous, and flight training, as Tom Wolfe would later document in *The Right Stuff*, was especially dangerous in the Navy. Its fliers landed on aircraft carriers – at all hours and in all kinds of weather. So eligible applicants were scarce, and the Navy, to meet its needs for the Korean conflict, had resigned itself to taking less than the ideal physical type. My heart murmur was no problem, but depth perception looked as though it might be. I was asked to peer into a tube and tell which of two objects at the far end was closest to me. All I could do was guess, but the medical corpsman obligingly repeated the test until my random selection yielded a correct answer.

There were other tests and interviews, and eventually I was approved for the program, sworn into the Naval Reserve with the rank of Navcad, the Navy's shorthand for Naval Aviation Cadet, and given some choice on the timing of my call to active duty. My cousin Ralph took the same path and chose an early activation. I opted for late summer or fall 1952. At last, I was out of the reach of Clay Center Local Board No. 11.

Preferring to wait for my call to service in Manhattan rather than going home to Clay Center, I went downtown to the *Manhattan Mercury-Chronicle* and asked Bill Colvin for a job. A former city editor of the *Topeka Daily Capital*, Colvin had gone to work for Faye Seaton, who had been content until then to publish a mediocre but profitable daily. Now he wanted to upgrade the paper with some good journalism. Al Horlings's *Manhattan Tribune* was costing him some advertising, and it was time to give it a run for its money. Colvin hired me as reporter-photographer. He was making the paper lively and feisty, and I was thrilled to be helping. And I gained a new technical skill. The *Mercury-Chronicle* was an early adopter of the Fairchild electronic engraving system, which was making the old acid-etched zinc plates obsolescent. The machine took up less space than a desk, and it produced engravings on plastic sheets wrapped around a rotating drum.

Old-technology engravers like Gene Guerrant in Manhattan and Don Wilson in Clay Center were losing business because even small papers could afford the Fairchild machines. It was my first direct experience with the disruptive effects of communication technology. There would be many more.

The big running story of that summer was the fate of the Blue Valley. Manhattan had been built at the confluence of the Blue and the Kaw rivers, and the Corps of Engineers was convinced that a dam on the Blue River was critical to its program to prevent a repeat of the 1951 flood disaster. In the past, Rep. Albert Cole, Republican from the 1st District of Kansas, had successfully blocked appropriations for the Tuttle Creek Dam, as it was called, but the flood disaster changed his mind. With his opposition withdrawn, a House-Senate conference committee on July 5, 1952, approved a $5 million appropriation to begin construction. The residents of the Blue Valley began an extended campaign to unseat their congressman and prevent the dam from being built. Because it was too late to oppose Cole in the 1952 primary election, they had to support a Democrat in a district that had never elected one. The Democratic candidate was a farmer named Howard Miller, and he gladly took an anti-dam position. It made for an interesting summer, and I hated to leave with the outcome still unknown.

Another big story that spring was General Dwight D. Eisenhower's return to his hometown of Abilene, Kan., to announce his candidacy for the Republican presidential nomination. I took a Speed Graphic and rode the train 60 miles to Abilene to get the story in both words and pictures. It rained. After the speech, on June 4, I walked in the rain back to the train station, and Eisenhower's motorcade, driving slowly, passed me. Ike looked out of his limousine and saw me wet and bedraggled. He smiled and gave me an encouraging wave. If I had been carrying a Leica instead of a folded-up Speed

Graphic, I might have been quick enough to record that wave. Its picture is still clear in my head.

My social life that summer had not improved. The Navy's letter came in October. To report for active duty on the prescribed day, I had to break a date with a coed whom I had been hoping to get to know better after recruiting her to model gloves for a fashion piece in the *Mercury-Chronicle*. Then I informed my employer and landlord, assembled my gear, and went home to Clay Center. Packing was minimal, the Navy having made it clear that I would not need a change of clothes. On October 25, candidate Eisenhower made his major foreign policy speech. He promised to "forego the diversions of politics and to concentrate on the job of ending the Korean War until that job is honorably done."

That job requires a personal trip to Korea. I shall make that trip. Only in that way could I learn how best to serve the American people in the cause of peace.

I shall go to Korea.

That was good enough for me. I obtained an absentee ballot from my local election board and voted for Eisenhower for president. Then I said goodbye to my mother and brother, and my father took me downtown to wait for the Trailways bus to the Naval Air Station at Olathe. We shook hands, and I was off to war. At Olathe, I was processed and issued government transportation credentials. From there, I went by bus to Kansas City, made my way to Union Station and, on election day 1952, boarded the Louisville and Nashville train headed south toward New Orleans.

With only a coach ticket, I had to sleep as best I could. When we rolled into New Orleans, it was daylight, and I had a few hours before transferring to the eastbound train for Florida. To fill the time, I walked downtown and found a furniture store with a TV in the window. It was tuned to a news program, and that is where I learned that Eisenhower had defeated Adlai Stevenson in the election. As a Kansan and a Republican, I felt proud.

The train ride to Pensacola was short and scenic. I took a cab to the air station, and reported to the receiving center to meet my peers. Aside from being all approximately the same age, we were a fairly diverse group. Most of us were civilians, but there was a Naval Academy dropout, a few sailors and one marine. The marine, Jimmy North, expressed a longing for a cigarette. "Here you go, Jarhead," said a sailor, Johnny Haynes, offering an open pack. The marine was not offended by the nickname. Sailors and marines had long ago established an easy relationship.

Our backgrounds ranged from city to rural, Ivy League to agricultural college or no college at all. The only thing we had in common, we realized, was that the Navy, in its wisdom, believed that we had enough of the right stuff to become Naval aviators. We had our last evening meal in civilian clothes. The next day we were issued uniforms and cardboard boxes in which to place our civvies for shipping home. The adventure was on. Pre-flight school would be 16 weeks of military drill and orientation, physical training, officer training, and aviation ground school at the mainside base at Pensacola.

Mine was class 46-52, meaning that it was the 46th to start up in the year 1952. We were organized as Fox Company in Battalion Four, which was composed of cadets at various stages of the program. I quickly discovered one thing that I did not like about pre-flight. We were awakened in the morning by a bugle! Not a recording of a bugle, but a real live bugle, piped loudly through a battalion-wide public address system. It was jarring. Seeking to avoid that, I discretely inquired about the bugler, learned that his class was about to graduate from pre-flight school, and so I volunteered to take his place.

From Boy Scout experience, I already knew four of the

basic bugle calls used in pre-flight: Reveille, Assembly, To the Colors, and Taps. There was a fifth that I liked best of all. After assembly, and on a cue from the cadet battalion commander, the bugler would blow four notes, C, E, G, then a sustained E, sort of a ta-ta, ta-tum to warn the troops that the command "attention" was about to be called. And the entire battalion would snap from parade rest to attention. I felt powerful.

But the best thing about being bugler was being awakened at 5:15 a.m., 15 minutes before reveille, not by a bugle but by a gentle shake of the shoulder from the mate of the deck. I would get up, dress in the dark, and then go down to the office, pick up the bugle, and inflict reveille on my peers by blowing it into the live microphone. And then I walked casually down to the mess hall to be first in line for breakfast.

As battalion bugler, 1952

The battalion cadet commander was an energetic, intense fellow whose name I did not retain at the time, but whom I would encounter later in life. In my years as a Washington correspondent, I would cover oral argument in only one Supreme Court case, Shepherd v. Maxwell, where Dr. Samuel Shepherd, convicted of killing his wife, claimed that the trial hadn't been fair because of prejudicial publicity in the Cleveland newspapers. The minute I saw Shepherd's attorney, I recognized him as my cadet battalion commander in 1952. His name was F. Lee Bailey. He had become a Marine fighter pilot, then gone to law school at Boston University. He was building a national reputation as a criminal defense lawyer, and he won Shepherd's case.

Our basic military instructors were Marine drill sergeants. They had an expression that, I later realized, was one of the fundamental rules of life. "There's always 10 percent that don't get the word." I understood that it would be better for me to not be part of that 10 percent. Acts of daily life were broken down into closely regimented procedures, down to telling us how to fold our socks and which part of the drawer to keep them in.

Flying, we were told, was just a set of procedures, so it was good to get used to learning and following procedures. I found that it was more fun to try to enjoy the spit-and-polish aspect of military culture than to fight it. And not all of the drill sergeants yelled at us. One, who was new at the job, corrected the way I was holding my rifle and did it without raising his voice.

"It's a common mistake," he said. "Don't worry about it."

The part I dreaded the most, of course, was neither military training nor ground school, but the physical training. Jocks had an advantage, the head drill sergeant told us, because flying took athletic skill. It sounded like trouble ahead.

To enhance our athletic skill, we were programmed for training in different sports for two weeks each. But first we had to be toughened up with two weeks of outdoor exercise, mostly running and calisthenics. At the end of the first such period, we thought we were dying. After the last one, two weeks later, we felt so good that we double-timed back to the barracks. Swimming came next. There were a number of tests, but two were formidable. One was to swim a half-mile in 40 minutes. The other was to do four laps nonstop of the 75-foot pool using specified strokes in a specified order: breast, side, back, and crawl. Those who did not pass in the first two weeks would be assigned to sub-swimming class, which would substitute for the rest period between the end of the day's work and the evening meal.

The instructor, Lieutenant Martin, was a formidable athlete. Among ourselves, we called him "old frog eyes," and his teaching method included a lot of yelling. But he could swim like a snake, legs together and arms at his side, just wiggling through the water. He broke each stroke down to a set of procedures. The breast stroke was "kick, glide, pull, recover." The backstroke was "kick and pull together, then hold your glide."

I got those fairly quickly, but the crawl was daunting. I learned how to keep my face in the water except for brief twists of the head to get a breath of air. I learned how to stroke with one arm at a time rather than simulating a windmill. Executing the components was doable, but putting them together in a coordinated way was a problem. I was enrolled in sub-swimming.

After six weeks of pre-flight, it was time for Christmas leave. Instructors in ground school who wanted to maintain their flying proficiency had to fly a minimum number of hours per month, and some of these flights were available for free rides home. The Navy set up a lottery to determine who would get the limited number of seats. I signed up for a flight to Olathe and won. The aircraft was an R4D sub hunter, the Navy version of the Douglas DC-3. Seating was on aluminum and canvas benches facing a center aisle. It was fun, and I made the final leg of the trip home from Olathe by bus.

Any expectations I had that the war in Korea would bring the kind of respect enjoyed by military men and women in World War II were quickly dashed. Wearing my Navcad dress blues, I visited the K-State campus to find old friends. The first person I encountered was a female journalism student who looked up and down at my splendid uniform, frowned, and said, "What happened to you?"

But the uniform made my parents proud, and I wore it to the Christmas Eve service at St. Paul's in Clay Center. And I rather enjoyed showing it off when I had a dinner date in Kansas City on my way back to Pensacola. It was with one of my former journalism classmates, and she was in aviation, too – as an airline stewardess. This was a day when stewardesses were required to be young, pretty, and to light men's cigarettes. Betty Friedan's *The Feminine Mystique*, which would kick off the rebirth of women's rights, was still a decade away. If the disconnect between my friend's journalism degree, her intelligence, and the career she had chosen bothered me, I don't remember it. But it should have. I was still totally unconscious of the ways in which American culture of the 1950s was unfair to women.

We talked about literature. She was enthusiastic about Thomas Wolfe. I resolved to check him out when I got some free time.

After I left her at the front door of her apartment hotel in Country Club Plaza, I walked back across Brush Creek and caught a streetcar to my downtown hotel. There was a loud party on my floor. A door opened, and several nice looking folks my age saw my uniform and tried to wave me in. But the hour was late, and I had to catch the Navy flight back to Pensacola early in the morning. A chapter in my life was ending.

Back in Pensacola, something strange happened in the first swimming session. I described it in a letter home:

January 9, 1953 – *First swimming period after leave, I figured I was ready to try the test where you jump off a tower and swim 75 yards, three lengths of the pool. But the only test they were running was the 40-minute half-mile, so I tried it just for the practice. A half-mile is 18 laps of the pool, and when I'd tried it five weeks ago I'd only made one. Anyway, I swam one lap Thursday without even bothering to sound off my number to the checker, then got pooped out after swimming a couple more. Just to prove I could do it, I decided to swim one more lap, even though I was exhausted. When I finished it, I didn't feel much worse so I decided to do just one more. This went on for some time, and when it really did get worse, I had gone 13 laps. This was so close that I couldn't bear to quit, so I went on just guts. No one was more surprised than I at the end of the 40 minutes when I learned that I had finished the 18 laps, even without the one that didn't count. The longest previous time I had ever swum continuously was three minutes. At any rate, I think I'm the only sub-swimmer in pre-flight who passed the half-mile before any of the other tests.*

I had done it with the elementary backstroke, watching the lines in the ceiling to keep on a straight course.

Passing the remaining tests took another nine weeks, and I mastered the four-stroke test just in time to graduate from pre-flight with my class. And I was never afraid of the water again. Decades later, I would get caught in a rip current off the North Carolina coast and calmly swim parallel to the beach until I was free of it, just as Mr. Martin had taught.

The other difficult sport was boxing. After we had learned the basic moves, including standing sideways to reduce the target area, the instructor assigned us sparring partners. Mine was strong and skilled, and he very quickly landed a good blow to my face.

"Stop!" cried the instructor.

We did and looked at him.

"Your nose is broken!"

He was looking at me. A glance in the mirror verified that my nose was crooked, and there was blood coming from the bridge. I was dispatched to the infirmary.

The doctor studied my nose and expressed confidence that he could straighten it. He inserted something that looked like a spoon handle in one nostril and pressed from the other side. He pressed and pressed. Nothing happened. He stood back and took another look.

"What," he asked, "did your nose look like before you got hit?"

I was stumped. I had never been aware of having a crooked nose, but then I had never studied it that carefully nor carried a picture in my head of what a normal nose should look like. The doctor shook his head, pasted a bandage across my nose, and we let it go at that.

That evening in the mess hall, some just-arrived cadets in civilian clothes were sitting across the table from me.

"What happened to your nose?"

"It got broken in boxing," I explained.

A brief silence followed.

"Does everyone have to take boxing?"

As it turned out, Fox Company had to take boxing twice. Because of a scheduling mix-up, the wrestling instructor was unavailable for the two-week period that we were to have learned that sport. So, to fill the gap, we took another two weeks of boxing. This time, I was given a helmet to wear and paired with weaker sparring partners.

In February, someone sent me a newspaper clip about a conflict between Laurence "Moon" Mullins, the K-State athletic director and Coach Gardner. The coach had announced that he would take leave from the college to accept an offer to coach the college all-stars in an exhibition tour against the Harlem Globe-Trotters. Mullins announced that Gardner would do no such thing because it would be an illegitimate incursion of professionalism into college sports. Gardner tried to go over his head to the alumni. It didn't appear that anyone was taking Mullins's side, so I wrote him a letter:

———————————————

February 16, 1953 – Dear Moon: This is just to let you know that at least one K-Stater is applauding your stand in the matter of Jack Gardner and the Globe Trotters game. I think Kansas State is fortunate in having an athletic director who recognizes the dangers of encroaching professionalism in college sports and who is not afraid to say so in public ...

There should be no reason to regret the amount of publicity that the controversy has received. If you win now, the decision is likely to stick, and you'll have established something more important than whether Coach Gardner is going to take time off from school to work for the Globe Trotters – namely that the point at which to stop professionalism in college ball is right here and now; as well as the fact that the athletic department is run by the athletic director, not by the basketball coach.

And I think you'll do just that. Even if the choice is between a championship team and integrity, I'll count on K-State to pick integrity."

––––––––––––––––––

Mullins wisely took his case to the media, and the administration had to make the decision openly, so of course, it sided with the athletic director. Later, I was pleasantly surprised to hear from Mullins. It turned out that he was a commander in the Naval reserve and had training duty in Pensacola. We had a nice talk. He had deeply appreciated my letter. The pressure had been so great, he said, that it was sometimes hard to think straight, and my letter helped him feel validated.

When pre-flight training ended, we of Fox Company accepted our certificates and repaired to the Aviation Cadet Recreation and Athletic Club (ACRAC) to drink 15-cent glasses of draft Michelob and congratulate ourselves on our splendid physical condition. Most were like me: stronger, slimmer and, having replaced baby fat with muscle, heavier. The downside, we reflected, was that this was probably our lifetime peak; we would never be in such good physical condition again.

Weekend liberty in Pensacola introduced me to the folkways of the south, including "white" and "colored" drinking fountains and rest rooms. Once, on the bus back to the base, the driver looked in his rear-view mirror, stopped, and refused to restart the bus until a black woman in the front moved to the rear. "When will the South grow up?" asked one of the cadets. Otherwise, it was a pleasant town with movie theaters and a bar in the San Carlos Hotel where cadets liked to gather, plus a downtown USO that drew Navy folks of all stripes. I attended services at the Episcopal church in Pensacola but made no connections with anyone in the civilian community. Soon it was time to move on to another base.

11. Up in the air, upside down

Our next assignment was Whiting Field outside Milton, Fla., some 30 miles across Pensacola Bay, for basic flight training. The part of my day formerly spent in sub-swimming was taken up with a new activity. With Independence Day approaching, the base commander thought it would be nice to have a cadet band, and so I volunteered, and my parents sent the cornet down. As in high school, I was just barely good enough to get by, but the Sousa marches were all familiar, and we sounded okay.

My checkered musical background paid off in yet another way. Ralph Flanagan, a popular recording artist of that day, brought his band to Pensacola for a concert. Finding a seat in the front row, I was positioned to bound forward when he asked for volunteers to participate in a song recognition contest. He chose five of us: an officer, a WAVE, two sailors and me. The game was for the band to play a song and the contestants to identify it by writing its title on a slate and holding it up. It wasn't fair because I had played a lot of Flanagan when I was a student disc jockey at K-State. Most of his arrangements I could recognize from the first few notes, well before the melody started. I won easily, and the prize was a record album autographed by Flanagan. I still have it.

Our flight instructors, like our ground-school teachers, were a mixed lot of career men and involuntarily recalled reservists. Some were happy to be there and others were uninterested or overtly disliked it. I lucked out by drawing Lt. Cmdr. Jack

Sisk, a reservist from New Orleans, who was not at all bitter or unhappy about being recalled. I called him "Mr. Sisk" because Navy officers below full commander are addressed as "Mr." instead of by rank. He still enjoyed flying. And he was patient with my physical awkwardness. The first flight with him is still clear in my mind, leaving the ground, clearing the trees, seeing the flat Florida landscape below.

After the flight, he asked how I liked it. I allowed that it was more complicated and more work than I had expected. Everything a pilot did, even as simple as going from level flight to a climb, involved so many details – procedures again – adjusting propeller pitch, manifold pressure, trim tabs and so on.

"Yeah," he said. "For you, it'll be work, but for me it'll be pure sport." And he chuckled.

The SNJ had been an advanced trainer in World War II. Cadets then started out in lightweight Stearman biplanes that were simple to operate and could be soloed after only eight or nine hours of training. The SNJ was the third airplane those guys learned to fly, but for us it was the first. This was a complex single-engine craft, meaning that it had retractable landing gear and a variable-speed propeller. If you cut the power to land and forgot to lower the wheels, an auto horn positioned just behind your head would start blasting.

If you were too confused to notice the warning, a sailor holding paddles at the landing end of the runway would give you the wave-off signal, frantically crossing and uncrossing the paddles over his head. That almost happened to me once when, on the downwind leg of the landing pattern, I noticed that my air speed was too high, even when I throttled back. I was concentrating on that problem when Mr. Sisk took over, and only then did I notice the horn blasting behind my head. I had forgotten to lower the gear, and it was the reduced drag that made the airplane go too fast. We went around again before the wheel watch could wave us off.

For a cadet to be declared proficient enough to be judged "safe for solo" in the SNJ, the Navy required 18 or more dual flights, each with at least an hour of instruction and practice.

It was a big airplane for a two-seater: 42-foot wingspan and 29 feet nose to tail. Seating was tandem with the student in front. Communication with the instructor was by radio intercom where the Stearman had used a Gosport tube, basically a rubber hose. The SNJ's 600-horsepower Pratt & Whitney radial engine was really loud. We wore cloth helmets and parachutes. Hard-hat helmets would be introduced a few months later. The cockpits were covered by a greenhouse enclosure that could be opened for exit and entry. The parachute was just the right size to fit into the aircraft's bucket seats, so it doubled as a cushion.

The main topics for primary training after climbs and turns were stalls and spins, landings and takeoffs. I learned to induce a stall – after putting 6,000 feet of air space between the airplane and the ground – by cutting power and pulling the nose up. That made the SNJ fly slower and slower until it would give a terrifying shudder and fall with one wing pointed down. A quick, forward stick to lower the nose restored flying speed. Failure to make that correction would cause the aircraft to go into a spin. Both stalls and spins are easy to get out of, but you lose altitude, so I learned not to try either one close to the ground. And by practicing them, I learned to recognize the warning signs that one was about to occur.

For our touch-and-go landings, we used a field that left plenty of room for error: a square mile of closely clipped grass. When Mr. Sisk decided I was ready to solo, he booked me to fly with another instructor for a flight check. If this neutral third party thought I could do it safely, he would let me take it up alone for three touch-and-go landings on the grass field. If not, he would give a thumb down, and send me back for two more training flights.

I got a down on my first check because of a tendency to skid on landing. On the second time, to my chagrin, I drew a

Lt. (jg) Ricker who had a reputation for being hard to satisfy. After I showed him a couple of stalls and a spin, he told me to fly to Choctaw, a practice field north of Whiting. I promptly got lost in the haze and buzzed a couple of Air Force fields before I finally got my bearings while he sat back in amused silence.

My touch-and-go landings were only fair. I had a tendency to hit wheels first and bounce instead of landing three-point. After a particularly bumpy one, Mr. Ricker said, "Okay, make the next one a full stop."

So I did, bumpily. And he said, "I've got it," and started taxiing us madly toward the take-off end of the field *Uh-oh*, I thought, *another down*. Then he pulled beside the crash truck and said, "That's enough, I'm getting the hell out of here."

And he climbed out on the wing, pushed the goggles back on my forehead, and looked at me earnestly. "Okay," he said. "Take it up, and give me, let's see, five touch-and-go's. Yes, five." He climbed down to the ground and walked away with a cheery wave of his hand.

The standard number of check-flight solo landings was three! What was this about?

I closed the canopy, locked the tail wheel, ran through the pre-flight check, and then shoved the throttle forward to the sea-level stop. The tail went up, then the ground fell away, and I climbed into the pattern, acutely aware of the emptiness in the back seat. Leveling off at 500 feet, I looped back and shot a landing, the best I'd made all day. The next one was a smooth three-pointer, the best I had ever done. On the third, I stalled a bit high and dropped to the runway a little too hard. On the next two attempts, I hit on the wheels and bounced but corrected properly and made acceptable landings. Then I stopped, picked up Mr. Ricker, and took him back to Whiting, a pilot in my own right.

Afterward, I thought it over and figured that he had called for five go-arounds because my case was marginal, and he needed the extra demonstration of competence. In any event,

At Whiting Field, 1953

he cleared me to spend an entire hour in the air all by myself on the very next day, May 29, 1953. Mr. Sisk was beaming, as happy as I was, perhaps in anticipation of the bottle of whiskey with which we who soloed rewarded our instructors.

The evaluation system for student pilots in the Korean War was much different than the one for World War II. That had been a popular war, flying was glamorous, and there were more people who wanted to be pilots than the military needed. Those who couldn't perform up to standard were removed from the program or "washed out" in the term of that day to make room for more talented prospects. But for Korea, volunteers were scarce, and I never heard of anyone being washed out. Many of us had to repeat segments of the training, but the Navy assumed that if we had enough time and motivation, all of us who met the original selection criteria could, if we kept trying, make it. Misfits self-selected out of the program by taking a DOR – which meant "dropped at own request." That was shorthand for "dropped for clearly demonstrated lack of motivation," but all one had to do was ask. Most DORs happened in preflight or in the first few weeks of flying. If aviation was not for you, it was a good bet that you knew it by then. By qualifying for solo, I had passed into another Inner Ring.

By then, I was aware that this was a fairly dangerous occupation. Tom Wolfe in his 1979 *The Right Stuff* would cite a medical journal report that a naval aviator, over the course of a 20-year career, had a 23 percent chance of being killed in a flying accident. This did not include combat. I didn't know the statistics, but I knew what was happening around me.

There was a kid from Kansas whom I met in the transient cadet barracks at Pensacola mainside. I was checking in and he was checking out, enroute to Corpus Christi to make the transition to fighters. Later, I learned that on his first flight in the F6F Wildcat, he missed his approach and had to apply full throttle to take a wave-off. He wasn't prepared for the greater torque from the 2,000-horsepower engine, and he failed to counter it with enough sideways pressure on the stick. The plane rolled over into a fatal crash.

So I paid close attention when the next two weeks were taken up with learning emergency procedures. Mr. Sisk would, when least expected, cut the power and say, "Okay, you've got it. Now what?"

My task then was to spot a farmer's field that would be suitable for an emergency landing and then glide with a dead stick to a position where I could land on that field. The rule was that all landings not on an authorized field had to be done with wheels up. It was safer that way, because wheels can catch on a furrow or a stump and leave the aircraft standing on its nose or worse. Also, the friction of the airplane's belly on the ground slows it and makes a safe landing possible in a shorter space. I liked solving this sort of problem and learned during routine flights to keep an eye out for places that might serve for emergency landings.

The next phase was aerobatics. It turned out to be more

work than I had expected. I had envisioned floating in a carefree manner around the sky carving interesting patterns in the air, but there was nothing carefree about it. Every maneuver had its own set of procedures to memorize. For something as simple as a roll, the trick was to lower the nose, to gain speed, add left rudder and stick simultaneously, making the nose describe a circle around a point on the horizon. If you did it right, you came out at the original altitude, compass heading, and air speed.

Mr. Sisk took leave in late June, and most of my aerobatics were taught by others. One instructor was a recalled reservist who had developed a visible fear of flying and couldn't do a roll as well as a novice like me. I had only two sessions with him, and he cut both of them short. Maybe he was just afraid to fly with me.

Loops and Immelman turns were the hardest. An Immelman is a half loop followed by a half roll. It is a way to reverse direction in a hurry without departing from a straight line across terrain. I remember one attempt in particular.

Flying solo at 6,000 feet, I closed the canopy, made an S-turn to check for other aircraft in the area, then pointed the nose down to build up air speed. Then, gently, I pulled the stick back, watching the horizon fall away. Seeming to skim up the side of a thunderhead, I aimed at the zenith and then let the nose fall toward the opposite horizon. At that point, all I had to do was an easy half-roll to the left to complete the turn and get right side up again.

But just as I started that rolling maneuver, the aircraft gave a little shudder, and all the tension went out of the controls, as though a scissors had cut the cables. The horizon lost its lovely parallel alignment with the wings and started moving around in a jerky, unfamiliar pattern. I was disoriented, caught in a kaleidoscope of earth and sky moving in a pattern that made no sense.

Finally, the airplane settled into the wobbly-top pattern that

I recognized as a normal spin. Now I knew what to do: hard left rudder and forward stick. The spinning stopped, and I could see the details of the landscape below. The aircraft was diving toward a half-plowed field with a tiny tractor in the center. I watched the airspeed indicator until I had built up 130 knots, and then leveled off, fast enough to make my jaw sag and a gray border creep into the outer fringe of my vision. *Well*, I thought, *that wasn't wasted. Practicing spins was one of the things on my to-do list for this flight.*

What had gone wrong, I realized, was keeping the nose too high at the top of the loop and losing flying speed. It happened more than once. It was a good thing that (a) the SNJ was a very forgiving airplane and (b) I started these maneuvers at 6,000 feet, plenty of room for corrections.

But the airplane was not always forgiving. Heading back to base from another solo flight, I heard an instructor yell to the tower, "Airplane down! I see two parachutes!" My left foot started shaking but calmed as I entered Whiting Field's landing pattern. Later, I learned that an instructor and student had somehow gotten themselves into an inverted spin, one where the centrifugal force pulls you out of the seat instead of pressing you into it. The SNJ was balanced in such a way that it happened only on dual flights. In that particular situation, the airplane was quite unforgiving, for there was no way to get an SNJ out of an inverted spin, and the only recourse was to open the hatch, unfasten the seat belt, and let the centrifugal force propel you and your parachute out into the open sky. I saw the cadet the next day. He had two black eyes from the G-forces of that escape.

By July 1953, the members of Class 46-52 were spreading out as we progressed through the program at our respective paces. I passed my last aerobatics check on July 1. On July 4, I marched with the Whiting Field Cadet Band in a parade down the main street of Milton, Fla. And then I moved back to Pensacola to learn formation flying at Saufley Field.

Whenever an accident happened, detailed accounts circulated spontaneously through the base. More than morbid curiosity was involved here. If somebody died of a mistake, we wanted to be sure we understood it so that we could keep it from happening to us. A cadet whom I knew slightly made one as we were learning a new landing procedure.

For formation flying we were taught to make a carrier-type approach to return to the field. First we would fly upwind over the intended landing point at an altitude of 1,000 feet. There we would cut the power and put the airplane in a bank at just the right angle to lose the whole thousand feet in one 360-degree spiral. Then we would level off at the start of the runway, pulling up the nose to execute a full-stall landing, meaning that the airplane loses flying speed as it touches the deck (we always called the ground the "deck" in the Navy). When done properly, all three wheels touched down at the same moment. This type of landing is especially important for carrier pilots because it ensures that the tail hook will be down to catch the arresting cable.

My casual acquaintance was in the last stage of this approach and just a few degrees from lining up with the runway when a gust of wind caught a wing and pushed it down. As the rumor mill analyzed his problem, the student pilot applied opposite aileron, in an attempt at correction. But he picked up the wing too sharply, its angle of attack increased to where it couldn't fly, the plane stalled, spun in, and the pilot was killed.

I was thinking about his case while on a dual hop with a really sharp, fearless instructor who had seen combat in Korea. It was a windy day. Everything went just right until I was in that final turn about 40 feet above the deck. The wind seemed to grab the left wing and push it down. Afraid of over-reacting, I froze and let the wing stay down while I figured out my next move. Then I saw the 100-foot radio tower at the side of the runway. We were banking directly toward it.

There were two choices. I could pick up the low wing really

fast like my late acquaintance had and point the SNJ back toward the runway. Or I could increase the bank and try to squeeze past the tower on the side away from the runway. Either way would risk an aerodynamic stall.

There was no time to think it through. The lizard part of my brain took over and decided to tighten the existing bank. With my left hand, I jammed the throttle toward the firewall. We cleared the radio tower by inches.

I leveled off and held it there. The engine was roaring at full takeoff power in level flight 40 feet over the airbase, wheels uncomfortably close to the buildings. I was too stunned to move. After what seemed a long silence, there was a soft voice from the back seat.

"I've got it."

The instructor took us out of the area, climbed to 1,000 feet, and let me do the whole thing over from the beginning. He never yelled at me. When we were safe on the ground, he told me that he saw the wheel watch drop his paddles and run for his life. I had come that close to spinning in and killing us all.

"I flew 30 missions in Korea," my instructor said calmly. "I was in dogfights with MiGs. None of that scared me like you just did."

The only good news was that for such an awful situation, I had made exactly the right moves: full throttle and tighten the turn. Oddly, it made me a little more confident. If I was fated to die in a crash, it should have been then.

Formation flying itself was a fairly interesting set of problems. There was the problem of getting three or four airplanes to a designated meeting place in the sky and then joining up behind the designated leader: 15-feet to the starboard of the plane ahead, 15 feet below, and 15 feet behind. We learned to climb, dive, and turn in this formation. We even did wingovers – steep climb, bank, and steep descent. We were doing some of what the Blue Angels, the Navy's crack aerobatics team did – only they used fast jets and a five-foot interval instead of our 15.

By now, July was about over. President Eisenhower had kept his promise to go to Korea. As a military hero, he had both the knowledge to evaluate the situation and the confidence to do what needed to be done. On July 27, a Monday, the morning papers carried banner headlines. This one was in the *New York Times*: "TRUCE IS SIGNED, ENDING THE FIGHTING IN KOREA."

Today, it is known as the forgotten war. When the 50th anniversary of the truce came in 2003, the few celebrations went mostly unnoticed. Even in 1953, little attention was paid. But to me, it was a new game. If I wanted out of the Navy, I could leave now without dishonor. Before the armistice, taking a DOR would mean somebody else would have to do my share of the fighting. With hostilities over, I could leave with a clearer conscience and shorten my active duty obligation from four years to two. I could resume my newspaper career in little more than a year.

This development made it harder to concentrate on flying. On July 29, my instructor decided that my wingovers in formation were too sloppy, and I needed to repeat a lesson. I did so on Friday, July 31, followed it with a solo hop the same day, and then decided it was time to get away from Pensacola to think things over. I took weekend liberty and hitchhiked to New Orleans, which I had wanted to see ever since taking a folklore course at K-State and writing a term paper on the emergence of jazz as an American art form. I wanted to find its roots and clear my head at the same time.

The Roosevelt Hotel was my obvious choice because of all the nights I had listened to live music coming from its ballroom on WWL, the clear-channel station whose 50,000-watt signal followed the AM skip for long distances at night. It had been loud and clear in Manhattan, Kan., on nights when the ionosphere was right. Besides, the Roosevelt was walking distance from the French Quarter, where the Dukes of Dixieland were playing at the Famous Door.

What happened next is recorded in a letter I wrote to a woman friend who had been in that class.

As soon as I'd checked in at the Roosevelt and straightened the stars on my shoulders, I headed for Bienville and Basin, which, in the old days, was the site of Lulu White's Mahogany Hall, a gathering place for the old jazz kings. Nothing was there but a warehouse under construction, and down the street, a fairly modern apartment building. So I eased over a block to Iberville, looking for some vestige of the wild and racy spirit that was supposed to be New Orleans, and, finding none, walked east to Franklin Street to the corner that was occupied by Tom Anderson's annex, hangout of King Oliver, Sidney Bechet, and a lot of others. A filling station stood on the spot.

I stood on the same Storyville street corner where Louis Armstrong's early notes rang out against the bright New Orleans night and where Jelly Roll Morton first pounded out Tiger Rag and saw only a couple of dirty kids playing in the gutter. Basin Street was just like any other street in any other town in America ...

It was getting dark, so I turned east and headed to the French Quarter and Bourbon Street. I knew there would be music there ...

Bourbon Street runs slightly northeast of Canal, the main drag, bending off the cardinal heading to follow a bend in the Mississippi just four blocks away. All New Orleans jazz has migrated to that area. Concentrated in five blocks of a very narrow, very crowded and very dirty street are the bars, bands, and skin shows that are all that's left of New Orleans night life. My first shock after adjusting to the glare of the bright lights – it was by now quite dark – was to see the street teeming with prosperous looking, well-dressed people. These were the sightseers, the slummers, the people like myself, and it's for these people and for them alone that Bourbon Street exists today.

It was like a carnival. Everyone trying to do everything and everything at once ...

I eased into one of the holes and listened to a fat piano player. He was great, the crowd thought, and they shouted their requests, and I was shocked into gulping my 60-cent beer instead of nursing it along like I'd planned because he was playing trivial mush like Sweet Lorraine and Tenderly and even Doggie in the Window. Imagine! On Bourbon Street in New Orleans, birthplace of Tiger Rag and King Porter Stomp, these idiots are applauding Doggie in the Window. Someone finally requested Rampart Street Parade, but the guy didn't even know it. Later, however, he partially vindicated himself by pouring out a cool rendition of St. James Infirmary.

––––––––––––––––––––

With all thoughts of the Navy cleared from my mind, I went back to my room at the Roosevelt to consider the problem afresh. If I stayed in the Navy, my flying would be like my cornet playing: maybe good enough to get by, but with no prospect of becoming one of the best. The next afternoon, I went to one of the designated military hitchhiking stands and caught a ride back to Saufley field. Early Monday, instead of checking in for morning formation, I reported to the commander's office. My pre-flight classmate Bill Krause was sweeping the floor. He looked troubled when he saw me there. I told the CO that I was dropping the program. He wondered why it had taken me so many months into it to decide that I didn't want to fly. I gave an awkward answer without mentioning the armistice.

There followed a series of interviews, some psychological testing, and an appearance before a board of officers to explain myself. This time I did mention the armistice. I said I considered myself a citizen-warrior and was ready to resume my civilian career now that the war was over.

"And what career would that be?"

"I am a newspaperman, sir."

It was also suggested that if I required a war to stay in the service, one was under way at that moment in French Indochina. Yes, I said, I have been following that in the newspapers, and it is pretty clear that this administration will not get us involved there, at least not anytime soon. And so that chapter of my Naval service ended and another began.

12. Aboard the USS Pocono

I was issued a sailor's uniform and posted to Battalion X, the transient barracks at Pensacola mainside where DORs awaited assignment to the fleet. My new rank was seaman, the same pay grade as Navcad, but without the glamour. I got to keep my aviator's flight logbook, which I still have today. It shows 99 hours in the air, 32 of them solo. There were several other former cadets in my situation, and we were assigned menial chores to fill the time, but I had a better idea. I arranged an interview with the editor of the base newspaper, the *Gosport,* to volunteer my services. He was a naval aviator who had served in the early stages of the Korean conflict. He looked at my Navy GCT score.

"You have a lot of stuff," he said. And he took me on as a copy editor.

In the evenings I hung around the base library, and discovered William Butler Yeats, being especially drawn to his "An Irish Airman Foresees His Death." And remembering a not-so-long-ago conversation, I checked out *You Can't Go Home Again* by Thomas Wolfe.

I would have been happy to finish my hitch by working on the *Gosport,* but the Naval Air Training Command believed, reasonably, that its dropouts should not mingle with the active cadets, so it found assignments for us elsewhere. Eventually mine came through: to the flag allowance aboard the USS Pocono, an amphibious command ship based at Little Creek, Va. Somewhere on the street, I encountered Mr. Sisk who was

147

surprised to see me in an enlisted uniform, but he understood. The peacetime Navy, he said, could be tedious and frustrating. He was on the way out himself and planned to enter law school at Tulane.

Little Creek turned out to be a suburb of Norfolk, and the Navy was everywhere. I reported aboard the Pocono, was assigned a locker and a sleeping rack, but soon learned that my main duty would let me live and work ashore. The Navy in its wisdom had found me a job related to journalism – in the public information office of the Atlantic Fleet Amphibious Force. Flag allowance meant that I worked under the admiral's flag, i.e. on his staff, which was where public information was positioned on the organization chart.

My first job was writing press releases, mostly "hometowners," brief pieces about a ship's embarkation or arrival, each customized with the name of one of its sailors and sent to his hometown paper. There were other enlisted men with media experience. One was a former reporter for the *New York Journal-American*. Another had been editor of the Notre Dame yearbook.

I quickly observed that the men in the Radio Section had more interesting work. They produced public-service radio programs and were gearing up to create a weekly TV show in prime time donated by a new UHF station. Not many people had UHF sets then, but our admiral did, so he was the target audience. I spent time chatting with the head of the Radio Section, Chief Gunner's Mate John T. Spavin, a smart man with a working-class Boston accent. After learning that I had done undergraduate work in radio broadcasting, he got me transferred to his section, and I was given responsibility for writing continuity for the new TV production, "The Gator Show."

It was fun. We designed a musical variety show with Navy talent, of which there was a lot in the Norfolk area. Its master of ceremonies was Ron Carney, who had a natural broadcasting voice and aspired to be his generation's Bob Hope. Carney gave the lead singer in the group a stage name, Ann McFadden. She was a WAVE from Lowell, Mass., and she sang "Get Happy" with a charming catch in her voice.

It was in my barracks at Little Creek that I first learned the outcome of the Brown case that I had covered in Topeka three years earlier. Supreme Court decisions are announced on Mondays, and so it was on the front page of the Tuesday May 18 edition of the *Norfolk Virginian-Pilot* with a banner headline. Oliver Brown had won his case, and the nation's schools would have to desegregate "with all deliberate speed." There was some griping and swearing among the white southerners in the barracks, but the prospect of being in the south at the time of the change appealed to my newsman's sense of adventure.

From time to time there was an opportunity for temporary duty on one of the ships in our command, e.g. a free cruise. I took two: one to the Naval Gun Factory in Washington, D.C., and one 10-day trip to New York City, and Newport, R.I. One of the musicians on our show fixed me up with a blind date with a captain's daughter in Newport, and I smuggled civilian clothes in a duffle bag, then changed at the YMCA so as not to embarrass her by being seen with a mere seaman. I met her and her father in my badly wrinkled outfit, and then we had dinner and took a driving tour of the Newport mansions. The next day, I took a bus down to Cape Cod to check out a job that had been advertised at the daily newspaper in Hyannis. But my release date was months away, and the editor needed someone immediately.

My task on these cruises was to write press releases for the local papers about our ship and its role in amphibious warfare. The most interesting trip was the one that took us cruising up the Potomac and Anacostia rivers on a Dock Landing Ship to the Washington Navy Yard in southeast D.C. When we passed Mount Vernon, we assembled on the port deck and saluted. Once ashore, I walked around and looked at the monuments, the mall, and the National Press Building. I tried to picture myself working there.

In the spring, the Eisenhower administration looked for ways to cut federal spending, and the Pentagon cooperated by reducing active duty tours for reservists. My 24-month obligation was cut to 20 months, my country having decided that I could best serve it by getting off its payroll. I had some accumulated leave and enough money to buy a summer suit with two pairs of pants, and soon I was out of Little Creek and flying home in the back of a TWA Constellation with a round lounge area and a birdcage in the rear. I reached into the pocket of my new suit and pulled out a pack of cigarettes. A stewardess noticed the lack of a tax stamp and knew its significance. "You're smoking sea stores," she said. "You must be in the Navy." Perhaps the military generated more respect than I knew.

I had a subscription to *Editor & Publisher*, which gave me a good sense of the job market. It wasn't bad. I still had the advantage of belonging to a low-birthrate generation, so there was not a lot of competition. I had placed a blind situation-wanted ad and received inquires from Moorhead, Minn., Syracuse, N.Y. and Rock Hill, S. C. All offered the same starting pay, $60 a week. I decided that I belonged back in Kansas. My market value would be stronger, and there was another consideration. Chances were good that I would meet my future wife wherever I landed. On the whole, it would be nice to marry a Kansas girl.

My parents by this time had moved to Manhattan, job opportunities having run out in Clay Center. My father would soon switch careers and start selling mutual funds instead of cars, dealing with the same people in the same familiar territory, and doing quite well at it. But in summer 1954, he was selling cars for the Studebaker dealer, and he found a good buy in a 1952 Starlight Coupe with low mileage, manual shift and overdrive. The bank gave me a loan on the dealer's recommendation even though I didn't have a job yet. My mustering-out pay covered the down payment.

First I drove the Studebaker to Kansas City, walked unannounced into the *Star's* newsroom and asked John Colt, the new managing editor, for a job. Hemingway had worked there, and Kansas City was an interesting town, as I knew from growing up reading the *Kansas City Times.*

Colt liked my clips.

"But I don't expect to have an opening for another month or two," he said.

"I don't want to wait that long," I replied.

"I wouldn't either."

We parted amicably.

Then I went to Wichita where the *Eagle* editors seemed very interested. They asked me to spend some time looking around the town and come back in three hours. I went out for lunch and a matinee showing of *Niagara* with Marilyn Monroe and Joseph Cotten, who, before he took up acting, had been an advertising salesman for the *Miami Herald.* When I returned, the *Eagle* editors said that a reporting job had just opened and asked how much money I needed. Given my experience, I said, that would be $80 a week.

"The best we can do is $65," the ranking editor said. I reached for my coat.

13. The Kansas desk

In Topeka, Jim Reed was glad to see me, and he hired me at the *Capital* for $78 a week. Later, I learned that the *Eagle* editors had been so confident of snagging me for $65 that they used my three-hour absence to fire a marginal performer and make a slot available. I hoped they would give him his job back.

The *Capital* started me on the business beat and gave me the only desk open at the time, which happened to be in the women's department next to Constance Van Natta. We had some nice chats between deadlines, and I told her about my plans for graduate school after some immersion in the news business. The business beat was really dull: visiting the headquarters of the Santa Fe Railroad to get their car-loading totals for the period, checking in with Kansas Power & Light and the Chamber of Commerce. Business journalism then was mostly rewriting handouts. The idea of giving corporations the same critical attention that was applied to government had not yet occurred to most newspapers.

Weekends were different. Because I was the junior reporter and single, I worked Saturdays and Sundays and covered the police on those days, spending some time at crime scenes. The first was a murder case. A man had stabbed his wife's boyfriend with a paring knife. The wife was there with her small boy. When the police told her they knew that she wasn't involved and was free to go, the little boy solemnly led her away. Reporters, like medical workers, get case hardened after a while, but I wasn't there yet. After a few weeks of this, I was moved up to a more interesting job: number-two man on the state desk.

Jim Robinson, the hard-working state editor, was the most creative member of the staff. My job was to work the desk on his days off and spend the rest of the time out on the road digging up stories. This job took me back to the Blue Valley and the ongoing fight against Tuttle Creek Dam. The newsroom was interesting, but I loved getting out in the world armed with my pen and a camera.

One day between road trips I heard a musical laugh and looked up to see a pair of Irish blue eyes and a sweet smile next to Connie in the women's department. Being a good reporter, I quickly found out that they belonged to Sue Quail, and that she was a freshman at Washburn University of Topeka. She had a part-time job writing wedding stories for Connie, who was a close friend of her mother. Connie filled me in on details of her history. Her family had been through hard times, too. Her father, Frank M. Quail, had been diagnosed with diabetes when in law school and not much progress was made in his treatment until his uncle Frank A. Quail intervened.

Frank A. was a well-connected Cleveland lawyer, and he got Frank M. into the Cleveland Clinic, where doctors were using insulin, discovered in 1922, for diabetes. Frank M. recovered enough to hold a state civil service job, but never practiced law, and died at the age of 51 when Sue was 13. Her mother, the former Helen Peppard, had a secure job as a public school teacher, and the family's stability came from her strength. Sue's religious heritage was Irish Catholic on her mother's side, Protestant Irish on her father's. So she split the difference and joined the Episcopal Church. She lived at home with her mother and grandmother. Later I realized that Connie, also a good reporter, was working both sides and feeding details about me to Sue and her mother.

Sue Quail, 1954

My other preoccupation in this period was finding a graduate school. I had started writing letters of inquiry while still at Little Creek, but now it was time to get serious. And I quickly learned that my K-State grades, mediocre because of my preoccupation with the *Collegian*, would not be an impediment to gaining admission. It was yet another benefit of being part of the low birth-rate Depression cohort. But my grades did stand in the way of getting a teaching or research assistantship. Some typical responses:

"The transcript does not justify a graduate assistantship. In fact, your undergraduate record means we'd have to admit you here as a non-degree candidate at first." – Gordon A. Sabine, College of Communication Arts, Michigan State University.

"Yes, we have graduate scholarships and after you have been here a quarter to learn our ways, you might well qualify for an assistantship." – Kenneth E. Olson, Graduate School of Journalism, Northwestern University.

"As you will probably agree, your undergraduate grade point average was not impressive … We were somewhat concerned by the fact that your grade point average for your senior year was even lower." – Leslie G. Moeller, School of Journalism, State University of Iowa.

But I had an ace in the hole. My old professor, John W. McReynolds, had moved on to teach government and coach the swimming team at his old school, St. Benedict's College in Atchison, Kan. He was confident that he could get me an assistantship at Chapel Hill, although he refused to put it that way.

"I am not going to get you in," he said in a January 1956 letter.

You and God will get you in. Some people have it; others don't have it. It just so happens that I have it, and at Chapel Hill somebody who has it knows I have it. That means that when he looks for somebody who has it, he can ask me, and if I say Smith or Jones has it, that means Smith or Jones has it. You have it. You are what universities are for.

Today, we call that "networking." Further encouragement came through a back-channel communication from Chapel Hill, relayed through McReynolds, in the form of a suggestion that I hold off on accepting any offer that might come from another school unless it was exactly what I wanted.

That was easy advice to follow. A chance to study political science at Chapel Hill would be the best possible deal because I had little interest in earning a graduate degree in journalism. An assistantship in journalism would be fine, but I needed to learn something substantive, something to write about.

As preparation – and to supplement my newspaper pay with

some Korean GI bill money – I enrolled as a part-time student at Washburn, listing my career goal as "sociological writer." However, the classes that I remember best were in psychology and government. The first, in the fall semester of 1954, met at 8 a.m. on Tuesdays and Thursdays. It was called "Psychology of Adjustment," and it was taught by Bernard Hall, M.D. of the famous Menninger Clinic. Dr. Karl Menninger was a guest lecturer, and I finally got the importance of Freud's concept of the unconscious mind. And a memorable political science instructor was Marc Carson, a graduate of the London School of Economics who had a subtle way of making me question my belief in the total power of the free market. He never said I was wrong about that. Just consider the possibility, he suggested, that there might be cases where market failure would be serious enough that government intervention would be needed. In my newspaper work, I soon found such a case.

It became the most memorable story assignment in my time at Topeka. Three years after the flood, Blue Valley residents were still fighting Tuttle Creek Dam. Howard Miller, their Democratic congressman, had succeeded in blocking further appropriations, and construction had stopped. His Republican opponent in November, William Avery, was also against the dam, so the valley residents started to relax. Officially, the Blue Valley Study Association was loyal to Miller, but the members' hearts were not in it. With the urgency gone, the district reverted to its normal Republican ways and Avery won easily. In the minds of the residents, big dams were an affliction caused by big government, and the Republicans were the party that fought big government. That turned out to be a tactical error. Nationally, as usually happens in off-year elections, the party in control of the White House lost seats – in this case, enough to lose control of the House to the Democrats. As a freshman member of the minority party, Avery didn't have much clout.

When the Republican leadership backed an appropriation

for continuation of the dam, even though it was not in the president's budget, Avery announced that he would oppose it. Howard Miller, asked about the situation, said, "If he succeeds, he's going to have to do it with Democratic votes – and he's in an awfully poor position to ask for them."

My political views began to shift while covering the Blue Valley side of this struggle. I believed in rational decision making and planning, and I could see how the convergence of political forces was pushing Kansas toward an irrational response to its periodic flooding problem. The most rational view, I thought, was that of Walter Kollmorgen, a professor of geography at the University of Kansas. His succinct summary of the problem: "Flood plains sometimes flood."

In other words, anyone who has land in a flood plain owns it subject to the prior easement belonging to the river. From time to time, the river will assert its claim, and the rational strategy for humans is to find out where the river likes to go and then stay out of its way. Flood-plain zoning was one of the options on the table, but none of the interest groups took much notice of it. In my observer's view, it wasn't bigger or smaller government that we needed, it was smarter government. And that demanded a smarter population, which put the problem at my door as a journalist.

It was a stark example of market failure. The industries at Kansas City had sunk the costs of building their plants in the 100-year flood plain without taking into account any possibility that there might actually be a 100-year flood. No thought was given to who would pay its costs. The arithmetic for discounting future costs or benefits to their present value is straightforward. But it requires long-range thinking and many players in the free marketplace are interested only in the near-term consequences of their decisions. Making those calculations is especially difficult, emotionally if not mathematically, when the timing of the future costs or benefits is uncertain. In the long run, said John Maynard Keynes, we're all dead.

And so it became an issue of raw power: wealthy industrial interests in the downstream cities against the less politically involved residents of the upstream valleys.

The near-term benefits of big dams were attractive to Kansans on several levels. Besides flood protection, they could provide water resources for irrigation, power, and recreation. The latter was especially appealing in our fairly dry state. The newly created Kansas Parks Authority arranged an airborne tour of the proposed dam sites in Kansas plus visits to state parks built around federal dams in Oklahoma. I went along, and we traveled in a formation of small private planes. It was just after we had taken off from a meal stop at Kansas City and headed southwest that I looked down and saw the old John Henry Myers farm, recognizable by the stone quarry and the fence corner where the horse had almost thrown me. It was the last time I would ever see it.

The person who drove me to the Topeka airport to begin that trip was Sue Quail, the wedding writer. We were growing accustomed to one another's company. It is hard to manage a social life when you work for a morning newspaper, and seeing someone who has a connection to that newspaper is a definite advantage. The thought crossed my mind that she might not mind writing about a wedding of her own. To improve my chances, I took up pipe smoking. Her late father had been a pipe smoker, and from my psychology courses I knew that women were attracted to men who reminded them of their fathers.

The *Daily Capital* lived up to the journalistic standards that I had been taught at K-State – part of the time. At other times, it was too ready to use its power in its own interest and those of its advertisers. I stumbled upon a pretty good story: that the local television station, WIBW-TV, owned by Senator Capper, had quietly begun broadcasting in color. The city desk sent my story up to the general manager for review, and his advertising department killed it. The reason: local merchants had an overstock of soon-to-be obsolescent black-and-white sets,

Christmas was coming, and they needed to use this opportunity to unload them. At least Charlie Pearson, the city editor, was not shy in telling me what happened.

An equally brazen act of self-interest was revealed by Bill Colvin, my old boss in Manhattan, who was a former *Capital* city editor. Downtown Topeka had an odd arrangement of one-way streets. The newspaper was on Jackson Street, a block from the main downtown street, Kansas Avenue. Jackson was parallel to and west of Kansas, and it ran one-way going south. Quincy, the parallel street a block east of Kansas, was one-way headed north. Therefore if a motorist driving down the city's main street wanted to reverse direction, he or she had to make a left turn to get to the one-way street going the other way. A normal one-way pattern allows you to reverse direction with a right turn and avoid crossing opposing traffic.

Topeka did it this way, Colvin explained, to make it easier for the *Daily Capital* delivery trucks to make their daily runs to the railroad station. (The newspapers moved to another location decades ago, and, according to Google Maps, Jackson Street now is one-way northbound, as it should be.)

A newspaper in mid-century was a manufacturing enterprise, and it was so classified by the Bureau of the Census. It brought in raw material, added value to it with heavy machinery, and then transported finished product directly to consumers. The news-editorial staff was a relatively minor part of the operation, and its only physical product was wastepaper. We wrote our stories on manual typewriters, editors improved them with soft pencils, and the paper went to the back shop where linotype operators replicated our keystrokes to create two-inch slugs of hot lead type. Then the composing room locked these slugs inside metal frames called chases and rolled them to the stereotyping department. A paper mache mat was pressed against the chase to capture the impression of the type to create a flexible mold, and it in turn was used to create a rounded printing plate that fit onto a tubular press. If a late story broke, and the editor cried,

"Tear out page one for a re-plate," this entire process had to be repeated. It was hot, sweaty work.

The paper had its own in-house engraving department, and I got to show off my tech savvy on a winter night when the roads froze over and a gas outage cut off our heat temporarily. Without gas to provide heat for drying the photo emulsion on its zinc halftones, the engraving department couldn't operate. The nearest Fairchild engraving machine was at the *University Daily Kansan* in Lawrence, 27 miles away. I saved the day by driving there on icy U.S. Highway 24, making the plastic engravings on the university's machine, and getting them back to Topeka in time for the first edition.

Management was happy, but the engravers were not. Unions were not strong in Topeka, and the newsroom stylebook let us know where Capper Publications stood. It cautioned against the use of the term "labor leaders" to describe union officials because, it explained, most working people in our community did not belong to unions. The correct term, the stylebook advised, was "union bosses."

Despite its quirks, the paper still had some good, public service reporting. George Mack got evidence of a political kickback scheme in the state's purchase of gasoline. Acting on a tip, he compared vendors' bills with their campaign contributions and found they matched at exactly one cent per gallon. But the paper's social responsibility went beyond uncovering corruption.

Anna Mary Murphy was an activist reporter who intervened in a dispute between the local police chief and Boys' Industrial School, a state institution for the rehabilitation of juvenile delinquents. When a school official bragged about its rehabilitation rate at a civic club meeting, the *Topeka State Journal* asked Chief S. I. Purdue if things were really going that well from his point of view.

"There is something radically wrong" with the operation of the school, said the chief, adding that he and his men were tired of chasing after the frequent runaways who stole cars and damaged property. "We don't consider it fair to the city of Topeka or the police department to bring boys in from across the state and turn them loose on the city," he said.

When Murphy read that in the *Journal*, she screamed, "They're trying to set us back ten years for the sake of a headline," and grabbed her telephone. By the time the next morning's Capital went to press, she had arranged a meeting between police and BIS officials.

With Murphy tagging along, the police toured the school and learned about its operation. Everyone came away happy. Chief Pardue was impressed by the training program and agreed to help his fellow Kansas law enforcement officers understand the importance of sending troubled youths to a school instead of a prison. And he advocated more funding for the school.

Topeka was a microcosm of journalism's best and worst. And I got to learn about my home state while driving around in the Studebaker in search of stories. The most memorable was driving through the Blue Valley on June 16, 1955, collecting reaction to the renewed funding for Tuttle Creek Dam. The main reaction was disbelief. The valley residents were still in the first of Kubler-Ross's five stages of grief. But denial would soon turn to anger, and that would be a better political story.

I proposed to Sue while we were standing in the middle of Canterbury Lane in Topeka on a snowy night in January 1956. She said yes. The next day, I sought out her mother and said, "I guess you know I want to marry your daughter."

"Yes," she said, "and I approve."

It was clear by this time, that we were not likely to remain in Kansas. The influence of Professor McReynolds had paid off, and North Carolina had made an offer of admission plus a teaching assistantship. That and the GI bill would enable us to live in relative comfort. We set an August wedding date and planned a honeymoon trip to Chapel Hill to find housing. Then it would be back to Topeka for two more weeks on the *Daily Capital* before taking off for school.

My apartment on Topeka Boulevard had a gas fireplace, and that's where we guys threw the glasses after toasting the bride at the bachelor party.

Sue was still 19 when we married. She moved directly from her mother's house to mine – not unusual for women in the mid-1950s. Dropping out of school to get married was normal behavior. We were still in the postwar period of prosperity, and, thanks to a strong labor movement and a steeply graduated income tax, there was much less income inequality than exists today. A family could have just one wage earner and still enjoy a good middle-class living. So we went on together.

The wedding was a big one, bigger than either family could afford, held in Grace Cathedral. After the reception, we climbed into the Studebaker and pointed it toward Chapel Hill, stopping the first night at the Muehlebach Hotel in Kansas City. The Interstate Highway System was barely under way, with the first construction contract signed that very month. We found it slow going, especially when we reached the mountains. Our route took us through Asheville, so we visited the Thomas Wolfe house and his grave. When we entered Chapel Hill from the south, a red fox ran across the road in front of us. We took that as some kind of omen. And I would remember it 25 years later, when we moved back to Chapel Hill, and thought of Edna St. Vincent Millay's line, "I hunt the red brush of remembered joy."[13]

For our first home, we chose a brand new cinder-block duplex one mile from campus. All of the neighbors were married students. Sue found a part-time job in retailing. We had a wide choice of daily newspapers, and we took a home-delivery subscription to the *Charlotte Observer*. Jim Reed had been a fan of its aggressive news coverage and slick design, and I had enjoyed browsing it in the *Daily Capital* library in Topeka. But later, when the national school desegregation story got hotter, we would switch to the *Greensboro Daily News.* Its traditional design was less attractive, but the absence of decorative white space gave it more room for news. Moreover, the Charlotte editors were too reluctant to continue a page-one story to the inside even when big national stories needed more space and better detail.

We were not in Kansas anymore. Regional differences were quite pronounced in the mid-1950s, and southern accents were both more common and stronger than they are today. The standard greeting, "Hey, how you?" had an odd ring to our Midwestern ears. Racial segregation was present, but not as pronounced as I had seen in Pensacola or Norfolk. A black businessman, operating as Pete the Tailor, had a shop on Franklin, the main street, and he specialized in converting two-button sport and suit coats to three buttons, which had just come into fashion. Originally, it was called the "Edwardian" look, but was adopted first in the northeast, and so it became known as the Ivy look.

The undergraduates were overwhelmingly white and male. The university accepted females as freshmen if they declared nursing majors, but others had to start at North Carolina College for Women in Greensboro and transfer as juniors.

It turned out that I had a choice of jobs. I could be a research assistant for Roy Carter in the Institute for Research in Social Science, studying newspaper coverage of the still-young civil rights movement. Or I could be a teaching assistant for Charles B. Robson, the department head, grading his papers in a large lecture section of the course on the national government of the United States.

He had fond memories of my old professor, John W. McReynolds, and asked what he was doing now. I told him that he was at St. Benedict's College in Atchison, Kan., and one of his jobs was swimming coach.

"Oh? Does he know how to swim?"

"I don't know."

"Heh. Ol' Johnny, he wouldn't have to!"

The research job seemed too close to journalism, and it involved quantitative content analysis. Boring, I thought. On the other hand, it was bold of Robson to offer the grading job to me because he knew from my transcript that I had never taken a course in American government. And it was bold of me to accept it, but I did. We both figured that I could stay far enough ahead of the students in the book. It also helped that I was taking other courses in that first semester that bore on the topic. The synergy of learning and teaching would prove to be powerful.

14. Hark the sound

It felt comfortable to be in a classroom again. The introductory seminar for first-year grad students was Alexander Heard's History, Scope and Methods of Political Science. Heard was Ivy League in manner and appearance, evidently getting his three-button suits from one of the Julian brothers, Milton and Maurice, who pioneered the Ivy look in Chapel Hill and ran competing clothing stores on Franklin Street. Heard had earned his Ph.D under Harvard's legendary V. O. Key and received an "assisted by" credit on Key's most recent book, *A Two-Party South?* For the seminar, he had a list of term paper assignments that were designed to fit around a stellar array of guest speakers, and the first paper, "The Scientific Tradition," would be due in two weeks.

I volunteered for that one. I liked the adrenaline rush of working on deadline, the topic interested me, and I would be getting a head start on the semester. Wilson Library had the right books, and my undergraduate background in science wasn't so bad. I started with Plato and his metaphor of the shadows in the caves in *The Republic*, covered the scholastic period with *Summa Theologica* by Thomas Aquinas, and eased into the modern area with Sir James Jeans's The *Mysterious Universe*, an almost-poetic explanation of modern physics published in 1931. My carrel in Wilson accumulated 18 books, the most recent being Bertrand Russell's 1953 *The Impact of Science on Society*. I borrowed the office of Dr. Robson's secretary after working hours to type the final draft on a good typewriter. It came to 40 pages.

My classmates were impressed, but any of their paper topics would have been a disaster for me because they required more prior knowledge of political science than I possessed. Only a few were interested in quantitative methods. One of them was Jay Gates, a first-year grad student out of Williams College, who explained the chi-square test to us. It is a way of testing an apparent relationship between two variables, e.g. gender and presidential choice, to see whether it goes beyond what could reasonably be expected by chance alone. The formula seemed very complicated to me, and the calculation pure drudgery, although the department did have a Monroe calculating machine that could do multiplication and long division with a great deal of noise and vibration.

The number-crunching political scientists were a rag-tag minority on the faculty as well as among the graduate students, some of whom called attempts to measure political behavior "the new scholasticism." I found it easier to agree with them than to master the chi-square test, and I remained safely on the traditional, qualitative side. Studying the institutions of American government and how they worked would be more valuable in my goal of becoming a Washington correspondent.

It was a presidential election year, and I was late in requesting an absentee ballot from Kansas, so I called the registrar in Topeka and had one sent. The minimum voting age then was 21, so Sue was still too young. Ordering a ballot by telephone was a big deal because long-distance calls were expensive in 1956, and when the topic of voting came up in Professor Heard's class on political parties, he mentioned my novel effort and commented on my relative affluence.

The probability seemed very high that I owed my life to Eisenhower and his ability to fold a war, so I voted for him again, not suspecting that he was the last Republican I would ever support for national office.

Chapel Hill did not make me a liberal all at once. And I never lost my intuitive appreciation for the wisdom of markets. But studying the institutions of democracy made me realize that government is not the only source of abusive power. Private entities can accumulate and abuse power as well, and those abuses restrict markets. The checks and balances needed to limit government power also apply to the relationship between private and governmental power holders. Those who hold power will use it to get more power, no matter which side they are on. The Wagner Labor Relations Act of 1935, for example, was a depression-era attempt to use government authority to create a fairer balance of power between capital and workers.

Fred Cleaveland's course in recent national policy also taught me the difference between monetary policy and fiscal policy and helped me to understand Keynesian economics for the first time.

Prof. William Sumner Jenkins taught constitutional history in a drawl that originated from somewhere south of North Carolina, and it was a pleasure to read cases under his direction. The 1937 opinion of Charles Evans Hughes upholding the Wagner Act was an eye-opener for someone who had grown up with a pro-business, anti-government bias.[14] Its basis was that freedom of contract cannot exist without equality of bargaining power, and labor's attempts to organize needed to be protected for that reason.

Sue and I brought good luck to Chapel Hill. The Tar Heel basketball team had an undefeated season and went on to win the national championship with three overtimes in both the semi-final and final game. Local music entrepreneur Orville Campbell wrote a calypso song about it: "Three overtimes, two nights in a row; we'll never forget that TV show." In fact, we bought our first TV for the purpose of watching those games, and afterward we joined the undergraduates in dancing around their bonfire on Franklin Street. Music was supplied from a high-fidelity speaker wedged into a second-floor window of Battle Hall, which then was a men's dormitory.

Soon afterwards, Sue and I moved to better quarters, a new apartment building of modern design on Hillsborough St., a short walk from campus. It was a good place to have parties, and we helped improve social life for my cohort of grad students. When Sue told me she had been sexually harassed by her supervisor at work, I, uncharacteristically, confronted him in her presence and threatened him with physical harm unless he apologized. He did. And then Sue found a better job selling classic women's clothing at Elizabeth "Beppie" Branson's Little Shop on East Franklin Street.

When the academic year ended, we went back to Topeka for one more summer on the *Daily Capital*. It had changed in our year of absence. Arthur Capper had died a few months after the 1951 flood, and in 1956 his heirs sold the paper to Oscar Stauffer, owner of the afternoon partner in the joint agency, the *Topeka State Journal*. That ended the rivalry between the two newsrooms and led to consolidation of some of their operations including the photography department.

It was an awkward adjustment. I was working a late shift one rainy night when the police radio reported a flash flood on Soldier Creek in North Topeka. I picked up a Speed Graphic and sped to the scene, arriving just in time to grab a shot of police escorting a frightened family through knee-deep water. Making the picture was no simple task. There was nothing automatic about the Speed Graphic. It was too dark to use the rangefinder, so I had to estimate the distance and set the camera manually, choosing a combination of shutter speed and lens aperture based on the power of the flash bulb, then remove the film-holder slide, sight through the sports finder, and fire. Between shots, it was necessary to eject the bulb, put in a new one, and change the film. Hoping for the best, I took everything back to the office. It was after deadline for the morning paper, so I left the film holders and notes in the darkroom for the next shift.

It turned out beautifully. The picture was in focus and correctly exposed. It captured the frightened look of the family and the determination of the police to get them to higher ground. Roscoe Born, city editor of the *Journal*, liked it so much that he placed it seven columns wide under a banner headline at the top of the eight-column page of the afternoon paper. But he didn't give me a credit line. Remnants of the old rivalry lingered, and he didn't want to admit using *Daily Capital* work. More than half a century has passed, and I'm still sore about that.

Jim Robinson, my old boss on the state desk, had moved on to a reporting job at the *Detroit Free Press*, and left behind a file drawer full of documents relating to the fight over Tuttle Creek Dam: speeches, letters, transcripts of Congressional hearings, minutes of the Blue Valley Study Association, technical reports, a beautiful collection. I wrote to him in Detroit and got his permission to take the whole package with me to Chapel Hill. My master's thesis would be a case study of citizen political action in the fight against the dam. It was a wonderful find. I entered the name and date of each item on an index card, sorted them chronologically, and that created the time-line for my case study.

In theory, it was possible to earn a master's degree in one academic year. Figuring that this would be my last shot at higher education, I stretched it to two years, taking more than the required number of courses and earning a graduate minor in history. There was a shortage of teaching assistants, so I volunteered for a heavy teaching load my last semester instead of finishing the thesis. It included several discussion sections, and I was upgraded from teaching assistant to part-time instructor. This meant that I had one full course, for which I was solely in charge of both lectures and discussion. By that time, I had learned enough about American government to teach it with both enthusiasm and gravitas.

As the time approached to enter the job market again, I worried about my military status. The Soviet suppression of the Hungarian revolution of 1957 was a reminder that the cold war could get hot. And the new Eisenhower doctrine to resist any communist encroachment in the Middle East opened another dangerous possibility. I was obligated to remain in the Navy reserve until 1960. My rank was seaman, third from the bottom in the Navy's pay scale, and Sue was pregnant. If I were to be called back into service, I could support a family more comfortably as an officer, so I applied for a direct commission in the Naval reserve.

The direct commission program, then as now, provides for people with special skills to go directly to officer rank without the usual requirements for officer training. At that time, reserve officers were needed for Naval intelligence, and journalism was one of the qualifying fields. So I submitted the paper work and was interviewed by a board of reserve officers in Durham, N.C. We argued about politics and constitutional law, including Brown v. Board of Education. I passed the test.

For my civilian job, I cast a wide net. *Time* magazine invited me to drop by next time I was in New York, but made no offer of travel expenses. The *Denver Post* never answered my letter. The *Minneapolis Tribune* sent me a single copy of a complicated application form that had to be filled out by hand, in ink. I botched my first attempt, and gave up. Perhaps eye-hand coordination was part of the test.

My resume did generate an invitation from Alfred Friendly, managing editor of the *Washington Post*, to drop in if I happened to be in town. That was an easy trip, and so I recruited fellow student Kent Jennings, who would later become president of the American Political Science Association, to meet my class while Sue and I drove north. We stayed at the Harrington Hotel because it was cheap and within walking distance of the Post. As I waited outside Friendly's office, I overheard a secretary and a staff member talking about the sudden death of one of the reporters.

Friendly was more impressed by my clips than my education. He said an unexpected opening had just come up and wondered if I could be ready to start next week. I realized that he was thinking about asking me to take the dead guy's job!

"No, sir," I said. "I have a teaching commitment until May, and I need to finish my degree."

"May?" he said. "How would I know what my manpower needs will be in May?"

And that is pretty much how newspaper hiring was done in the middle of the 20th Century. If you walked in on the day that somebody quit, dropped dead, or was fired, you stood a chance of getting that person's job. Editors were tied to a 24-hour news cycle, and their planning horizon was not much longer than that.

But one company was different. Acting on Jim Robinson's advice and citing his recommendation, I wrote to Lee Hills and told him that I wanted to work for a Knight newspaper. At that time, Hills had the title of executive editor at both the *Detroit Free Press* and the *Miami Herald*, but his influence was company wide. The other Knight newspapers of that day were the *Charlotte Observer*, the *Akron Beacon Journal*, and the *Chicago Daily News*.

Hills was an early adopter of psychological testing to screen potential employees, using a system created by Byron Harless, who had established an industrial psychology consulting firm in Jacksonville in 1946. Eventually, Harless would join Knight Newspapers as a vice-president. Hills arranged for me to visit the *Charlotte Observer* to be interviewed by editor C. A. "Pete" McKnight and take some psychological tests administered by Sam McKeel, the *Observer's* human resources director. I knew a little bit about psychological tests, having experienced them both at K-State and Washburn. And I had read William H. White's 1956 best-seller, *The Organization Man*, an examination

173

of corporate conformity and its role in postwar America. Its thesis was a good fit to *Time's* concept of the passive Silent Generation with its impulse to fit in and sacrifice individuality for security. And the volume contained a delightful appendix titled "How to Cheat on the Personality Tests."

But White's advice proved to be of major help to me on only one of McKeel's instruments, the draw-a-person test. It is one of a class of diagnostic tools called "projective methods." You are given a blank sheet of paper and a pencil and told to draw a person. The psychologist interprets it as a self-portrait and looks for signs of weirdness. Drawing a person with any characteristics of the opposite sex was considered particularly aberrant. I drew a casually attired male figure in an open, welcoming stance and put a smile on its face. Years later, after projective methods had been found to be seriously unreliable, I was surprised to learn that the corporation was still using them.

I must have done well on the tests because Hills soon indicated a strong interest in finding me a job, probably at the *Detroit Free Press*. That led to some encouraging correspondence with Frank Angelo, the managing editor.

"It is very difficult for me to anticipate what the situation may be next summer," Angelo wrote. "However, I would like you to know that we have your name very close to the top of our list."

But the economy was in recession, and it was hitting the automobile industry especially hard. The *Free Press* put new hiring on hold. The dogwood was still blooming in North Carolina when a letter with a job offer arrived from George Beebe, the managing editor of the *Miami Herald*. It was positioned as a temporary summer job, but with a possibility that I would be asked to stay on. Being young and confident, I was not worried in the slightest. The *Herald* promised to pay our moving expenses, something it wouldn't do for someone who was unlikely to stay for more than the summer. It was time to settle down, too, because we would be arriving with a six-week old baby. The job paid $100 a week – only a little more than $39,000 a year in constant 2010 dollars, but one had to start somewhere. I was headed for big-town journalism.

Professor McReynolds had a cryptic word of advice when I told him of my plan to move to a tougher market. After my *Mercury-Chronicle* summer, he and Bill Colvin had compared notes on my prospects. There was a consensus.

"We agreed that you won't take any guff from anybody," he said. "Your problem is that you won't give anybody any guff."

It would be some time before I understood what they meant by that.

15. Getting sand in our shoes

I drove the Studebaker down to Miami alone and found an apartment on San Remo Avenue in Coral Gables while Sue and the baby waited in Topeka. Our furniture was already in storage in Miami. After a certain amount of driving around in circles, I decoded the Miami street system and found the *Herald* building at 200 South Miami Ave. George Beebe introduced me to the assistant managing editor, an energetic young Midwesterner named Al Neuharth who briefed me on the *Herald* and its culture. Vigorous rivalry with the afternoon *Miami News* was part of that culture, and the *News's* owners had just expressed their confidence in their paper's future by building a fancy new plant on the south bank of the Miami River.

"We thought their city editor was too good for the *Miami News*," said Neuharth, "so we brought him over here." And he took me over to meet John McMullan who turned out to be a natural newsman full of ideas that he liked to press with relentless vigor, whether they were good or bad. He sent me out to learn about the area by accompanying Gene Miller on the rounds of his beat, which at that time was the city of Miami Beach.

McMullan was a sharp judge of good writing, Miller told me. "He likes to reach way down into your story and find a buried lead there and bring it to the top."

Miller had been there less than a year, coming from the *Richmond News Leader* after two years in the Army Counter-

Intelligence Corps. He loved the *Herald* for its emphasis on writing, and he convinced me that Miami, with its odd array of characters, was a wonderful news town, practically a journalist's theme park. He would stay at the *Herald* for nearly 50 years, win two Pulitzer prizes and contribute to a third.

In rained a lot in Miami in the summertime, but in 1958, nobody carried umbrellas, although their use had been common in Chapel Hill. I learned of this cultural quirk when I walked into a bar with my big, black Chapel Hill umbrella during an evening thundershower. Conversation stopped as everyone turned to look at me.

"Well," said a patron, "here comes Mr. Chamberlain."

I was old enough to recognize the historical reference to Neville Chamberlain, the prime minister of England who negotiated what he thought was "peace for our time" with Adolf Hitler at Munich in 1938. His symbol for newspaper cartoonists was his umbrella.

Being fairly immune to social pressure, I continued to use my umbrella and rejected the clear plastic raincoats that were sticky and hot in Miami summer thundershowers. Then, on one muggy afternoon I was out with photographer John Walther to cover an accident, when it started to rain.

"Damn," said Walther, who had no way to protect his camera. I opened my umbrella and held it over him and the camera while he got his shot. After that, Walther started carrying an umbrella and other photographers followed his example. Eventually, reporters noticed the utility of umbrellas and acquired their own. I had become, early in the Miami part of my career, an agent of cultural change.

McMullan soon revealed what the Herald had in mind for me: to fill a vacancy on the education beat. "Since you just came from an educational experience, we thought you'd like that," he said. And he sent me out with Joy Reese Shaw, who had been filling in on the beat, to cover a meeting of the Dade County School Board.

"This is a good beat," said Joy, "because it involves the two things that are the most important to our readers: their money and their kids."

She was right, but there was one problem. The *Herald* had more reporters than desks, and as the newest on the staff, I had to float from one unoccupied desk to another. It was a serious inconvenience. After my second School Board meeting, I returned with a large stack of documents, all related to various aspects of ongoing stories.

"Where should I keep these?" I asked McMullan.

McMullan led me on a stroll around the perimeter of the newsroom, looking for an empty file drawer. There weren't any.

"You know," he said, "the education reporter really needs a desk."

And I was assigned one in a cluster of four with Gene Miller, Dom Bonafede, and Mike Morgan.

Despite the recession, South Florida was in the middle of one its periodic building booms, fueled by the steady arrival of sun seekers. The school board's building program was creating the equivalent of a new classroom every week. The *Herald* had a fat Sunday real estate section that chronicled the sprawl of suburban home building, mostly south and west of the city. Keeping up with the growing pains was one of the education beat's ongoing stories.

There were two others. The Soviet Union had beaten us in the space race by launching Sputnik 1 the previous October, and that raised concerns about the education system in the USA. All sorts of reform movements were springing up. Miami, in the process of being transformed from a sleepy Southern town to a booming melting pot of people who had been socialized somewhere else, was a good place to try new things.

The third running story was Florida's response to Brown v. Board of Education. Four years had elapsed, and there had been no move to desegregate anywhere in Florida, despite the high court's directive that segregation be ended "with all deliberate speed." When I arrived, the county had 12 senior high schools, 32 junior high schools, and 107 elementary schools that were all white and four senior high schools, five junior high schools, and 19 elementary schools that were all black. On this issue, Miami was still part of the traditional South, but local activists, led by Theodore Gibson, an Episcopal priest in the Coconut Grove section of Miami, had legal action pending in federal courts to get the board moving. At the state level, political leaders judged that desegregation would be more acceptable in Miami than elsewhere in the state, and were quietly encouraging the Dade board to act.

And so it was a good time to be the education writer. Digging in with gusto, I plotted ways to beat the *Miami News*. One big break was the chance to work general assignment on Saturdays, the one day of the week when both the *News* and *Herald* published on the same schedule, for Sunday morning delivery. George Beebe and Lee Hills routinely put both papers side by side on Sundays and paged through them, comparing the Herald stories with those in the News. My challenge when covering breaking news was to visualize what the *News* would do and then try to go it one better.

Gene Miller had been right about the *Herald*. For the first time, I was working for a newspaper that operated the way my first journalism textbook, Curtis MacDougall's *Interpretative Reporting*, said newspapers were supposed to operate. It gave the news clearly and boldly. The editors were quick to give feedback. Once, when I was on rewrite duty, John McMullan summoned me to his desk with his standard invitation, "Got a minute?" and showed three of my carbons spread out on his desk.

"You turned some nice phrases here," he said. "Good work."

It took only a few weeks to earn a raise and a permanent job. Sue and I used a GI loan to buy a house in a new development, figuring we wouldn't be bothered with expensive repairs and upkeep for the first few years. It was built from concrete block covered with stucco, and the roof was anchored by metal tie-down straps as provided by the new hurricane code. The development was called Pool and Patio Estates, and a few of our neighbors had actual 25-foot pools. I marked off a badminton court in the backyard, which led to some merry Sunday afternoon gatherings.

The downside was that there was no shopping within walking distance, and I often needed a car in my job, so Sue and the baby were stuck in the neighborhood all day. I worked out a routine where, at least one day a week, I could ride a Greyhound bus to work or carpool with John McMullan, who lived in the vicinity. There was no way we could pay for a second car on a *Herald* salary.

Newspaper pay was poor everywhere. Russell Baker was a reporter for the *Baltimore Sun* in that same decade, and when he wrote his memoir, he said it seemed that the *Sun* had the mysterious power to calculate, to the last penny, exactly how much money his family needed to survive week by week. Then it set his salary at a dollar less than that. That reminded me of the *Herald*, where the raises always came barely in time to save us from one disaster or another. A little bit of income from the Navy Reserve kept us solvent.

My direct commission had come through, my cousin Ralph gave me his old Navcad uniform, and I purchased an officers' bridge cap and ensign's insignia from the Donald Lavigne uniform shop. I joined a reserve unit that drilled on Thursday nights, taking the uniform to work on a hanger and changing in the *Herald* men's room at the end of my shift. I was supposed to drill with an intelligence unit, that being my designated military specialty, but that unit met on Wednesdays, the same day as the School Board meetings. To avoid a conflict, I found a telecommunications censorship unit that would take me. Besides meeting on Thursday nights, it offered good summer duty, consisting of annual two-week training periods on Church Street in New York's financial district, and living at the Tower Hotel in Brooklyn, a short subway ride to Wall Street.

The worst problem was that censorship, as John Milton pointed out in *Areopagitica*, is seriously boring work. My unit's main task was learning how to eavesdrop on overseas telephone calls and cut them off if anyone mentioned weather or ship movements. But at least, I finally had a commission in the United States Navy. I thought about that medical corpsman at Olathe who had told me I would never get one because of my overbite. I wanted to track him down and make him salute me.

Placing the school beat ahead of the Navy provided exactly the opportunity that I needed at that point in my career. To me, the school board was just another political body and should be covered as a political story rather than collections of anecdotes about cute things the kids were doing. This perspective gave me an advantage over my opposition at the *Miami News*, a gracious and caring woman named Louise Blanchard. She took getting beaten stoically, and we remained friends despite some dirty tricks that I pulled.

McMullan got promoted that fall, first to a new position of executive news editor, and then to assistant managing editor on a par with Neuharth. An assistant city editor, Derick Daniels, succeeded him. Derick was only 29, and that led to some bulletin board humor, e.g. "All *Herald* executives must show proof of age before being served liquor."

He was a grandson of Josephus Daniels, who had been secretary of the Navy and head of the Raleigh, N.C., *News & Observer* publishing company. His news instincts were as good as McMullan's, his competitive drive was as great, and he projected a more reasonable persona. He could use his personal charm to con you into doing unpleasant and difficult things.

I had a second raise, to $115 a week, by then, and I adapted to the Herald better than I adapted to Miami. Writing to my old high school buddy Lee Sheppeard, still in Kansas and reporting for the *Lawrence Journal-World*, I said, on December 8, 1958:

I recommend the Miami Herald *as a place to work. I do not recommend Miami as a place to live. Of course the latter depends on your taste, and most of all on your adaptability. For one thing, Miami is not only far away from Kansas, it is far away from everywhere.*

It is different, and there's the rub. .... Down here, nothing is the same. They don't even grow the same kinds of trees. They don't bother to put curbs and gutters on the streets. You want to grow a lawn, you don't worry about the rain, you worry about the chinch bugs. They don't build houses out of wood, hurricanes would blow wood away. But you can huff and you can puff, and a hurricane can't blow our house down.

It is not a small-town, friendly, everybody-likes-everybody sort of place. It is anti-intellectual, and nobody has time to read a book. On the other hand, as you stay here, you get used to sitting out on the patio even if it is December (today's temperature: 80 degrees). And you get so you like palm trees and think of planting one in your own backyard next to the poinsettias. ...

We compete fairly fiercely with the afternoon Miami News, *and then there is the internal competition, with everyone maneuvering for promotion. This can wear you down if you let it, and a good many people, about as many as get promoted, quit for public relations or go back to the old hometown newspaper. It affects me to the extent that I intend to finish the damn thesis so I will have the degree as an escape hatch to the quieter, realer world of college teaching should I ever have the need for it.*

The competition with the *News* was at its most intense on

the civil rights story. These were perilous times for blacks in the South. In the fall of 1957, the governor of Arkansas Orval Faubus had called up the National Guard to block the entry of black students into Little Rock's Central High School. A federal judge told the governor to order the Guard to either escort the children into the school or withdraw them. The governor withdrew them, and rioting ensued until President Eisenhower sent the 101st Airborne Division in to disperse the mobs and get the children to school safely.

Florida officials were under a federal court order to begin the desegregation process, and they wanted to avoid a scene like Little Rock, but some nasty characters were converging on the state to stir up trouble, along with some homegrown rabble-rousers.

The School Board's choice for starting the process of desegregation was Orchard Villa Elementary School in central Miami. Its neighborhood was already a well-established target for real estate redlining – designating traditional white neighborhoods for conversion to black. Real estate sales people could make money on that because whites would panic and sell cheap while quality housing for middle class blacks was scarce and could be sold at a premium. That process had already begun in the neighborhoods that fed students to Orchard Villa Elementary School. Therefore, assigning black students to the previously all-white school would be obviously meaningless. And that is where the School Board planned to focus public attention.

The School Board's Wednesday meetings were usually in the afternoon. But the vote to authorize the first school desegregation in Florida would draw a large audience and could take some time, so a morning meeting was scheduled for February 18, 1959. I cursed this decision because it meant the vote would happen on *Miami News* time. Louise Blanchard chuckled in anticipation.

The board met on the stage of an auditorium in a former

184

school building close to downtown Miami. Two tables were located in the wing at stage right. The first was for the board attorneys so that they could provide instant legal advice. Behind them was the reporters' table. To its right, out of sight of the audience, was a locked cabinet in which a working telephone was stored. Before each meeting, a secretary would unlock the cabinet, place the telephone on its counter top, and leave the door ajar with the key still in the lock. This arrangement allowed the reporters to call in breaking news without leaving the room.

The desegregation issue had already been discussed enough so that events moved fairly quickly. The *Miami News* home delivery deadline had passed, but there was still plenty of time to replate page one and get the story in part of the home delivery run and the entire final street edition. While Louise leaned forward in anticipation, I quietly rolled my chair back, returned the telephone to its cabinet, locked the door, and put the key in my pocket.

The question finally came to a vote, and it was unanimous. Louise reached for the phone that wasn't there. She stood up and ran out into the hall, her arms moving above her head in counter-rotating circles. She found a phone in someone's office, of course, and called the story in, but my dirty trick had probably kept it out of several hundred copies of the press run. Back at the *Herald* newsroom, I confessed my bad deed and was roundly congratulated. And the episode had a long-term benefit. It protected me to some degree from sounding sanctimonious when I lectured on journalism ethics many years later. Confessing my own bad deeds made my teaching credible.

In the summer of that year, school officials let me in on the other part of their plan. They had designed a misdirection. The first significant desegregation of public schools in the state of Florida would take place at a brand new school in the south part of the county, near Homestead Air Force Base. To minimize its recognition as a public school, the board had named it "Air Base Elementary."

I took this news to my editors at the *Herald*, and we decided to play along with the board's pacifying strategy. We would report the facts about Air Base Elementary, but keep it low key and below the fold of the front page while directing our readers' attention – and that of the racist troublemakers – toward Orchard Villa.

On August 23, a Sunday, two weeks before the first day of school, I began a three-part series explaining the School Board's decision to desegregate. It ran two-columns wide on the front of the local section, and it was designed to calm the community. I emphasized the unanimity of the board's decision and compared it with the unanimity of the Supreme Court in the Brown decision five years before. I reminded Miami readers that six of the seven board members favored segregation but felt a duty to follow the law of the land. I mentioned the local litigation led by the Rev. Theodore Gibson that was putting added pressure on them. I did not mention Air Base Elementary School until the second day of the series.

That story was more specific, and it stressed the exceptional nature of Orchard Villa Elementary School because of its location in a changing neighborhood that was expected to become all black. The first mention of Air Base Elementary was postponed until the 15th paragraph, well below the fold in the page.

I portrayed the move as a clever strategy by the School Board lawyers to delay legal action.

———————————

At military bases in the state, schools operated by the armed services for children of military personnel are wholly integrated. Because Florida residents are not involved, this has been accepted without strong criticism from most segregationists.

Though no such schools have operated at bases in Dade

County, a similar situation will exist this fall. Air Base Elementary ... is a new school which will be attended exclusively by children of Homestead airmen. Among them probably will be children of 20 Negroes in the Air Force.

The assistant city editor who processed the story was Bob Swift. When he got to that sentence, he said, "The hairs on the back of my neck stood up." The story continued:

Such a situation would be the same sort of integration already accepted at other Florida military bases. But there is one technical difference which could give School Board attorney Edward Boardman a strong legal weapon in future integration suits.

It is the fact that Air Base Elementary is operated by the Dade School Board instead of the Air Force. Attorney Boardman could use it as an example of good faith the next time the NAACP complains to a federal court that the Dade School Board is failing to heed the 1954 Supreme Court ruling.

The decision to treat the story in this manner clearly violated the non-consequentialist rule of journalism, that of presenting the facts without caring where the chips fall, and every time I tell the story at seminars on media ethics, the *Herald's* action is roundly denounced. But you had to be there. Little Rock was fresh in our minds. I knew from police and related sources that some genuinely evil people were converging on Miami to try to make trouble. And we had our homegrown troublemakers, too.

One was a blue collar worker named Fred Hockett who claimed to represent the White Citizens Council in Miami. He was arrested for burning a cross on some piece of property associated with the civil rights movement, and we kept that story out of the paper fearing that publicity would encourage imitators. (Many months later, Hockett thanked me for that. His daughter, he said, would have been horribly embarrassed and teased by her schoolmates if they knew that her father was the perpetrator.)

Dade County integrated two schools as planned that September. The night before, Daniels and I went to a public speech given by one of the visiting troublemakers, a die-hard segregationist named J. B. Stoner. It was full of the standard racist clichés and appeals for white supremacy. Daniels allowed that he had heard the same speech many times when he had been a reporter in Georgia. We did not publish a word of it.

On the first day of school, Stoner was out in front of Orchard Villa elementary along with Fred Hockett and the usual cluster of TV cameras. The expected four black students showed up, and there were only eight whites. Stoner scrutinized each white student carefully.

"That one's not really white," he would say, "look at her nose." And he found a reason to deny the whiteness of every one of the eight. Then he claimed success in stopping integration.

Only brief mention of Stoner and Hockett made the paper. Meanwhile, Herald reporter Rose Allegato monitored Air Base Elementary, and it opened without incident. It had 21 blacks and 732 whites. We reported that fact in the fourth paragraph under our joint byline, but put the main emphasis on Orchard Villa. No one complained about the lack of segregation at Air Base Elementary, and Florida met its first test of the Brown directive.[15]

I confessed to Derick Daniels that I was a little bit uncomfortable covering civil rights because my Chapel Hill-formed attitudes were so much more liberal than those of most of the people that I wrote for.

"I don't care if you are the most liberal reporter in Miami," Daniels said, "so long as you are the best at hiding it."

A core of southern racism was built into the *Herald's*

operation. Once when I was taking rewrite from Henry Reno at the police station, he told me about a story that sounded like Greek tragedy. A rejected mistress had taken revenge on her former lover and his wife by killing their child.

"We can't use it," Reno said. "All the parties involved are colored."

It was true. Black on white or white on black crime was reported, but black on black was ignored.

There was more. Every September, on the first day of school, a photographer was assigned to take a picture of children entering an elementary school. We never put black children in that cliché photo. My task was always to select a white school that was in the same vicinity as the photographer's next assignment of the day.

Not all of the journalistic racism was as benign as that. I played a major role in the development of a promotion conceived by George Beebe called the Silver Knight Awards. The purpose was to choose the outstanding high school student in each of a number of fields, and the program was so successful that the *Herald* still sponsored it as recently as 2011. On the first time out, cartoonist Al Capp, the creator of *Li'l Abner*, was the featured speaker at the award ceremony, and a black student won the prize in journalism.

A few weeks later, I was attending a meeting of the Miami chapter of Sigma Delta Chi (now the Society of Professional Journalists) to select a recipient for its annual college scholarship. I suggested the Silver Knight winner.

"No," I was told. "That would be hypocritical of us, because we know that (being black) he wouldn't be able to get a job."

I did not make a fuss. Decades later, I attended a reunion in St. Petersburg of people who had worked in the early days of the Florida civil rights movement. I told some of these stories, and said that I felt like Henry David Thoreau, who summed his career by saying, "If I repent of anything, it is very likely to be my good behavior. What demon possessed me that I behaved so well?"

One of the old-timers in the movement tried to make me feel better. "We knew you were on our side," she said.

Well, sometimes I misbehaved. After Jack Gordon came home to Miami Beach from World War II, he recruited some investors and founded Washington Federal Savings and Loan, opening it in 1952. That made him financially secure enough to turn his attention to public service, and in 1960, he ran for the School Board.

Don Shoemaker, a 1934 Chapel Hill graduate and liberal by southern standards of the day, was editor of the *Herald's* editorial page, and he came to me for advice on an endorsement. I spoke highly of Gordon. Shoemaker looked at the list of board members on my desk and tapped the name of Anna Brenner Meyers.

"Don't you think this person adequately represents that point of view?" he asked. I gathered that by "that point of view" he meant some combination of liberal, Jewish, and Miami Beach.

"Mrs. Meyers is good," I said, "but she could use some help."

But the editorial board endorsed Jack Gordon's conservative opponent. Without telling anyone, I decided that Gordon would be better for Dade County, and I made my coverage of the campaign straightforward and factual while taking care to report every smart thing Gordon said and every dumb thing his opponent said. Gordon won, took a leadership role in desegregating the schools, and was later elected to the Florida senate. Today, there is a Jack Gordon Elementary School in southwest Miami-Dade County, as it is called now.

Miami was a good place for the civil rights movement to get a foothold in Florida because of its population mix and the leadership of two good newspapers. When four students at North Carolina A&T University staged a sit-in at Woolworth's lunch counter in Greensboro, on February 1, 1960, they created a demonstration effect that was felt across the south. The Florida legislature had passed a law that allowed a restaurant manager to evict, with police help, any customer that he or she did not choose to serve. A group of black ministers, inspired by the Greensboro four, sought to test the law by sitting in at downtown department store lunch counters. They hoped to get arrested, but, while they were not served, no one bothered them. Afterward, an interracial commission created by Governor LeRoy Collins worked quietly to persuade four downtown department stores to desegregate their lunch counters.

That August, the Committee on Racial Equality (CORE) chose Miami as the site for a training program in nonviolent resistance. It brought 21 blacks and 14 whites down for an experiment in interracial living plus training in the theory and practice of nonviolence. Wearing dungarees or Bermuda shorts, they clutched soft-cover copies of The *Autobiography of Mahatma Ghandi* and moved into the Sir John Hotel in what we then called the Central Negro District, now known as Overtown.

Their first major target was a whites-only restaurant at Shell's City, a block-long supermarket in an older section of town. Seventeen trainees and their leader marched into its glass-enclosed café and occupied four tables, sitting in racially mixed groups. The manager called police and invoked the new law.

A Miami police sergeant visited each table in turn and advised them politely that the manager had asked them to leave. With equal courtesy, all refused. Then, in what must have been the most congenial mass arrest in Florida history, all 18 were led to a paddy wagon singing "Battle Hymn of the Republic." I interviewed their leader, James P. Robinson, in the county jail.

"Law is supposed to be a reflection of justice," he said,

echoing Thoreau. "So if the law is unjust, the only place for a just man to be is in jail."

The trial was swift, and all were placed on probation with a promise that if they stayed out of trouble for a year, their convictions would be erased from the record. Robinson decided that Miami was too liberal to form a real training ground for his activists. "Next time," he grumbled, "we'll go to a really southern city."

The Rev. Martin Luther King Jr. showed up toward the end of the CORE program, and I got a chance to interview him at the Sir John Hotel. He was 31 then, barely older than I was, and it was already five years after the Montgomery bus boycott that brought him to the forefront of black leadership. His famous letter from the Birmingham jail was still three years in the future.

We talked about an incident in Jacksonville where, the previous week, a lunch-counter sit-in had led to violence, and blacks fought back. That demonstration was quickly suspended. The suspension was the right thing to do, he said, but it should be temporary.

"The first thing a non-violent resister realizes is that he may be the recipient of violence," he said. "But he does not retaliate."

I made that my lead, having little idea what an important figure King was already becoming.

16. Becoming an investigative reporter

Important though it was, the civil rights story was merely an adjunct to my main assignment, keeping track of the Dade County school system. The first hint of a major story unrelated to civil rights came in the late summer of 1959, overlapping the desegregation story and, for a while, overshadowing it.

At a routine board meeting, Superintendent Joe Hall asked for an appropriation of $10,000 for an independent study of the board's method of purchasing fire and windstorm insurance on its school buildings. The board voted it down with only cursory discussion.

Louise Blanchard and I looked at each other.

"Something is going on with school insurance," she whispered. "But nobody will talk about it. I've tried. It's a dead end."

Thus challenged, I found the administrator who oversaw the insuring of school buildings, and he was glad to brief me. Because the insurance industry is regulated by the state, he said, costs were pretty much fixed and the only problem was how to allocate the business among the various local agents. A system had been worked out that was considered fair to all concerned.

One agent, H. Stilson Brannen, was designated the insurance servicing agent and was in charge of getting all the buildings covered. He chose the insurance company, and, to make it fair, he shared the commissions with the other agents in the county.

Brannen was quite forthcoming when I went to see him. He was proud of the system he had put together. "America is wonderful," he said. "You can build a mechanism for doing something useful, and it works so well, that you might as well have nothing left to do but pull a lever," – and here he made a dramatic two-handed gesture of pulling a very large lever – "and the money comes pouring out."

The agents who shared the commissions, he said, were designated by individual board members. I went back to the office to think it over.

It was time to get analytical. No-bid contracting didn't smell right. The model in my head was a patronage-reward system. To make a story, I had to prove two things: that the School Board was paying too much for insurance, and that the members were getting something in return. Louise had hit a dead-end because she was stuck in the hunter-gatherer model of reporting. She needed to find someone to tell her that the system was flawed, and, of course, none who were involved would do that. The puzzle had to be assembled one piece at a time, and the story would be in the pattern, not the pieces.

As a political science student, I had heard about the concept of "operationalization," but with limited understanding. Now, I could see how practical it was. Social phenomena can be complex and obscure, but some aspect of the interesting stuff will usually surface in a way that is visible and measurable. The premiums were measurable, as were the values of the insured buildings. What I needed was something to compare them to, what social scientists call a control group.

I found one.

The recently established Metropolitan Government of Dade County had the same geographic definition as the School Board, and it owned buildings that were subject to the same fire and windstorm hazards. I walked over to the courthouse and learned that Metro had a very different method for insuring its buildings. It did it by competitive bidding. And the winners

194

were always members of a class of insurance companies called "factory mutuals." They specialized in insuring buildings for large institutions, and they were able to underbid the traditional stock companies significantly. I talked to a factory mutual agent. He was paid a straight salary instead of commissions and so had no motivation to inflate costs.

Comparing what Metro paid for fire and windstorm insurance to the School Board's costs, I found that schools' costs per value insured were about triple those of the county. Insurance premiums were $200,000 (more than $1.5 million in 2010 dollars) too high. Yet this system had persisted for years. Now all I needed was evidence of a payoff.

Florida lawmakers had pioneered in mandating open records with "sunshine laws." Strict reporting of political campaign contributions was enforced at the county level. But before I went to the records in the courthouse, I obtained the A.M. Best directory of Florida insurance agents, and made an index card for each officer of each agency in Dade County. This was the hardest part. If it had been 10 years later, I would have used a computer.

When the cards were assembled, I sorted them alphabetically, took them to the courthouse and checked the name of every contributor to the school board election against the cards. When I found a match, I entered the name of the recipient and the amount on the donor's card.

With that done, it became a simple matter to discover, with some hand sorting of the cards, that more than half of all campaign contributions to school board members came from owners or officers of insurance agencies. I wrote a story for Sunday morning's paper, but waited until late Saturday to contact the board members, one at a time, tell what I had, and get their reaction to put in my report. This delay was standard *Herald* procedure for exclusive stories. It was calculated to limit the ability of the *Miami News* to try a fast catch-up. My story led the Sunday local page and became the first of a three-part series.

A grand jury was convened to investigate. After retracing the steps in my investigation, it recommended that the school board follow Metro's example and put insurance out for competitive bidding. The board complied. When the next budget cycle came around, Superintendent Hall surprised the board by including a raise for teachers.

"Where did you find the money?" a member asked.

Hall shuffled some papers, mentioned several sources, then added, "and, of course, we saved a good deal on insurance."

It was around then that Louise took me to see Jack Roberts, her city editor at the *Miami News*. The meeting had been his idea. "I just wanted to meet the best reporter in Miami," Roberts said. "You should be working for us."

I listened carefully for him to drop some hint about making me the best-paid reporter in Miami, but heard nothing. I thanked him, admired the new building, and left.

Reporting for the *Miami Herald* made it possible for me to meet one of my early literary heroes, Philip Wylie. He had published six more novels since I read his *Opus 21* in college, was in his late 50s by then, and lived in South Miami. He was a quick thinker, had a slight speech impediment, and he was always good for a lively quote on controversies involving either of his two favorite issues, the environment and civil liberties.

I turned to Wylie in the spring of 1960 after somebody, possibly the mother of a high school student, skimmed through two books that were on a required reading list and found references to sexual activity in both of them. She complained in an anonymous phone call to the school, the matter was referred to the director of senior high schools for the county, and he shared the offending passages with Joe Hall, the county superintendent. They decided to remove the books from required reading at that particular school.

This decision was reported at the next monthly meeting of

the 17 senior high school principals, and, with each apparently acting on his or her own, they went back to their schools and withdrew the two books from circulation.

Now here's the irony. The offending books were the two great dystopian novels of the Depression and postwar years, George Orwell's *1984* and Aldous Huxley's *Brave New World*. Many of the book-banning principals had read neither one. When the story broke, I called the person whom I knew would have a colorful reaction. Wylie said the school officials' action was "ignorant and craven."

"To take *1984* and *Brave New World* away from high school seniors is to cripple them intellectually for the rest of their lives," he said. "They are the two most satirical and valuable – and in Huxley's case hilarious, and in Orwell's case grim and instructive – books that exist.

"If you haven't read *1984*, you can't talk to any intelligent person. To take it away is to bring 1984 dictatorship closer, and do just what the book was written to try to stop."

As it turned out, I was able to reach nine school officials involved in the book banning, and not one of them had read either book, except for the passages pointed out as offensive by the anonymous caller.

Wylie was still outraged the next day, and he wrote a letter addressed to "Phil or whomsoever," two typed, single-spaced pages with hand-edited corrections and underlining for emphasis in brown ink. First he thanked me for accurately representing his views in the paper, and then he went on.

———————————

One of the now-banned books, 1984, *is the most powerful anti-communist book ever written. So the "anonymous tip" may well have come from a communist who was trying to keep Dade's high school seniors from reading Orwell's hideous portrait of a world that universally followed the present Red methods.*

The alleged "obscenity" in that book is a scene which

merely shows that "The State" Orwell portrays watches even the most intimate acts of every citizen. The book appeared long ago.

Huxley's Brave New World *is a very funny spoof of the poor sex attitudes most common nowadays – among other common and dismal conventions and social antics. That book – now available everywhere in paperback and published nearly 30 years ago – particularly kids our widespread notion that sex-for-pure-pleasure is an adequate idea of the meaning of man – and woman.*

The community reaction generated by the *Herald's* attention was swift and effective. The 17 principals restored the books as quickly as they had removed them.

But I didn't always beat the *News.* One Saturday I was taking what I believed to be a routine obituary of a young woman when the funeral director gave me the time and place for the service and then added, offhandedly, that her wedding had been scheduled for that same church at that same time. *Whoa!*

I called the home and found a family member willing to tell the story. The fact that the deceased had a terminal illness had been intentionally kept from her. To keep up her morale, her fiancé and her relatives continued with the wedding plan as though she were going to get well. He had tried as many excuses as he could think of for moving up the date of the ceremony, but she had been adamant about sticking to the planned date. So he had to choose between telling her the truth and respecting her wish. Nurturing the illusion of impending recovery was his last gift to her.

It was in the course of reporting this story that I realized how casehardened I was becoming. I fidgeted impatiently whenever the woman on the phone interrupted her account to weep. I realized that the story needed a photo. I asked if there were a photo of the couple that the *Herald* could borrow. Yes, she said. I thanked her and dispatched a copy boy to pick it up.

I should have gone myself. By the time the copy boy arrived on the scene, the *Miami News* had been there and swept up the only available photo of the couple. A more gracious person would have given up, but I called my family source back and asked her to beg the *Miami News* for the return of the photo. I said we would send a copy boy to the *News* in their name. I said the deceased deserved to have her story illustrated in both papers. She demurred, we sent the copy boy anyway, but the *News* was not forthcoming. I had demeaned myself for nothing.

On Sunday morning, both papers had the story, and only the *News* had the photo. The *Herald* story, however, was better written.

There came a day when the School Board scheduled a highly unusual closed meeting to discuss a new hire. Daniels advised me to show up at the meeting, demand a vote on closing the session, and visibly take notes during the vote. I had a better idea.

Roaming the halls of the school administration building, I found a copy of the board's agenda that revealed the name of the candidate being discussed. And I chatted up a secretary who didn't see any harm in mentioning the town and state where that person lived. I went back to the office and called the newspaper librarian in that town and found that the person had gotten into some embarrassing legal trouble serious enough to make him want to move far away. Digging further, I found a hint that he had a connection to one of our School Board members.

Was the public interest served when the *Herald* published my story and killed that particular opportunity for the man's rehabilitation? We didn't think about that. Gene Miller expressed our ethos the most succinctly: "Publish, publish, always publish." We were non-consequentialists like Immanuel Kant. Following the rule was more important than its result.

By now, the School Board had begun to regard me with some wariness. It had hired a security administrator named John Tyler, a former FBI agent, primarily to sniff out troublemakers responding to the desegregation moves. A friendly man, he invited me to his office, made casual conversation, and asked me if I had ever been in military service.

"Two years in the Navy. Why?"

"Oh, I just wondered," he said. "You don't seem old enough."

Months later, Joe Hall, the superintendent, told me the rest of the story. The board members, worried about losing control of their own information, had started to mistrust one another. They assigned Tyler to collect each member's copy of the report on the proposed hire that had been the basis of the closed meeting. The reports had plastic covers that would have retained clear fingerprints. Tyler knew that the FBI files held copies of all fingerprints of former servicemen and women, and he was determined to find out which board member had let me handle a copy of the report.

I was flattered. My reporting had been so accurate that they assumed the information must have come straight from a written report handed to me by a board member! I kept quiet, hoping they would think I had been clever enough to read it while wearing gloves.

Not all of my work at the *Herald* was so serious. We needed some comic relief. One of the assistant city editors, Bill Phillips, later named feature editor, had a good mind for stunts that would yield goofy news copy. For example, on the day before Lincoln's birthday, he assigned me to stand at Lincoln Road in Miami Beach and stop passersby:

"Hello. I'm with the *Miami Herald*, and tomorrow is Lincoln's birthday. We're trying to find out how many people know how President Lincoln got to Gettysburg to give the Gettysburg Address. Can you tell me?"

After a bit of hemming and hawing, the subject would

confess ignorance, and I would dramatically point to the Lincoln Road street sign over our heads.

"Lincoln rode," I would say.

Groan.

On the day before April Fool's Day, 1960, I stood at the corner of Miami Avenue and Flagler Street holding a piece of transparent fishing line tied to a purse lying on he sidewalk. A five-dollar bill was sticking out of the purse. Whenever a passerby bent to pick it up, I jerked it out of reach and yelled "April Fool" while Doug Kennedy took a photo of the transaction. I saved his photos and would show them years later to students to illustrate the extremes to which a dedicated reporter will go to generate news.

The mixture of light and serious reporting at the *Herald* was energizing. One of Phillips's better ideas was a project we called "Phone Fun." Readers were invited to write to us about a celebrity with whom they would like to have a telephone conversation, and we promised to set it up for the most meritorious entries.

The most meritorious were, of course, those asking for celebrities whom we could persuade to participate. Phone calls were expensive then, so we put the arm on Phil DeBerard, the Bell South public relations executive in Miami, for free calls. We set them up on a speakerphone, a new technology at the time, in George Beebe's office. The only celebrity I remember clearly from that project is Eleanor Roosevelt. She was expecting serious talk from an informed citizen, but about all she got were questions from a woman who wanted to know about President Roosevelt's stamp collection. It was one of the shorter conversations in the series.

Speed-reading was fashionable in the early 60s because President Kennedy had taken a speed-reading course. I enrolled in a course sponsored by the Dade County schools. It was taught by a smart young instructor named Jim Schiavone, and I dreamed up a way to create a newspaper promotion out of it.

We prepared a how-to series on speed-reading for the *Herald*, and we created a self-administered testing system so readers could track their progress. The clever part was using existing newspaper content as the material to read for the test. We were improving our readers' reading skills and driving them to features in the paper that they might not already know about.

The *Herald* helped us self-syndicate it. We sold it to about a dozen papers including the *Dallas Morning News, Cincinnati Post*, and the *St. Petersburg Times*.

My education beat included the University of Miami, and interesting research was happening at its medical school. So I gradually acquired medicine as a secondary beat and started covering the many medical conventions held in Miami Beach hotels. This work led to a moonlighting job with a new magazine aimed at physicians called *Medical World News*. The first assignment it had for me was a meeting of the American Academy of Orthopedic Physicians at the Americana Hotel in Miami Beach. Being fat with drug company advertising, the magazine paid well, $100 per magazine page ($592 in 2010 dollars), and I was able to expand and refine my Herald medical stories for its more specialized audience. It was a timely move, because the old Studebaker had taken to burning a quart of oil every 200 miles, and my new free-lance earnings enabled me to trade it for a previously owned red Hillman Minx convertible.

In September 1960, we experienced hurricane Donna, our first. It came at an awkward time because Sue was eight and a half months pregnant. Instead of riding out the hurricane at the office like almost everybody else at the *Herald*, I stayed home with my wife and our two-year-old. Our house had been built to the standards of the new hurricane code, but the windows were still vulnerable to wind-blown objects, so I bought a large piece of plywood and covered the lone window of my study with bolts anchoring the wood to the concrete block walls. We put a mattress on the floor, and rode out the night there.

When the power failed and our battery radio gave out, I

crawled out to the carport on the leeward side of the house and got an updated weather report on the car radio. Donna was striking only a glancing blow. The baby arrived two weeks later, and we considered naming her Donna, but chose instead two family names.

Newspaper ethics were relatively undeveloped in those days, and one of the fringe benefits for reporters was access to freebies. I was assigned to take a free trip to Mexico City to publicize the first jet service between there and Miami, and, to keep it honest, I avoided writing about the airline and instead covered a student uprising at the University of Mexico City.

Guests on the trip included reporters from the wire services and Hal Hendrix of the *Miami News*, along with some public officials. Our Mexican hosts took us to fancy ethnic restaurants, including French and Chinese. We were guided by the public relations representative of the airline, an attractive young woman named Beverly, and an official of the Mexican tourism agency took an interest in her, seating himself at her right at the French restaurant while I was on her left. After a couple of tequila-spiked Dos Equis beers, he began making crude suggestions to her. She was obviously uncomfortable, and I tried to defuse the situation with a jest: "Sir, if you persist in these remarks to this fine young lady, I shall be forced to punch you in the nose."

I was speaking softly and smiling while I said it, but the official reached across the woman's plate, grasped my jaw with thumb and forefinger and turned my head to the side as if looking for a spot to land a blow. Then he excused himself to go the men's room. An aide followed and came back alone.

"It would be best," he said, "for all of you to leave."

We did. I had gotten us thrown out of a high-class restaurant without even raising my voice. That was my main adventure in Mexico.

Every Christmas season, messengers would arrive in the *Herald* city room bearing gift packages shaped like whiskey bottles to reporters whose beats affected important economic interests. Alas, the school beat was not one of them.

But there were the parties. Miami Beach was still the scene of at least one new hotel opening almost every year, and each was the occasion for a major outlay of free food and liquor for the press. The Orange Bowl was played every year in Miami, and on New Year's Eve, the Orange Bowl Committee would throw a huge party at the top of the Columbus Hotel on Biscayne Boulevard. The city editor controlled the tickets, and I was usually awarded a couple as recognition of my good work or my low pay or both. On one such occasion, I had an accidental meeting with my old nemesis, Dean M. A. Durland, who represented K-State on the Orange Bowl Committee. We had a friendly, liquor-fueled conversation about the state of the world and never once mentioned the Student Union architecture case.

My insurance series won two awards, a citation from the National Education Writers Association and a public affairs reporting award from the American Political Science Association. It had not been entered in the Pulitzer competition. When Al Neuharth happened by my desk, reporter Tom Lownes asked him why the promotion department had passed up that contest when my story was such an obvious contender.

"Can't win 'em all," said Neuharth.

The political science award entitled me to a weeklong seminar with other winners at Eagle Rock Ranch, near Austin, Texas. The most memorable of the visiting professors was Warren Miller from the Survey Research Center at the University of Michigan. He explained probability sample in an intuitive way that I never forgot.

"The sample is drawn," he said, "so that each member of the underlying population has an equal chance of being included."

Of course! That would explain how error margins could be calculated. The equal-probability design would eliminate systematic bias. Miller also recommended that reporters learn scientific interviewing technique. He would become a major news source for me just a few years later as I started to cover national election polls. I chatted with Howard R. Penniman of Georgetown University, who encouraged me to apply for the association's Congressional fellowship, which pays for an academic year spent working on Capitol Hill. It was designed for both academics and journalists, to further their understanding of the workings of Congress. Penniman knew of my ambition to be a Washington reporter, and the fellowship, he said, "would be a good way to turn a corner."

"And if you don't make it the first time you apply," he said, "try again."

Another seminar speaker was Neale Copple, former city editor of the Lincoln, Nebraska, *Journal* who had left to teach at the University of Nebraska. Later, he would use my insurance series as an example in his 1964 textbook, *Depth Reporting: an Approach to Journalism*.[16] He and DeWitt Reddick, dean of the University of Texas School of Journalism were concerned about the effect of the new technology of television on newspaper journalism. Copple warned us that although newspaper circulation was rising, it wasn't growing as fast as population, and that trend could become dangerous. He and Reddick both argued for more sophisticated reporting.

With traditional reporting methods, Reddick, argued, we wait until a crisis develops or until something gets into the public record before we report on it. By that point, TV or radio can easily beat us on it. What broadcasting can't do well is provide the analysis that illuminates the structure and pattern of important social and political trends. I recorded these thoughts in a five-page memo for my editors.

The ranch was isolated from urban temptations, so we spent evenings drinking and playing poker – except for one memorable evening that included a horseback ride and, at trail's end, feasting on a roast of freshly slaughtered goat.

It was normal for journalists in those days to drink a lot, and I feared that my use of alcohol was starting to take a darker turn, and when I got home I announced to friends and family that I was taking a one-year sabbatical from the stuff. I would give my brain cells a break.

In 1961, Leo Adde, who covered the Metropolitan Government of Dade County, left for a job in television, and I was assigned to his beat while continuing to cover schools, science, medicine, and civil rights. In November of that year, George Beebe went outside his budget to give me a raise to $150 a week. "Meyer has developed into one of our top reporters," he said in his request to the business manager. "He is in demand by other newspapers."[17]

17. Washington D.C.

David Kraslow, the Herald's Washington correspondent, won a Nieman fellowship at Harvard University for the 1961-1962 academic year, and Lee Hills decided to fill the temporary vacancy by letting interested members of the newsroom fill the Herald slot with one-month duty tours in Washington. I immediately started lobbying for one of those assignments. I had followed Howard Penniman's advice and applied for the Congressional fellowship the previous year and made it only as far as the final interview stage. My application for the current year was in the works. Management knew about my effort, and was willing to send me on temporary duty, hoping I would get Washington out of my system. It took some advance planning because there was no obvious person to fill in on all of the beats that I had been covering. My month finally came in the spring of 1962.

Knight Newspapers maintained a small bureau in Washington with a suite facing an airshaft on the 12th floor of the National Press Building, one flight below the Press Club itself. Room 1286 opened to a reception area with a secretary and private offices for Bureau Chief Edwin A. Lahey and the senior correspondent, James Haswell of the *Detroit Free Press*. In the adjoining room were cubicles for Robert S. Boyd, reporter at large; Chuck Hauser of the *Charlotte Observer*; a recently vacated space for the *Akron Beacon Journal*; and Kraslow's temporarily empty *Miami Herald* cubicle. A Teletype in a corner gave us the Washington reports from United Press

International, and it was equipped with a bell that would ring to indicate news that was especially urgent.

When our stories were not time related, we sent them to the Knight papers by mail. The bureau's secretary typed them with five carbons. When a story had time value, we would hang the copy on a hook by the door and ring a buzzer that sounded in the Western Union office, five floors below. A pleasant African-American woman named Jane would arrive in minutes and take the story downstairs to be dispatched. I was very glad to be there, and especially glad for the chance to get to know Ed Lahey.

Already a Washington legend, Lahey had grown up on the south side of Chicago, entered the work force at 14 as an office boy, then became a shipping clerk, hod carrier, and clerk in a railroad yard before landing a job, at age 25, on a suburban weekly. The *Chicago Daily News* hired him two years later. His Irish wit made him an engaging writer, and he could combine human interest with clear exposition of complex policy issues. For that reason, he was given the labor beat at just the moment in history when the Depression inspired the Wagner Labor Relations Act and made collective bargaining feasible. His success led him to close friendships with union figures, including labor lawyer Arthur Goldberg, who would later become a Lyndon Johnson appointee to the Supreme Court.

Although largely self-educated, Lahey cured himself of "the worst damn inferiority complex about college you ever saw" by gaining membership in the inaugural class of Nieman fellows and spending the 1938-1939 academic year at Harvard. His salty wit made him popular with the faculty, including law professor Felix Frankfurter, who joined the Supreme Court after that fall semester. Decades later, part of the orientation of new Nieman fellows was a recounting of Lahey anecdotes, such as the time he deflated an intellectual who appeared to be talking down to him by cracking, "Ah, Shakespeare! I'm nuts about him. I read his stuff as fast as it comes out."

Although Ed always spoke fondly of that year, he confessed to me once, "I wish I could do it again sober." In 1940, he joined Alcoholics Anonymous, and burned surplus nervous energy by playing bridge, piano, and, on annual trips to Miami, the horses. His Washington insider credentials were sealed by membership in the Gridiron Club, which he described as "amateur hour," because the club invites newsmakers to an annual show of music and political satire featuring press corps talent.

When I got back to Miami, I looked under my own name in the library files and found an envelope containing clips of all the stories that I had written in my month in the bureau. Apparently, I was being evaluated for Washington. I had also made it to the finals in the Congressional fellowship competition while I was still on temporary duty in Washington. George B. Galloway of the Library of Congress conducted the interview over lunch at the Cosmos Club. "I think you'll get it," he confided.

Soon it was late spring, Jack Knight was still in Miami, and I received an unexpected summons to George Beebe's office for a meeting with the boss. Knight, I was told, had a tip on a development in a recent news story about a burglary at a prominent citizen's home in Miami Beach. They needed a reporter to take some notes from him.

He recounted some details of the case, explained his relationship to the family, and allowed that it might have been an inside job. I dutifully wrote it all down and asked, "How should I source this."

"You can't tie it to me," Knight said, laughing, and the interview was over.

Puzzled, I took my notes to Al Burt, an assistant city editor, and asked what I should do with them.

"Just type them up and give them to me as a memo," he said.

A couple of days later, Al confided to me, "I think you're

going to Washington." It was then that I realized the point of the Knight interview. It was so the old man could size me up, decide whether I presented myself in a way that would reflect well on Knight Newspapers in the nation's capital.

My next important meeting in Beebe's office was with Ben Maidenburg, the editor of the *Akron Beacon Journal.* Maidenburg was tall, lean, and surprisingly youthful for someone who had been a *Herald* legend as the Knight brothers' first news-side representative to join the staff after their purchase of the paper way back in 1937. He asked about my interest in possibly representing Akron in Washington.

"Ohio has some really interesting people in Congress," I said. "It would be fun to follow Frank Lausche."

Lausche was a former mayor of Cleveland and governor of Ohio. His family had come from Slovenia, and he paved the way for other ethnic Democrats seeking office in Ohio. When he first went to Washington in 1957, he threatened to caucus with the Republicans in a closely divided Senate and thereafter earned a reputation as highly unpredictable. The strategy was designed to give him leverage, but instead it merely made him seem untrustworthy, as I would later learn. I knew a little bit about Lausche because my Republican friend in graduate school, Jay Gates, came from Cleveland and was constantly bragging about Lausche's obstructionist talents.

"I'm glad to hear you say that," Maidenburg said. "I've been having a lot of trouble getting the Washington Bureau to pay attention to Lausche."

Before I left Beebe's office, I had the job, a new salary, and a starting date. I quickly wrote a letter withdrawing from the Congressional Fellowship competition. It crossed in the mail with a letter of rejection.

Maidenburg had asked me not to waste the company's money with a lot of back-and-forth travel between Washington and Miami during the transition. So I engaged a moving company, left Sue to supervise the packing, and drove the Hillman Minx to D.C. to start house hunting. I quickly found a somewhat run-down 19th century, Victorian-front row house on SE Seventh St. in the Capitol Hill neighborhood. It was walking distance to the Capitol, the Library of Congress, the Eastern Market, and some Pennsylvania Ave. shops. Its owner was a Foreign Service officer, and the neighborhood was just starting to gentrify. As Ed Lahey put it, gentrification at that time meant, "a new coat of paint, a brass door knocker, and double the rent."

The house was pretty much in original condition inside. It had non-functioning gaslights protruding from the walls. But there was a nice walled courtyard in back and a skylight over the stairs. It would do as a place to park while we looked for a house to own. Sue and the girls arrived by train, beating the moving van by a day.

Ed Lahey gave me a clue to the company's reasons for sending me.

"I asked Lee Hills if we was sure about picking you for the job," he said. "'Washington is tough and competitive,' I told him. 'Meyer is so quiet and mild-mannered.'

"And Hills said, 'Yes, but he's steel inside.'"

After that, whenever Lahey sent me on a potentially difficult assignment, he would say something like, "I figure I'd better send my man of steel on this one."

And he showed me a letter from the Herald's John McMullan mentioning my transfer.

"Phil Meyer leaves Friday," McMullan said, "and it's leaving a helluva hole in our city staff. However, I think he ought to add to the bureau strength, and we stood to lose him anyway."

The second year of the Kennedy administration was an exciting time in Washington. Kennedy's campaign pledge had been to "get America moving again," and all sorts of initiatives were afoot. I joined the National Press Club and started to feel like a Washington insider, and then the reality hit. Washington reporting is nothing like covering the courthouse or the school board. I was in the majors now, competing for attention against a lot more talent than the *Miami News* had ever been able to put up against me.

Even worse, the mission of the Washington Bureau, as I had sensed during my one-month tryout, was unclear. Washington journalists behaved liked the school children on that soccer field back in Edgerton, Kan., everybody clustering around the ball and trying to get a foot on it. If we joined the cluster and covered the day's major stories, our editors would complain that we were duplicating the wire services. If we came up with something original, the editors would suggest that it couldn't be important or the wires would have had it. The result of that conflict was a tendency to work around the edges of the news, staying relevant to the big stories, but going more for sidebars or related developments or explainers – and, of course, the local angles.

National journalism's group mentality was especially evident when covering political campaigns, as I would discover, when, in 1964, I got to spend some time with Barry Goldwater's whistle-stop rail trip through the Midwest. At every station, we would pile out and listen to the candidate's latest speech. Then the wire and national media reporters would huddle to decide on the facts to use in the lead. That way, no one would have to explain to his editor why his news judgment was different from the others.

But there were not too many reporters going after Ohio angles. To help me become familiar with the state and its politics, Maidenburg teamed me with reporter Robert Kotzbauer and asked us to drive around the state and conduct a public opinion poll. Its goal: to predict the outcome of the coming November 1962 election contest for governor. Democratic Governor Mike DiSalle was up for re-election, and was challenged by James Rhodes, the state auditor. Having studied political science at Chapel Hill, I was pretty confident that we could do this. Kotzbauer assembled precinct maps from the major population areas, and I designed brief interview forms that were color-coded for gender: pink for female respondents, green for males. They had spaces for recording voting intention plus some basic demographics.

For two weeks, we ranged across the state, picked inviting looking neighborhoods and knocked on doors. Each evening, we would file a story giving our qualitative assessment of voter mood in that day's location. Then we looped back to Akron, spread our paper forms out on a library table and started counting. Crosstabulation by hand proved too daunting. We could easily separate the pink and green ballots, but sorting by age category, education, and other variables was too time-consuming. So we recast some of our qualitative findings and led the story with our election forecast: the election was too close to call.

We were wrong. DiSalle won in a landslide. Our error should have been painfully obvious. We were drawn to nice-looking neighborhoods. There are more Republicans in those neighborhoods because they tend to be more affluent than Democrats. Our casual sample had an obvious bias. I had forgotten Warren Miller's advice at that ranch in Texas: for sampling to work, each member of the target population must have an equal chance of being included.

I wish I could report that we learned from that mistake. Maidenburg liked our stories despite the bad call, and he sent us out two years later when Robert Taft Jr. was challenging Senator Steve Young. We wrote the same kinds of colorful stories and predicted that Taft would "win handily." He lost. At least, by then I knew a lot more about Ohio. And I learned another Ed Lahey aphorism:

"The greatest virtue is humility, and the shortest route to humility is through humiliation."

In Congress, the predominately Republican Ohio delegation turned out to be fairly dull, not for lack of talent, but for lack of power. The presence of a Democratic majority in both houses meant that I did not have any committee chairmen on my beat.

Akron's delegate in the House was William H. Ayres, a former plumbing and heating contractor with an ebullient personality and a fondness for martinis with lunch. He was the ranking minority member of the House Committee on Veterans' Affairs. On our second meeting, he told me that he and his administrative assistant had discussed our previous encounter and decided, "We can trust you." For a reporter schooled in the need to keep sources at arm's length or more, this was not an entirely good thing to hear. In fact, I liked Ed Lahey's advice: "Pee on your source's legs at least once a week. It keeps them from getting too close."

It took me a while to learn what news was considered important enough to justify the expense of sending by Western Union. When Senator Stephen Young made a speech calling for U.S. recognition of red China, I put a strong lead on the story and filed it by Western Union. That yielded an irritable response from Maidenburg.

"Steve Young calling for recognition of China is like the Cleveland Indians crying 'Next year,'" he said. "It's not worth the wire charges."

I received an unrelated complaint from John McMullan in Miami:

This is a protest.

The last copy you sent us was a carbon that was almost completely illegible. Fortunately, the second and third sheets gave me enough clue to the contents that I was able to decide that it probably wasn't worth using anyway.

But stop playing games with us. Please find some onionskin and carbon that will make it possible for us to understand what you are writing about even when we are on the bottom of the list.

Otherwise, no complaints. You seem to have dug in and

got the feel of Washington, and we have used many of your stories.

Drop a note sometime. We are entering the rainy season, and you are often in our thoughts as we see bumbershoots emerging from closets again.

Our two daughters were not yet school age, so we took an October vacation to visit the grandparents and enjoy the Kansas fall colors. My parents had finally realized their lifelong dream of home ownership. Uncle Lester, the last Meyer on the original farm, had died in 1961, and so my father inherited a share of the farm for the third time. They applied the proceeds to a bungalow on Moro Street, an easy walk to Aggieville, and used it to generate retirement income by renting the basement rooms to students. And that's where we were visiting when the Cuban missile crisis erupted, I cut my vacation short and left the family in Kansas. Jets were in more common use by airlines then, and I was back in Washington quickly, reflecting that if there were a nuclear exchange, our house, seven blocks from the Capitol, could be part of Ground Zero.

My 32nd birthday fell on the darkest day of that confrontation, Saturday, October 27, 1962, when such a fate seemed possible.

It was one of those big stories where the function of a small bureau seemed especially uncertain. I was posted to the Justice Department so I could keep an eye on Attorney General Robert Kennedy and write about his participation in the crisis, and then it was off to the Pentagon to attend the briefings on the Kennedy-ordered blockade of the Cuban coastline. The *Beacon* was an afternoon paper, and, knowing its deadlines, I could phone with just-in-time updates.

I was home alone between deadlines when I heard Sander Vanocur report on NBC that Soviet Premier Khruschev had agreed to withdraw his missiles. I arranged for Sue and the girls to fly home. And I covered a background briefing – meaning that the attribution had to be veiled. It was led by Secretary of State Dean Rusk. He urged us not to strike a triumphal note in our stories for fear that it might upset the delicate and still fairly tenuous agreement with the Russians.

Sources in Washington were not like sources in Miami, where the *Herald* held most of the power. With so much going on and so many journalists chasing the same stories, doing original reporting often required a delicate and usually unspoken market transaction between source and journalist. To persuade a fully cooperative source to give you information that no one else had, you needed to give something in exchange. And what did the reporter have that the source wanted? A favorable slant, of course, so the implied contract was a story framed the way the source wanted it in exchange for the exclusive information. For this to work on a national story, you had to represent a news medium that was large and visible enough to have agenda-setting power and/or the power to initialize a frame that would stick.

Basically, this meant a major advantage for those media that were read in Washington. I quickly realized that, outside the Ohio Congressional delegation, not many politicians or bureaucrats in Washington cared what the *Akron Beacon Journal* said about them. However, the fact that our bureau fed its national stories to the *Chicago Daily News* wire service helped. The *Washington Post* was a client.

With the Democrats in control and no committee chairs on my beat, I had no obvious sources to turn to. I soon realized that if I were going to contribute original material to the Washington conversation, I would have to work more from documentary evidence. So I applied my political science training and looked for patterns.

Lee Hills was aware of the bureau's frustrations and the ambiguity about its function and attributed some of the problem to Lahey's mostly hands-off leadership. Ed preferred to lead by example rather than direction. So Hills, on one of his periodic visits to the bureau, announced that he was creating the position of news editor, and that it would be filled by my former city editor John McMullan.

The only worry that Ed expressed about this arrangement was revealed in his question to Hills.

"Who are we supposed to call to say, 'My mother's drunk again, and I can't come to work today?'"

Hills assured us all that Lahey was still in charge, although we all knew that McMullans' stronger personality would bring changes to our operation.

John was a fertile source of ideas, good and bad, he was quick to recognize the good ideas of others, and he provided support for my strategy of data-dredging and pattern recognition. And he gave us the courage to cover spot news without worrying about duplicating the wires. That is how I got to be present in the Senate Press Gallery when the Limited Nuclear Test Ban Treaty was ratified on September 25, 1963. The Senate was a more civil and rational deliberative body than it is today, and the treaty passed with support from both parties. After the 80-19 vote was tallied, Senator Mike Mansfield of Montana, the majority leader, and Everett Dirksen, the minority leader from Illinois, reached across the aisle and shook hands. I wondered how often I would see that.

My first important data-dredging story came after Tennessee Senator Estes Kefauver died in 1963 and his estate was probated. It revealed that he had been a heavy investor in the shares of drug companies. This news was a surprise because investigating price-fixing by drug companies had been one of his major endeavors as chairman of the Senate Anti-Trust and Monopoly Subcommittee. That story made some front pages and then died, but I wanted to know more. I called the estate's executor and found out who the senator's broker had been, then called that broker and asked for the trading dates of the drug stocks that had been in Kefauver's portfolio. I tried to sound skeptical, as though I didn't really believe he owned drug company shares. To prove that the estate inventory was correct, the broker gave me the buy date for each company.

With that list in hand, I went to the *Congressional Record* for those dates and found the pattern. Kefauver would denounce a company on the Senate floor, wait for the market to punish its shares the next day, and then buy. Why? The only logical conclusion from this pattern is that the investigations were mere political theater, and the senator knew that no regulatory or punitive government action would result. This might have been insider wisdom, but it probably wasn't specific enough to qualify as illegal insider knowledge. Yet, it was newsworthy. It was one of the few times that the *Washington Post* ran my bylined story from the *Chicago Daily News* wire service.

Sue and I spent many weekends of our first year in Washington scouting the area for a permanent home. It wasn't easy. Elite journalists liked to blend in with the elites of official Washington, but Knight pay levels wouldn't allow us to live in those more desirable neighborhoods. Correspondents of our ilk endured commutes from the far suburbs like Kensington or Upper Marlboro in Maryland or Falls Church in Virginia. Lahey, whose children were grown, lived in a fashionable apartment on Chevy Chase Parkway near the Maryland-District line. We liked the convenience of Capitol Hill, but worried about the restoration cost. Then a story in the *Washington Post* about a fair-housing movement in northwest Washington caught my eye.

As was common in many cities, there was a shortage of housing for middle-class black families, and the real estate industry thought it could make some money, by "red-lining." This strategy meant drawing a line on the map to designate an all-white area for conversion to all-black. It was accomplished by persuading one or more white owners to sell to blacks. The next step was to stir panic among the remainder so that they would sell out cheaply, just as I had seen in Miami's Orchard Villa neighborhood.

The red-lined area was called Manor Park, and one of its residents was Marvin Caplan, whose day job was reporter for Fairchild Publications, a publisher of trade journals. He had been a civil rights activist, working to desegregate lunch counters and other public facilities, and he saw an opportunity here to fight segregation in housing. He organized a citizen's association to work toward building a stable, racially integrated neighborhood. It was called Neighbors, Inc., and it countered the industry decision to show for-sale houses only to blacks by recruiting volunteers to work in real estate sales on behalf of black and white buyers alike.[18] The panic had started in 1958, but in 1959, Neighbors Inc. succeeded in finding one white family to buy in the redlined area. It cast some doubt on the speculators' claim that no white person would move into the neighborhood.

But the panic selling continued and moved northward. The association tried to get ahead of the game by extending its recruiting of white families to three more neighborhoods, Brightwood, Takoma, and Shepherd Park. It struggled for two years to get racial designations removed from real estate advertising.

Sue and I loved the concept for two reasons. In Miami, I could never join an activist group because it would violate my reporters' neutrality. But in Washington, this was a local story, of no interest to my Akron readers, and I could get involved as much as I wanted. Moreover, I knew from the history of block-breaking efforts elsewhere that the decline in prices would be temporary. By moving quickly, we might find a bargain. We focused our house hunting on the most attractive of the four neighborhoods, Shepherd Park, occupying the triangle between NW 16th Street, Alaska Avenue, and Eastern Ave., just north of Walter Reed Hospital. It had been developed in the depression years, and the houses were well-built, faced with solid brick and stone, and roofed with slate. It had mature trees and a traditional grid pattern that promoted walkability and neighborhood interaction.

Our oldest daughter was ready for kindergarten, and we found a house across the street from Shepherd Park Elementary School. The house was an impressive brick colonial with a finished, walk-out basement that had been designed for use as a physician's office. With the help of a bequest from Sue's lawyer uncle in Cleveland, the house was affordable, and we moved in the summer of 1963. I made the doctor's examining room my study while the reception room became a guest bedroom with a private side entrance. We quickly began to make our first close African-American friends, most notably Chuck and Louise Stone who lived a few blocks away and threw memorable parties. Chuck was assistant to Rep. Adam Clayton Powell, and he had stonewalled me when I tried to get a story about his boss's rumored vacation in Bimini with an attractive female staff member.

"I don't know where he is," Chuck had said. "I don't call him, he calls me."

But in Shepherd Park, we were comrades in arms. Now Sue and I could feel like real participants in the civil rights movement. Sue joined the neighborhood corps of volunteer real estate guides, showing houses to interested buyers of all races. When houses started to sell without agents, the real estate industry reconsidered its strategy.

We held frequent business/social gatherings that always ended with attendees joining hands and singing, "We Shall Overcome." We held an annual holiday house tour and borrowed the Coolidge High School gymnasium for a yearly book sale. And the strategy worked. Like-minded whites as well as middle-class blacks moved in. Some of the whites were journalists who thought like us, including John Pomfret of the *New York Times*, John Averill of the *Los Angeles Times*, and Laurence Stern, the national editor of the *Washington Post*. We also had Associate

White House Press Secretary Andrew Hatcher, plus lobbyists, lawyers, and a few diplomats, including Fern Baguidy, the ambassador from Haiti. One journalist wrote in 1965 that the residents "have shown the way to other communities; they have become, whether they wanted to or not, a model."[19]

Shepherd Park eventually stabilized, and it was still a meaningfully integrated neighborhood, about one-third white, in the 2000 census. However preservation of racial balance in its elementary school was less successful over those decades. The school population became 95 percent black as younger white families stopped moving in or sent their children to private schools.

We were still adjusting to the move when I met one of my boyhood heroes, Fulton Lewis Jr., the right-wing broadcaster with the deep voice. He was one of the guests at a garden party at the home of an Ohio congressman from the western suburbs of Cleveland, Oliver P. Bolton. My political views had moved considerably to the left since I was a boy listening to Lewis's broadcasts on our old Philco radio back home in Clay Center, but I think I still would have had an unfavorable impression. He was loud, overweight, and had a coarse sense of humor. When the conversation turned to the recent suicide of Philip Graham, the *Washington Post* publisher, Lewis had a ready theory.

"I know what that was about," he said with a vulgar chuckle as ice cubes tinkled in his glass. "It was a broad." I walked away.

My other early broadcasting hero did live up to my expectations. The Knight bureau owned a small, portable wire recorder, advanced technology for its day, and we were encouraged to record long interviews and edit them to appear in Q-and-A format. I managed an hour with Edward R. Murrow a year after President Kennedy had named him head of the United States Information Agency. He still had his broadcaster's precision. I was ushered into his office at what seemed like the exact second of my 3 p.m. appointment.

Our conversation went quickly to the parallel between his convincing journalistic technique, a balance of showing and telling, with what he was doing for the agency. For example, to show Fidel Castro's inconsistency, a USIA broadcast contrasted tapes of the dictator's early denials that he was a communist with his later admissions. The same technique was used with the Soviet Union, which had resumed nuclear testing after officially deploring such testing.

"This is a technique you have borrowed from your own broadcasting days, isn't it?" I said. "Selecting the critical quotes that tell your story?"

"The technique has a lot of conviction," said Murrow. "It's a little difficult for anyone to contend that he was misquoted when it's right there in his own voice."

I asked him if he ever felt uncomfortable in his role as an advocate instead of one dedicated to journalistic objectivity.

"No," he said. "I don't think there is a basic conflict. I don't even mind being called a propagandist. I think the propagandist is sort of like a lobbyist. If he is lobbying for something with which you agree, then he is a public-minded, noble citizen, who is concerned only with the public welfare…

"There are times, to be quite candid with you, when I would like to sort of swing free again as an entirely private citizen – but not very often."

I always envied the ability of broadcasters to speak off the cuff in complete, coherent sentences. In the Q & A interview as published in the *Miami Herald*, I seem as polished and coherent as Murrow – but only because of my post-interview editing. (To be fair, I gave Murrow the opportunity to edit his side of the interview, too, even though it didn't need it.)

With John McMullan taking responsibility for day-to-day coverage, we gained confidence and convinced ourselves that we wrote better than the wires. Wire-service reporting had to serve a great variety of clients, and that forced it toward average, down-the-middle accounts. Representing only five papers and one owner, we were freer to take some risks, interpret the news, and go beyond dry listing of facts. The job became more interesting.

President Kennedy liked frequent and live press conferences. So did newspaper correspondents, because it gave them a chance to be on television. The meetings were held in the State Department auditorium to accommodate the heavy demand for seating. In October 1963, the *Charlotte Observer* called the bureau with a request. Governor Terry Sanford had been lobbying to get a proposed national environmental health research center placed in North Carolina's new Research Triangle Park. The park was an expanse of land between Raleigh, Durham, and Chapel Hill designated for research activity, but no research ventures had been launched there. It needed a catalyst. Because of disagreement over where to put the environmental center, its approval was stalled in Congress. The *Observer* needed a reporter to get the President on record about the possibility of putting it in North Carolina. I was available.

The procedure was orderly. The President, wearing a three-button pin-stripe suit and narrow tie, entered from stage left, stood behind a lectern, and went right to work. He started at his right, recognizing the senior correspondent, Merriam Smith of United Press International. Then, for the next half hour, he worked his way from right to left. Reporters in his line of vision would stand up if they had a question, and he would recognize one of them with a point or a nod. The situation was more dignified than your average press conference today. No one had to raise his or her voice because the acoustics were good, and a sound technician with a directional microphone stood on the stage to pick up every syllable for the live television audience.

I sat to the President's left so that I would have time to compose myself. About 22 minutes into the conference, he got to my sector. When he pointed to me, there was an awkward pause while I turned and looked at the reporters seated behind me, thinking he might mean to recognize somebody more important. Then I looked back, and the President nodded at me, a little impatiently. I asked my question.

"Mr. President, as you know, the plan to build a National Environmental Health Research Center has been hung up in Congress. Apparently they can't decide where to build it. There is a report that you would like it built in North Carolina. Would you?"

To the surprise of some, he had a detailed and specific answer.

"North Carolina would be very acceptable," he said. "I think the Budget recommendation was Maryland, but North Carolina does have the facilities. But I think in our recommendations we made, HEW made, the first recommendation was Maryland. The site in North Carolina is a good one, as there is a triangle there of colleges and hospitals and medical facilities. I have indicated that that would be satisfactory, if that was the judgment of the Congress. I think our first choice was Maryland."

Some of my cynical colleagues believed the question was a plant, that Kennedy had been warned about it in advance. No, no, I said, this was spontaneous. But much later, after I was more knowledgeable about the ways of Washington and politics as theater, I changed my mind. Governor Sanford had visited the White House a few days before to press that very issue, and it was probably he who made the suggestion to the *Observer*. Political theater or not, it worked, because the stalemate in Congress quickly ended in favor of North Carolina, and the Environmental Health Research Center became the first institution to open its doors in Research Triangle Park, which, in time, became an important economic driver for the area. Now that I live in North Carolina, I like to brag that I had something to do with that.

A few weeks later, I missed my usual bus and had to hail a cab for work. Its radio was playing a melody by Irving Berlin from a rather lame Broadway musical called "Mr. President."

The name of the tune was, "The Secret Service Makes Me Nervous."

After lunch and a quick trip to the Press Club library, I walked down to the 12th floor, and found Lily Murdoch, our secretary, weeping in the hall. "Oh, Mr. Meyer," she said. "The President has been shot."

We had no one traveling with the President in Dallas that day, but we could get the Washington reaction. I went outside and walked toward the White House. A crowd was already gathering in Lafayette Park. Inside, all the journalists were gathered around TV sets – in the lobby of the West Wing, in Pierre Salinger's office, and in the press room. We were in the White House, but like everyone else in the country, we got the news from Walter Cronkite. First there was a crescendo of unofficial, unconfirmed reports that the president was dead – from a CBS affiliate in Dallas, quoting a physician, then from Dan Rather at the hospital with a report that was "confirmed but unofficial," and, finally, Cronkite put on his reading glasses and looked at a bulletin that had just been slipped onto his desk.

"From Dallas, Texas, the flash, apparently official, that President Kennedy died at 1 p.m. Central Standard Time, 2 o'clock Eastern Time. Some 38 minutes ago."

He took off the glasses, was quiet for a few seconds while he composed himself, and went on. In the West Wing, one correspondent muttered an obscenity and turned away. Others just rubbed their eyes. Outside, the bell at St. John's Church in Lafayette Square began to peal. That and the lowering of flags at the White House and surrounding government buildings were the first external signs. I went back to the office and wrote about that scene, and then did a sidebar on the Secret Service and the difficulty of its historic mission to protect the president.

Like many other Americans, I woke up the next morning cherishing a secret and irrational hope that it had all been a dream. But the radio quickly confirmed that it was real, and so I went back to Lafayette Square and joined the hundreds of people just standing there in the rain and looking at the White House. They wanted to do something, and this was all they knew to do, to come and bear witness. After a while, I used my press pass to enter the White House and looked at the candle-flanked casket in the East Room. Pierre Salinger held a press briefing in another room. The Kennedy children, he said, had been told of their father's death at 7:30 p.m. the previous evening.

Some idiot asked, "How did they react?" and was quickly shushed by his peers.

The next morning, when the president's casket was placed on public view in the rotunda of the Capitol, I got up in the dark and drove down North Capitol Street to visit with the people standing in line. Like those in the park, they weren't sure why they were there but felt they had to do something, and wanted to be there. I felt useless, too. It wasn't the kind of reporting that I was good at. It was a relief when the mourning period ended and we could turn to reporting on the transition.

The Johnson administration never quite caught the glow of the Kennedy years, despite its legislative productivity. The Ohio delegation continued to be dull, although Akron's Bill Ayres provided some comic relief. On one occasion, while I was visiting in his office, Senator Barry Goldwater dropped by.

"Say, Bill," he said, "Where are those Stompin Rockets?"

Ayres kept a cabinet full of Akron-made toys. The Stompin Rocket consisted of a large rubber bulb attached to a rubber hose and a tube into which a cardboard toy rocket could be inserted. When you stomped on the bulb, air compression propelled the rocket out of the tube. Ayres opened his office window so that he and Goldwater could try to make a rocket hit the Longworth Building, across the street. Goldwater aimed while Ayres stomped. They hit the building on the fourth try, but the Arizona senator wasn't satisfied. "Last time I was here," he said, "we got them over the building."

I later arranged a Q-and-A interview with Goldwater. He

admired the little wire recorder and said that his department store should use that technology for training sales people.

Lacking much important news from the Ohio delegation, I strained for a little color. Frank Lausche, the old Slovenian, had no visible influence in the Senate, and he had a habit, almost a nervous tic, of always prefacing his remarks on the floor with a lament that he would be punished at the polls for speaking out so courageously. He did this no matter how bland the topic.

So I wrote the following for the *Beacon Journal* of May 10, 1964. It shows how desperate I was to get readable copy out of the delegation.

WASHINGTON – Who is the noblest senator of them all?

If public self-assessment were the guide, a gold medal would have to go to Senator Lausche.

This otherwise loveable Ohioan has fallen into the habit of sprinkling his speeches with flowery tribute to his own courage and devotion to high purpose.

It is not conceit. It is only that Lausche persists in viewing the world in Shakespearean terms.

Life's stage is to him packed with conflict, struggle, and moral dilemma. It is full of personal dangers that you would not expect to be sensed by a politician who won his last election by 700,000 votes.

He ponders these dark problems aloud in the Senate chamber, bushy head darting from side to side as he soliloquizes. The setting is somehow wrong. He ought to pace behind a castle parapet in flowing robes illuminated by torchlight and the occasional flicker of distant lightning.

The Ohio senator bared his soul to the galleries a few weeks ago. The subject was a member of the Negro lunatic fringe who had said members of his race were arming themselves to battle for civil rights.

To most senators, denouncing a crackpot would be routine

business. It wasn't to Lausche. "This matter is grave," he intoned. Then, Hamlet-like, he told how he had mustered the bravery to make that statement.

"Before I entered the chamber, I pondered whether I should speak on the subject. The devil within me said, 'keep silent. You will be hurt politically if you speak.'"

The stage thus set, he then resolved the conflict.

"I will act, but it will not be in fear. It will be in furtherance of justice and decency. If I were to act otherwise, it would be better to drop my head in shame and run for cover so that the eyes of decency would not look upon me."

Lausche, who is justly admired for his rugged independence, brought the subject up again a few days later. He indicated a fear that the voters would throw him out in 1968 if they recalled his position against screwball gunmen. He said his speech might cause "my demise from public life."

But, "I shall feel the better for it," he said, "that I have not been an abject coward fearing to speak what I believed to be the truth."

Senators are notably polite to one another. Lausche's fretting about his possible "demise" was hailed as a "fearless speech" by Senator Spessard Holland of Florida.

But tempers were growing short in the civil rights filibuster last week, and Lausche suddenly found himself rudely snapped at.

It happened during a highly technical debate over contempt-of-court penalties in the bill. Lausche is an expert in this field, having taught it and practiced it as a judge.

He launched into a brilliant analysis of the point at issue, cited precedents, and stuck to the issue without a single self-accolade.

He might have left it at that if Senator Sam Ervin of North Carolina hadn't interrupted him to offer a compliment.

"At this point," said Ervin, "I should like to say 'amen' to everything the Senator from Ohio has said."

228

It triggered Lausche's color-me-noble reflex. "I do not care whether the Senator from North Carolina says 'amen' or not," he said. "I have only one purpose to serve. I must be true to myself."

John Pastore of Rhode Island couldn't stand it any longer, and senatorial courtesy went right out the window.

"How does the Senator from Ohio feel we are all motivated," he thundered. "We have just as much responsibility, just as much conscience. Each of us has just as much love for America as has any other member of this body.

"If any one senator wishes to put a halo over his head, he should pause for reflection."

Pastore, like Holland, Ervin, and Lausche, is a Democrat.

The ever-independent Lausche clung to his pedestal. "I could accept those words with great grace, favor, and belief," he said, "if the deeds of the past conformed to the words spoken."

It may not be the world's most quiet brand of bravery, but there it is.

———————————

The executive branch side of the Akron beat was also quiet most of the time. Getting a new federal building, to house all of the government's Akron outposts at a single address, was a major concern of the *Beacon.* So I made frequent contact with the General Services Administration to see if the project was still edging toward approval. When the building was finally authorized, funded, and built, I felt so involved in the process that I joked to my peers that the building should be named for me.

And there were the non-journalistic functions in my job, such as lining up tickets to Washington attractions for friends of the Beacon's business manager. I supposed they were advertisers, but didn't ask. Of course, there were also opportunities to do a favor for a friend, and that more than balanced the drudgery.

At one point, acting on a tip from Ayres, I did a favor for my father. The only financial benefit for World War I veterans was a disability pension, but it did not have to be service-related, and the VA defined disability so broadly that just about anybody over 65 could qualify. I told my dad, he applied, and received a small monthly stipend for his remaining years.

In 1965, *Miami Herald* reporter Al Burt and photographer Doug Kennedy were covering a civil war in the Dominican Republic, when they were shot by U.S. Marines as their taxi approached a vehicle checkpoint. Kennedy's wounds were serious, and the Marine Corps flew him to Walter Reed Army Hospital for long-term treatment of a badly injured leg. Our house was walking distance from the hospital grounds, and we had plenty of room, so we invited Doug's fiancé, Eileen Fulford, to live with us while he recovered. She was Canadian and worked at the *Detroit Free Press*, where they met, and she had a cheerful, outgoing personality. We were glad to have her around.

I visited Doug frequently, and it soon became apparent that he was going to have some degree of permanent disability. He stayed in a Foster orthopedic bed, which was a double canvas frame that could be pivoted to turn the patient over with a minimum of effort. Without mobility, he had a lot of time to think, and he kept asking what would happen to him and his job after he was discharged. The company had only vague, noncommittal answers. Were the Knights worried about liability? I couldn't understand the failure to give him some kind of encouragement, some assurance that he still had a future with the company.

Doug and Eileen got married in the hospital. For once, I was the one who got to write a wedding story. They more than amply repaid us for the use of the room by letting us borrow Doug's house on Key Biscayne for a Miami vacation. The only sour note came after his discharge when Lee Hills sent me a substantial check as a reward for helping out in that difficult situation. I got the feeling that we weren't being rewarded for our humanitarian concerns so much as for possibly having saved the company some money. Still irritated by the Knight's failure to give Doug better assurance about his future, I sent the check back with a poorly drafted note that tried to explain my objections. I should have waited a day or two and tried some rewriting. Hills was offended, Bob Boyd told me later.

But the story turned out about as well as it could have given the circumstances. Doug walked again, although he needed a cane. And the Herald gave him a desk job, running the photo department, for which he was well qualified. They settled down on Key Biscayne, and Eileen bore him a son.

My most interesting assignment of 1965 was joining the National Aeronautics and Space Agency in chasing a comet across the Pacific Ocean. My name was drawn for a small pool of reporters to fly with NASA scientists 37,000 feet over Hawaii to get a look at comet Ikeya-Seki, named for the two Japanese astronomers who were first to detect it as a faint, moving object. Calculations of its orbit suggested that it would approach the sun and become extremely bright in late October.

This was pretty good duty. The small press pool was billeted at the Hilton Hawaiian Village Hotel on Waikiki Beach. We slept and went sightseeing by day and flew with the scientists at night in their airborne observatory, a Convair 990 named the Galileo. But the comet's arrival was later than predicted, and one by one the pool reporters were called back by their editors. I looked for unrelated stories so my office would know that I was busy.

One fairly obvious topic was Pearl Harbor's strategic position in the Vietnam war. It was a station for refueling, mostly airborne, for aircraft headed west for action. The Navy's public information officer at Pearl turned out to be my old boss from Little Creek, Paul Trahan. He took me to headquarters to meet Admiral Roy L. Johnson, commander of the Pacific Fleet. From his office, overlooking the harbor, he showed me the mountain pass through which the Japanese torpedo bombers had flown on the morning of December 7, 1941.

And now in 1965, this idyllic setting contrasted sharply with awareness of the new war in Asia. The beach was lined with palm trees and bars and young women who danced and sang, and the muffled, roaring counterpart to the laughter and the music was the sound of jet tankers taking off from Hickam field. I thought of a short story by Thomas Heggen, the troubled author of *Mr. Roberts*. It was about a World War II Navy veteran who tried to recapture the poignant tension of sitting in bars like these while he contemplated the war raging beyond the breakers. But once the war was over, the music never sounded as sweet.

At last, in late October, we sighted Ikeya-Seki. When it finally came into view, I was the only journalist still aboard. I waxed poetic.

——————————————

First a dark sky, almost black, accenting the brilliance of the stars. Then at the horizon a wisp of light, something like the beam from a far-off searchlight pointing at the sky.

From the left-hand windows of the Galileo, the view is probably the second best in the world. The best is from the Gemini Six capsule where astronauts Stafford and Schirra can see it undimmed by the atmosphere 16 times a day.

But the Galileo, at 37,000 feet, has an altitude advantage, too, with 85 percent of the earth's atmosphere below it. That's why the sky is black. There is nothing to scatter the light.

The first wisp of light is the tail of the comet, and as it begins to rise in the sky you can see that it bends in a graceful curve. This is a whiplash effect caused by turning the corner around the sun.

The light keeps rising. Soon it stretches from the horizon to a point about as high as your fist held at arm's length. It angles to the right. Last to appear is a tiny pinpoint of light at the lower tip. This is the nucleus, and some of whatever it is made of has come off and is flowing away from the sun to create the glowing tail ...

I observed my 35th birthday while packing up to leave Hawaii, glumly aware that I was now closer to 50 than 20. It felt like I was leaving my youth behind on that beautiful island. I never touched down in Hawaii again except once, in the middle of the night, to change planes enroute to Australia.

To further cost-justify the Hawaii trip, I stopped in California on the way home, tracked down some former Watts rioters for their current perspective on race relations, and then toured a few vegetable farms in response to an editor's query about the high prices for produce.

Back in D.C., I picked up a hint that the *Beacon* was getting ready to post me to an editing job in Akron, i.e. send me down to the minors. It was only a hint, and nothing would come of it, but it reminded me of the instability of my situation. This was a frequent concern for correspondents. Ed Lahey liked to tell the story of a *Kansas City Star* Washington correspondent who was recalled. When he encountered the man several years later, Ed asked how he was doing.

"I'm doing fine," was the answer. "I have my own column now."

"Congratulations," said Ed. "What's it called?"

"Other Kansas City deaths."

So, quite understandably, the Akron rumor made me assess my situation. Washington felt like home, disappointing as the job had been. But I knew that my situation was inherently unstable. My appointment as the *Beacon's* man in Washington had led to some understandable resentment in its city room. Lee Hills had been using the job as a placeholder while he figured out what to do with me. There had been a sign of trouble, but I had been too dim-witted to pick up on it.

It had come the previous spring at the Washington bureau's annual breakfast with editors, including John S. Knight, at the time of the annual meeting of the American Society of Newspaper Editors (now the American Society of News Editors) in Washington. There was the usual chatter about Washington events, and then, out of the blue, Jack Knight began complaining about a story I had written.

The story was a McMullan assignment, based on a Brookings Institution report, about the surprisingly high number of very rich people who had paid no income tax at all in the most recent year for which full records were available. Normally, there is a limit on charitable deductions, but a loophole had been created so that if you could arrange your charitable bookkeeping to show that you gave away all of your income in a given year, you paid no income tax for that year. (Congress would not enact an alternate minimum tax until 1969.) Knight did not complain about any specific detail of the story. He apparently just didn't like the fact that it had been written at all.

"You wrote that story, didn't you, Phil?" said the boss. I nodded and waited for McMullan to come to the defense of his assignment. But John just sat there speechless. So did I, and the conversation moved to other topics.

A cloud of gloom settled over me for the rest of the day. It wasn't until years afterward that it dawned on me this had been another of Knight's field tests. The first one had come in George Beebe's office when he gave me useless tips about the Miami Beach burglary just so he could size me up. This second one had been to see whether I was bold enough to talk back to him. I flunked – without even knowing it was a test, probably a test of whether I could handle the give-and-take of a management job. Lee Hills liked to promote smart people, and he knew from the Knight Newspapers testing program that I was smart. But my emotional intelligence was in doubt.

I should have given Jack Knight some guff.

18. Escape to Harvard

At least, I was smart enough to grasp that my Akron situation was shaky, and I decided that the time had come to try for a sabbatical. I had first learned about the Nieman fellowships when someone sent me a copy of *Nieman Reports* while I was in the Navy. My double strikeout with a parallel program, the Congressional fellowships, did not discourage me because, for this one, I had a hole card: Ed Lahey liked my work and, he still had close connections to the Harvard program.

When I told Ed about my ambition, he approved, and remarked confidently about what a great year I would have.

The next endorsement I needed was Ben Maidenburg's. He expressed support but advised me that Bob Giles of the city staff was already well into his own application. The Nieman Foundation had never chosen two fellows from the same newspaper in the same year.

So I decided to wait a year, and I told everyone who would listen about my plan to apply for a Nieman the following year. Spreading the news, I figured, would discourage competition from within the company. And it was a good thing that I did wait. Giles would eventually become curator of the Nieman Foundation and guide it deftly into the 21st Century transition to digital journalism. The delay would prove to work in my favor as well.

I was now beyond the median age for Nieman Fellows, so I would probably not get multiple chances as I had with the Congressional fellowships. The most important factor under my control would be the study plan. It needed to deal with a societal need, it had to fit what Harvard had to offer, and I had to make a convincing case that I would be good at it. Mrs. Nieman's will had indicated only that she wanted her bequest used to "promote and elevate the standards of journalism, and educate persons deemed especially qualified." To Harvard, that meant finding a few good journalists with good ideas and giving them access to the university to design their own programs.[20]

My good idea had already formed. It built on my graduate work in political science, applied to current events. Eugene Burdick had published *The 480* in 1964, a novel that warned about the possible malevolent consequences of using public opinion polls and computerized simulation models to guide presidential campaign strategy. In the closing scene, the central character imagines the late Senator Joseph McCarthy "watching the tapes and spools and lights and buttons and planning some masterful manipulation of the American public so that it would embrace his kind of madness."

As Burdick explained in a preface to his novel, it was based on a true story, that of the Simulmatics Corporation, whose scientists had put several years of Gallup poll data into an election model to guide campaign strategy for John F. Kennedy in 1960. The title came from the 480 voter categories created from the aggregation of Gallup data, and the brain behind it belonged to Ithiel de Sola Pool, professor of political science at Massachusetts Institute of Technology. It seemed to me that reporters who covered politicians who used these tools needed to understand them at least as well as those who stood to benefit.

That I did not fully understand survey research was clear from the two Ohio efforts that Bob Kotzbauer and I had produced in 1962 and 1964. But knowing that you don't know can be an early sign of wisdom that I hoped Harvard would appreciate. I framed my proposal with that in mind:

A year at Harvard would be for me partly a patching job to fill in the educational gaps that I feel most acutely in my work. These gaps cover a number of areas in economics, history, and government. But to the extent that I would focus on a particular field, that field would be political behavior.

My limited information on this subject comes mostly from half-remembered conversations at Chapel Hill a decade ago. At that time, I didn't think it was important. Now, however, I think it is necessary for a reporter who covers national government and politics to understand what is happening in this developing branch of political science.

There are two basic reasons for this view. One is the obvious need to understand and keep up with the substantive findings now being made in the area of voting behavior. I write a lot of copy on this subject – without calling it that, of course – every election year, and my methods of investigation are strictly seat-of-the-pants. I don't suggest that reporters should necessarily imitate social scientists, but I do think they should know what they are doing and be able to interpret their findings to the public.

We should also know something about their methodology. Total reliance on intuitive analysis in political reporting was adequate when politicians operated the same way. But, increasingly, they do not. Therein lies the second reason for studying this field. There is a big and mostly unreported story – because nobody understands it – in the use of behavioral science methods by political candidates and political parties. The White House has a continuing input of information on public attitudes from opinion polls. The major parties are turning to computerized information retrieval systems to give them data on voters and voting patterns.

The reporter who examines these new procedures ought to be sufficiently well backgrounded to understand and interpret them and also to make some kind of judgment about their validity ...

Finally, study of this field would have a fringe benefit. Since 1962, I have participated in semi-scientific newspaper surveys, which sought to predict the outcome of various elections. All have been embarrassingly inaccurate. It may be that I could learn enough to avoid such disasters in the future ...

The application also required a narrative description of my work history. To show some sense of progress, I started with the railroad experience that led to my first newspaper job in Clay Center in the hot summer of 1950. I proofread the package and sent it to Cambridge on March 10, 1966.

An encouraging response came two months later. I had made the first cut. A meeting with the selection committee was scheduled for 11:30 Sunday morning, May 22. "Please ask at the desk of the Mayflower Hotel for Mr. Dwight E. Sargent."

It was time for some more research. First, I had to investigate the backgrounds of the committee members.

One whom I thought would be friendly was Bill Pinkerton, the news officer for Harvard. He had been a member of the third class of Nieman Fellows in 1940-1941 and was a good friend of Ed Lahey. John Colburn, editor and publisher of the *Wichita Eagle* and *Beacon*, Malcolm Bauer, associate editor of the *Portland Oregonian*, and Eugene Patterson, editor of the *Atlanta Constitution*, represented the industry. The faculty was represented by Bruce Chalmers, professor of metallurgy, and Sargent presided as curator of the foundation. I studied the Harvard catalog so that I could drop the names of faculty members relevant to my proposed course of study.

Other preparations were more mundane. I went to the barber one full week before the interview in order to ensure a good haircut, but one that would not be obviously fresh on the day of the interview. In that same spirit, I wore a shirt that had been laundered once – new but not obviously so. I shaved that morning with a slightly used blade – sharp enough for a close shave but not so sharp that I would cut myself.

On the Friday before the interview, I used a stopwatch to time the walk to the Mayflower, starting from the east gate of the White House, four blocks away. I wanted to arrive at the precise second of 11:30 a.m., thus confining any nervous pacing to the trip itself. Also, the exercise would pump some stimulating blood to my brain, making me more alert.

It seemed to work. The interview went pretty well, I thought, although Saul Friedman, the new Detroit man in the Bureau and a 1963 Nieman Fellow, had warned me that subjective impressions of the interview were not at all predictive of the outcome. When Pinkerton asked me who at Harvard had the knowledge I needed, I was able to mention Seymour Martin Lipset, a quantitative political scientist who had recently arrived in Cambridge. And I expressed regret at the recent death of V. O. Key whose work I had read and admired in Chapel Hill. John Colburn was especially interested in my plan to study the effect of polls on campaign strategies and voter behavior, and I thought that was a good sign.

Then came the waiting. It was still May, about two weeks later, when Sue called me at the office. A letter had arrived from Harvard.

"Please open it," I said.

It got quickly to the point. "The Nieman Selection Committee has chosen you as a Nieman Fellow."

I jubilantly took the news to Ed Lahey and Bob Boyd, who was now second in command of the bureau, McMullan having gone back to Miami to run the *Herald.*

"Ed, you are a better fixer than anyone of us thought," cracked Boyd. "First you got me into the Gridiron Club, and now Phil is a Nieman Fellow." Lahey smiled benignly.

Only one little detail remained, and that was how to pay for it. The Nieman stipend was $7,360, but $1,760 of that went to Harvard for tuition and health insurance. That left us with

$160 a week to live on during the 35 weeks we would be in Cambridge. My *Beacon Journal* pay was $225 a week. And we now had another mouth to feed, daughter number three having arrived the previous February.

Lee Hills said that my request for a stipend to cover the difference was inappropriate because I was presenting him with a "fait accompli." I never did figure out what he meant by that because he had known about my Nieman aspiration, and the company had agreed in writing to grant me the leave of absence if my application should prove a success. But I knew that some companies subsidized their Niemans, and some did not. And the Knights were well known to be parsimonious. So Sue and I decided to go into debt rather than drastically reduce our living standard. I had a life insurance policy to borrow against, and we had other sources of collateral. It would be an investment. At the first opportunity, I took the Boston-Washington shuttle to look for housing.

Sue listed our home on Kalmia Road with the White House Fellows program, whose schedule was also based on the academic year. She found a family to live in our house, and I located an academic-year rental in the Boston suburb of Arlington, near a bus line that ran directly and frequently to Harvard Square. It was a colonial house like ours, it had early-American furniture like ours, and there was a bonus: a sun porch with a player piano. We would have some great parties there.

I took our 1963 Valiant to a welder to have a trailer hitch installed, and we moved ourselves, with three kids and a cat in the back seat. Boston was too far to drive in a day, so we overnighted in Connecticut, sneaking the kitty into the motel room inside a pillowcase.

The new Nieman fellows gathered in Harvard Yard for orientation. While waiting for the tour to start, we compared notes on the career histories that had brought us here. Seven of us were Washington, D.C. reporters: Tony Day of the *Philadelphia*

Bulletin, Dana Bullen of the *Washington Star*, Remer Tyson of the *Atlanta Constitution*, Joe Mohbat of the Associated Press, David Hoffman of the *New York Herald-Tribune*, Al Shuster of the *New York Times*, and me from the *Akron Beacon Journal*. Somebody asked Shuster where he worked before he went to the *Times*.

"Nowhere," he said. "I started as a copy boy in the Washington Bureau and never left."

There was an awe-stricken silence. Who could top that? I tried to break the tension.

"But, Al," I said, "the trouble with that is, you'll have to live out your entire career without ever knowing if you could have made it on a second-rate newspaper!"

We all laughed and relaxed. Several years after Harvard, when Shuster became the foreign editor of the *Los Angeles Times*, I kidded him about working for a second-rate newspaper.

The concentration of Washington journalists was unusual. To represent the rest of the USA, we had William F. Woo, feature writer from the *St. Louis Post-Dispatch*, Ken Clawson from the *Toledo Blade*, Jim Whelan of United Press International, Dewey James, from the *Florence Morning News* in South Carolina, and Dick Stewart of the *Boston Globe*. Woo, born in Shanghai, was a University of Kansas graduate who had started his career on the *Kansas City Star*. And there was a small group of foreign Niemans from Asia and South Africa.

The Nieman program in the 1960s had the virtue of simplicity. The way to succeed in an enterprise, some management expert once said, is to find something useful to do, and then do it simply, do it well, and never fail to do it. That is how Dwight Sargent managed the program he inherited from the revered Louis Lyons. The Foundation had a staff of two, Sargent, the curator, and Mary Ann Pratt, his assistant. Fellows were free to attend any classes that we found useful or interesting. We would not be graded, and we could sample, dipping in and out of courses at will. The only requirement was that we do all the work in at least one course.

Nieman fellows could hang out at the headquarters on Dunster St., and we met with some degree of regularity at two kinds of functions: Tuesday afternoon beer-and-cheese seminars with faculty members and Friday dinners with interesting people outside of Harvard. One of the dinner guests was James Bryant Conant, who had been president of Harvard when the Nieman Foundation was created. And it was at such a dinner that I first met Leo Bogart, the research director for the Newspaper Advertising Bureau of the American Association of Newspaper Publishers. My classmates greeted him skeptically because he was identified with the business side, but I was impressed with his knowledge and his PhD in sociology.

Another notable dinner speaker was Vermont Royster, editor of the *Wall Street Journal*, a newspaper that did not allow its journalists to be Nieman fellows. When Joe Mohbat challenged him on that, Royster replied that specialization was a bad thing for a journalist.

"A reporter should be a professional amateur," he said.

I thought about that observation from time to time as I poked into more and more esoteric fields at Harvard. A few years later, Royster retired from the *Journal* and returned to our shared alma mater, the University of North Carolina, to be a Kenan professor. He must have been doing something right.

One of the perks that went with the fellowship was membership in the Senior Common Room of one of the Harvard residential houses. I was assigned to Quincy House, just outside the Yard, a fairly new building with a clear midcentury modern influence in its design. I remembered Professor Layman at K-State praising Harvard for its ability to preserve traditional architecture without inhibiting its use of modern design for new construction. William James Hall and Quincy House were good examples.

The Senior Common Room was a gathering place for

faculty and graduate students, and I was awarded a key to its liquor locker and the privilege to entertain guests there. The chance to interact socially with faculty members would prove valuable.

Quincy House was a magnet for theatrical talent, and in the spring semester, its residents produced, on their own stage, the Leonard Bernstein musical "On the Town." It was beautiful, but the best part came after the final curtain. Bounding out of the audience came Leonard Bernstein himself to mount the stage and sit down at the piano.

And he pounded out a louder and faster version of the first-act song, "I can cook, too," to show the students how it should be done. Harvard was full of surprises.

And so it went. Just enjoy the intellectual and cultural buffet. Spouses were not invited to the official Nieman seminars and dinners, but they were allowed to attend classes, and Sue found a baby sitter so that she could attend art history classes and enjoy some of Bernard Bailyn's lectures on American colonial history.

There was one other thing, an early sign of mission creep in the Nieman program. Louis Lyons's last class had decided to honor him in a way that seemed simple and inexpensive: create an award in his name. The award carried no stipend, only a plaque. There was no application procedure, the members just sat around and discussed overlooked examples of journalistic excellence that deserved recognition. The only costs were stationary and the plaque, which was financed by fellows who volunteered to judge newspaper contests and contribute the honoraria. They expected future classes to carry on that work in perpetuity, but our class balked. We liked and respected Louis Lyons, but we were not interested in judging contests while we were busy soaking up the wisdom of Harvard. Sargent wisely put no pressure on us to continue the Lyons award. Succeeding classes followed our lead until 1981 when the Lyons award was revived under the curatorship of Jim Thomson. Lyons died in 1982, and the award has been given in most years since then.

We had moved to Arlington well ahead of the start of classes in order to get our two older children enrolled in public school, which began ahead of the Harvard semester. That gave me time to do some legwork. I remembered the words of my old professor at K-State, John W. McReynolds: "Find the person who has the knowledge you want, and make him teach it to you." So I studied the Harvard catalog, and tracked down professors who taught courses that sounded like they would fit my study plan. My first and most obvious interview was with David Armor who taught a graduate seminar in quantitative methods in the social sciences. As holder of a master's degree, I thought I would be most comfortable at the graduate level.

It took only 10 minutes of conversation with Armor to disabuse me of that notion. At his advice, I began instead with Social Relations 82, a course designed for sophomores and juniors getting ready for their senior research papers. Taught by an untenured assistant professor, Chad Gordon, its lectures were augmented by a discussion session led by a graduate student.

The course provided a clear overview of social science research methods and an introduction to Harvard's simplified computer language, DATA-TEXT. This assemblage of machine-language instructions for the IBM 7090 was organized into a programming system with syntax resembling everyday English. You told the machine, "compute correlations," specified the variables you wanted correlated, and the 7090 would do it.

Each student in Gordon's class was allocated three minutes of 7090 time for the whole semester. It was more time than it sounds like, because those minutes were measured by the central processing unit, not the wall clock. But it was limitation enough that we spent the first three quarters of the semester planning our analytic strategies. The data set was an attitude study of high school students. Our task was to find whether a student's self-conception affected his or her behavior. It was here that I started to see expanded possibilities for operational measurement. As I learned in the Florida school insurance case, whatever you are trying to measure might not be accessible to direct observation, but you can get close enough by finding a place where some piece of it, or some manifestation of it, surfaces in the visible world. An example used in one textbook: you can estimate the ages of previous viewers of a museum exhibit by finding their nose prints on the glass and deducing their makers' height by measuring the distance from the nose print to the floor.[21]

For the first time, I grasped the difference between reliability and validity in evaluating a measurement of some social phenomenon. A measure is considered reliable if it gives you the same answer with repeated attempts. It is valid if it's the right answer. If your paperboy always throws your paper in the gutter, he's reliable, but not valid. It is easy to test for reliability by taking repeated measures. Validity is harder to verify, and sometimes you have to settle for face validity, i.e. if it looks right, maybe it is. A more reassuring check on validity is to see if the phenomenon being measured correlates with things that you know should be related.

One way these concepts are applied in survey research is by asking different questions relating to the same phenomena. If the answers tend to be consistent, i.e. are intercorrelated, you have a good sign of a reliable measurement. And if they are predicted by theory – or are themselves predictors – it's a sign of validity. This triangulation reminded me of newspaper reporting, where an investigator will approach a difficult issue from as many different directions as possible. But this was less seat-of-the-pants. About a third of the way into the semester, listening to Chad Gordon describing the many systematic tools for measuring intangible things like trust in government, a thought struck me.

A journalist could do this!

I thought of all the newsroom conversations where we had discussed the possibility of reporting on some interesting social phenomenon. We always ended with a shrug and a lament that there was no way to measure it. We thought we were limited to tangible things. Now I began to wonder.

Journalists and scientists, I realized, were basically in the same business, discovering and imparting the truth. Now I saw how statistical tools could dredge meaning from large bodies of data, and I grew confident that I could learn to collect and organize such bodies of data on my own. I thought of the earnest attempts Bob Kotzbauer and I had made to predict Ohio elections. And Harvard's DATA-TEXT software instantly made computers accessible to people like me. As a graduate student, I had avoided quantitative methods because of the drudgery. But here was a machine that could do the heavy lifting. As long as I understood what went into the black box and what came out, I could apply statistics to interesting questions. It would not give me X-ray vision like Clark Kent, but it did seem like a kind of superpower.

Nevertheless, to be sure that I would have an intuitive understanding of what went on in that machine, I bought myself a slide rule at the Harvard Coop and learned to do chi-square tests by hand.

Harvard had cross-registration with MIT, so I took the subway to Kendall Square, and visited Ithiel Pool to get permission to attend his course in public opinion. Pool's work for John F. Kennedy had led to such key campaign decisions as the West Virginia speech where he faced down the religious bigots and made the case that a Catholic could be president. Back then, computer simulation seemed esoteric and dangerous. Today, you can do its simpler forms with an Excel spreadsheet. Pool's Simulmatics project for Kennedy had used an IBM 709 computer, which ran on vacuum tubes and was already becoming obsolete. The 7090 was its transistorized version, faster and more compact.

Even so, the 7090 took up a large room at the Harvard Computation Center because it needed 10 floor-standing tape drives to handle all the input-output operations that were required to get the most out of its tiny core memory. Today, the chip in your cell phone stores more information than that computer's core did.

With great enthusiasm, I devised intricate indices built from questions in the high school survey and showed them to the teaching assistant.

"Too complicated," she said.

Okay, I get it. Just because a computer could do complicated stuff didn't mean that complicated was good. I came up with a simpler plan, wrote a DATA-TEXT program on grid-lined paper, punched it into IBM cards, slapped a binary boot on the top of the stack, and took it to the computation center. The 7090 could do only one thing at a time. So the operator batched the jobs, and you had to come back a couple of hours later to find out how yours turned out. If you got back a short stack of paper, you knew it contained an error message. That computer was programmed with hundreds of different ways to insult you. If it was a thick stack, the computer had blessed it, but there still might be substantive mistakes that you would find when you pored through the output.

It took me several tries to get the thick stack of continuous-feed computer paper. It was late in the day, so I took it to Signet House where one of our evening events was about to be held. Dave Hoffman, the *Herald-Tribune* science writer was there, and I dramatized my achievement by placing the output on the floor and unfolding it into one long sheet that stretched the length of the room. Dave was impressed.

"Package it and sell it," he said.

Later, I saw Gordon's teaching assistant on the bus. "Isn't it a shame," she said, "that you'll never actually use any of these methods that you are learning?"

Useful or not, I had to know more. For second semester, I

247

participated in a graduate course on quantitative methods in political science taught by H. Douglas Price, a skinny bundle of nervous energy, who had been V. O. Key's graduate student. He revealed the good news that each student would get a full hour of computer time and the bad news that it would cost us $100. I couldn't spare that kind of money.

So I went to Dwight Sargent and asked if the Nieman Foundation had any funds for laboratory fees and the like. It didn't, but we struck a deal. I would write a piece for *Nieman Reports* about the strange things I was doing with my fellowship, and he would pay $100 for the article. I wrote it quickly. It was called, "Social Science: a New Beat?"[22] Its premise was that the computer had made intricate statistical tools accessible to anyone interested in data, and that its effect was revolutionizing the social sciences. I was nowhere near ready to say that it might revolutionize journalism, but the thought was beginning to form.

In Price's class, I got deeper into the analysis of cross tabulations and built up the nerve to try more complicated statistics, including factor analysis, which is a data-reduction tool, using the power of the computer to look for a few common factors around which a large number of variables might cluster. It made me feel nine feet tall. I might still be just a mild-mannered reporter, but I was gaining command of a tool that could provide a tremendous advantage in my highly competitive field.

The freedom to roam Harvard classrooms at will made it possible to approach some of my most pressing questions from different angles. I spent a good many hours in Owen Gringich's Natural Sciences course. Unlike the comprehensive courses at Kansas State, it did not try to survey the findings of the natural sciences in general. Its goal was to help us grasp the nature and methods of scientific research, including learning the technical details for a few selected cases. Thinking about what Chad Gordon was teaching and putting it in the larger context that

Gingrich was explaining was most helpful. I liked the example of the Copernican model of the universe, which puts the sun at the center instead of Earth. It had the virtue of simplicity.

The flaws in the earlier system of Ptolemy were revealed only after astronomical measurements got better. To explain the wandering of the planets against the background of the fixed stars, Ptolemy had proposed a system of epicycles, each planet revolving in a little circle of its own as it revolved in the big circle around he earth. Each time an error was uncovered, he would fix it by postulating a new epicycle within the previous one. In other words, his theory was not falsifiable, and if you can't test a theory for error, it's not much good. Verification is a journalist's quest, too.

I sampled two other courses that involved quantitative concepts that first semester. One taught by John V. Lintner, a Harvard Business School professor and fellow Kansan, was called Managerial Economics. Because of the traditional church-and-state wall between editorial and business sides of the news enterprise, I was woefully ignorant of how business decisions were made. To some news people, such ignorance was a virtue. I disagreed, believing that if we could understand the business side, we might do better in the inevitable conflicts that we have with it.

Al Neuharth had provided an example at the *Herald*. When a big story came along, the editor would ask publisher Jim Knight to add pages to the paper to make room for all the extra reporting. Knight would ask the production department how much the additional pages would cost. And the production manager would look at the total production cost for the previous year, divide by number of pages produced in that year, and report an average cost per page.

"Wait a minute," I could imagine Neuharth saying. "It's not the average cost that is important here, it's the marginal cost!"

He was right, however he said it. Average cost includes all

the fixed costs, such as salaries, taxes and depreciation on the plant, utilities and everything else that does not change when production increases or decreases.

Marginal or incremental cost includes just the things that change as the result of the decision to add more pages: mainly, ink and newsprint.

Neuharth made that case, Jim Knight bought it, and getting his okay to boost the size of the paper for a big story was much easier after that.

In the managerial economics class, I learned about using fixed and variable costs to calculate a break-even point, plus such things as make-or-buy decisions, and discounting a future sum to its present value. Those tools have everyday life applications as well. Professor Lintner would present real data, introduce problems, and say, "Now what's the best way to make a buck? Let's scratch the bear and see if he growls." Then he would urge us to "push the pencil" until we got the answer. Today, of course, we would use computer spreadsheets.

One other course in applied economics drew my attention: Thomas Schelling, who would win the Nobel Prize in 2005, taught a course called Games and Strategy. I had been vaguely interested in game theory ever since I heard Professor McReynolds talking about it at Kansas State, but with only a vague idea what it was for or how it worked. Schelling explained it clearly and with intuitive examples. And he was a member of the Quincy House senior common room. It was there that I had the opportunity to ask him about a personal application of game theory.

Sue and I had been driving along Route 128 encircling Boston when we saw a car at the side of the road with the hood up and man holding a sign, "Send help." We argued a bit about whether we should stop and call the police or, given the density of traffic, just assume that somebody else would do it. You see the problem. If everybody stopped, the phones would jam. But if we assumed somebody else would do it, how could we not expect everyone else to make the same assumption and leave that poor man stranded?

Applying game theory, we left it to chance. If every tenth car stopped, a call would surely get through. We had no way to compel every tenth car to stop but our personal moral obligation was clearly just one-tenth of a phone call. So we agreed that at a signal from Sue, I would look at my watch, and if the second hand were between 0 and 6, we would stop. It wasn't, and we did not stop.

I asked Schelling if we had done the right thing.

"Yes," he said, "given two requirements: that you did not feel guilty at not stopping, and that you would not have felt resentful if the decision rule had compelled you to stop."

I took the lecture notes from Schelling's course to my carrel at Widener Library, and pounded out the first draft of an article on game theory that I would later sell to *Playboy*. My twist: using game theory to compete for attractive women.[23]

Like most newspaper people in our age bracket, we Nieman fellows dreamed of writing our way out of the news business with a best-selling novel. There were two examples from Washington: Allen Drury had published *Advice and Consent* in 1959, and reading it had sharpened my desire to go to Washington. Then Fletcher Knebel and Charles W. Bailey II had brought out *Seven Days in May* in 1963. Both books were best sellers and became movies. Some of us looked and said, "I could do that."

And a Nieman year seemed like a good time to try. Theodore Morrison was a kindly, white-haired, soft-spoken teacher of creative writing. He had mentored A.B. Guthrie, the 1945 Nieman fellow who wrote *The Big Sky* and published it in 1947. Guthrie's sequel, *The Way West*, won the 1950 Pulitzer Prize for fiction. Morrison also referred frequently to George Weller, who published a novel of Harvard undergraduate life, *Not to Eat, Not to Love*, in 1934. Weller went into journalism, won a Pulitzer Prize for war correspondence in 1943, and became a middle-aged Nieman Fellow, class of 1948. Weller's Pulitzer story, about an emergency appendectomy in a submarine, in wartime with no physician present, remains a classic.

None of the Niemans in my class got rich enough from writing to leave the news business, but we enjoyed Morrison's advice, which came in the form of, epigrams, e.g. "Show, don't tell," "Will he or won't he?" and "A parallel with a difference." We enjoyed his anecdotes about Guthrie and the trouble that the author took to gather realistic detail, e.g. finding a folk remedy for gonorrhea that had been used on the western frontier.

Morrison's primary teaching technique was to read the work of students in class, then lead a critical discussion. My hopes were aroused when he wrote the following on one of my early submissions:

Neatly, cleanly, and sharply done. For what it is, it can't be faulted. But this particular kind of limited story or sketch – a biographical sketch in form – isn't a test of how you will operate in other kinds of fiction. Let's see what comes next!

It was not until the second semester that I produced something worthy of being read in class, and my work as a whole did lead to an accurate evaluation of my talent for fiction: not so much. I wrote well enough, but I didn't get far enough under the surface of my characters' thoughts and actions. Better, said Morrison in his gentle way, to stick to non-fiction.

I took that advice and never regretted it. Twenty years after *Esquire* rejected my railroad story, and thanks to Morrison's encouragement, I would finally make it into the magazine with a non-fiction piece on psychologist Stanley Milgram and his experiments on human obedience. I found out about Milgram when one of his Yale students visited a Harvard seminar, and I chanced to hear his description of what Milgram was up to. When unrelated events took me to New York City while Milgram was teaching there, I tracked him down and got several interviews. My *Esquire* piece was the first popular interpretation of his work, and it is still reprinted in both psychology and sociology textbooks. It is even included in one collection of exemplary nonfiction writing.[24]

We had other sources of writing advice. William J. Lederer, the career naval officer who co-authored *The Ugly American* with Eugene Burdick, lived in Kirkland House as writer in residence. One of our classmates talked him into meeting with us on Wednesday nights to talk about fiction writing.

His most memorable lesson was the one that relayed the wisdom of Ernest Hemingway. As Lederer told the story, he was based on an island in the Pacific early in the World War II era, when Hemingway knocked on his door. He had been drawn there by a rumor that Lederer owned the only supply of whiskey on the island. Lederer did indeed own a case that he had won in a poker game, and he offered to trade it for writing lessons. Hemingway agreed.

My notes paraphrased a few highlights of Hemingway's wisdom as relayed by Lederer.

A writer is not a writer unless he writes every day, like learning to kill or to screw.

You must conquer your story, which is a beast. All of your tenderness, love, hate, and anger go into the story. If you dilute your writing, it is not writing. Truthful writing is a huge beast. It eats you.

As soon as possible, give the problem and the main character. A majority of leads are dull because they are description without motion. A stream of consciousness is a mark of a lazy man. Write your lead, then resume your novel in one page.

Have the active verbs do he work, not is's and was's. Not, "He was tall," but, "He looked down on others." Show, don't tell.

In rewriting, consciously vary the length of sentences and paragraphs. Throw away the first 25 percent of your dialog. Keep it to "he said, she said," no synonyms for "said." But change the order: "He said, ..." or "... , he said." Keep the rhythm of speech so that you don't have to keep mentioning who it is. On each page, make clear how many miles or minutes have gone by. See that every sentence and page moves the story ahead.

In getting started, it helps to pretend that you are telling the story to your intimate friend, who knows nothing of it.

Write from daybreak to lunch. Then drink and screw.

After dispensing this sort of wisdom over a period of several days, and with one more lesson to go, Hemingway failed to show up at the appointed time. Lederer went to look for him and was told the great writer was leaving the area. Gunning his Jeep and pointing it toward the airstrip, Lederer intercepted Hemingway just he was about to board an airplane whose engines were warming up.

"What about the last lesson?" he said. "You said it would be the most important lesson of all. After all, you do have my whiskey."

"It's not whiskey, it's tea," said Hemingway. "You got done in. Everybody from here to Chung King has been pulling my leg."

"Then, why did you give me writing lessons at all?"

Hemingway looked at him.

"Compassion. Until you learn compassion, you'll never learn anything. And that's the final lesson. Goodbye, you sucker son of a bitch."

And he turned and climbed the steps of the airplane.

Years later, teaching news writing to journalism students, I would share Hemingway's advice, and congratulate them on learning about writing from a man who had learned about writing from a man who had learned about writing from Hemingway. Only two degrees of separation!

But I also came to doubt Lederer's account. He said he had preserved Hemingway's voice on a wire recording that was stored in a bank box in Honolulu. Eventually, he told us, he would get around to publishing it in full. To my regret, I never tracked him down to ask about it. Lederer died in January 2010 at the age of 97.

So I searched for evidence that Hemingway had been in the Pacific theater at some point in World War II. Finally, with the help of a Chapel Hill scholar, I found an account of a 1941 trip to China, before Pearl Harbor, where Hemingway accompanied his third wife, Martha Gellhorn. She was on assignment from *Colliers* to report on the China-Japan war. So an encounter with Lederer could have happened.[25]

My enterprising classmates organized a number of seminars outside the official Nieman program, most of them held at Dana Bullen's house, walking distance from Harvard Square. Dana was single at the time and affluent enough to rent a house with a good-sized living room for such gatherings. Al Capp, the creator of *Li'l Abner*, was one of a number of guests who came to Harvard on other business and were kind enough to spend an evening with us.

Some of my peers thought that Dwight Sargent wasn't doing enough to keep us busy, but I had no complaints. As a fund-raiser for the program, he was excellent, and that skill was badly needed because the value of the endowment had shrunk under Lyons's supervision. "All I require of my curator," I said, paraphrasing Ed Lahey, "is that he keep the program solvent." The intellectual riches of Harvard were there for the taking by anybody aggressive enough to go after them. We were reporters, after all. We just needed to use our brains to move our feet.

A good venue for meeting interesting faculty members was the weekly sherry hour held on the top floor of William James

Hall by the Department of Social Relations (which combined psychology and sociology). It was there that I met Thomas Pettigrew, author of the newly published *Profile of the Negro American*, a volume based on survey research. I never sat in on his courses, but we had some good conversations, and he clarified some concepts in statistics for me. David Armor, who was playing an important role in updating and improving DATA-TEXT, was also a regular at sherry hour.

In the second semester, I sampled some lectures on Southeast Asia by John K. Fairbank and Edwin O. Reischauer. I learned from Seymour Martin Lipset why the few Republican votes in North Carolina were concentrated in the mountains. It was because the Whigs had built the roads there.

Toward the end of the semester, Professor Price showed me a conference program that he had received from "those crazy pollsters." It was the American Association for Public Opinion Research, and a session on polling for election campaigns was included in the program. The conference was set for a long weekend at the Sagamore Hotel in Bolton Landing, New York, on Lake George in the Adirondacks. Scraping the bottom of our cash reserve, I flew from Boston to Albany, rented a car, drove north and arrived just in time for the opening dinner. I found a welcoming table with a man who turned out to be Burns W. Roper, the son of Elmo Roper, who had pioneered in broadcast audience measurement in the 1930s. Bud, as he was called, filled me in on the culture of AAPOR.

It was family friendly, Bud Roper said, and the presence of his children and their sheep dog bounding through the halls proved that point. Leo Bogart gave the presidential address, and Oliver Quayle had some intriguing comments on the value of factor analysis in analyzing voter characteristics. Quayle was a pioneer in applying survey research to the development of campaign strategy.

At one point, during a break in the proceedings, I looked up from the lawn of the Hotel Sagamore and saw Elmo Roper,

George Gallup, and Archibald Crossley standing on the porch. They were the pioneer pollsters of the 1930s, and I should have gotten that picture. From that weekend on, AAPOR meetings and publications became a regular source of knowledge and inspiration for my reporting career.

When leaves began to fill out on the tree that was visible from my basement carrel, I knew that the year was about over. The transition from Nieman fellow to working journalist was abrupt. I remember the exact moment. We were packed and ready to load, so I drove to the U-Haul dealer and hooked a trailer to the hitch on the Valiant. The coupling made a little clunking noise, and we were no longer free to drive anyplace but home. But we were older and wiser – and considerably poorer – as I looked forward to the challenge of finding ways to demonstrate my newly acquired superpower.

19. The Detroit riot

Bob Boyd had written on May 25 about my new assignment.

I think this bureau can do some damn important and interesting things, and you're going to be in the enviable position of a free-lancer on a steady payroll, looking for the best . . . Knight Newspapers, as you may know, is expansion-minded as hell, making money by the potful, and interested – as long as the dough holds out – in excellence, not adequacy. It ought to be a good period.

And so I returned to the Washington bureau as a national correspondent. My replacement from Akron, Bob Feldkamp, got to keep my old job. The bureau had expanded and moved down one floor to 1195 National Press Building, on the outside ring of offices with a nice view of Pennsylvania Avenue and the Washington Monument. (Eventually, a Marriott Hotel would rise next door and block that view, but not in my day.) I got to share a good-sized office with Ed Lahey, but his health was failing, and he was not often present. Bob Boyd was in charge.

Still, it was pretty much the old routine except for being free of Ohio concerns. And then on Monday, July 24, a major story from Detroit appeared in the morning papers. Rioting had broken out in the central city starting in the early hours of

Sunday. It was reminiscent of that riot in the Watts neighborhood of Los Angeles two years earlier. On Wednesday, July 26, I was alone in the office at lunchtime when the phone rang. The caller was Derick Daniels, who by then had left Miami to become executive editor of the *Detroit Free Press.*

"My staff is exhausted, and this stuff is still going on," he said. "Send us two fresh people."

I have often wondered what might have happened if somebody else had been there to answer the phone. The two people that I chose to fly to Detroit that afternoon were Saul Friedman and myself. And that night, we were in the riot area, riding with the National Guard, seeing the flames of 12th street and hearing shots in the night. The next day, I started piecing a chronology together, getting police reports of shooting incidents and fire department reports and mapping them, looking for a pattern. When the shooting and burning stopped, I roamed the area collecting eyewitness – and participant – accounts. By interleaving the official and participant accounts, I was able to create a long narrative -– too long. It could fill more than a full eight-column page.

While I was writing it, editors, including Lee Hills, strolled casually by and looked over my shoulder. I got my full page. Its headline: "Putting the Riot's Pieces Back Together."

This narrative was different from the prevailing one, set mainly by television, which held that most of the shooting in the night had been the work of snipers. The newspapers had bought into it, too. "Troopers Seal Off Nests of Snipers," said a page-one banner in Wednesday's *Free Press.* "New Tactics Flush Out Snipers," was the top line on Thursday. I spent most of Sunday going over police reports and writing a piece suggesting that sniper reports had been erroneous. The medical examiner discounted some of them by finding that the bullets had traveled horizontally, not from above. Other reported sniper fire proved to be stray bullets from guardsmen or law enforcement officers.

That Sunday evening, after deadline, we talked in the city room about going even deeper into the analysis of what had happened and why. A Sunday magazine collection of narrative pieces on the riot area and its problems was proposed. There were 43 deaths, and we had conflicting accounts about the causes and circumstances behind them, so an investigation into each of those cases was scheduled. My contribution to the conversation was to propose a scientific survey of attitudes and grievances in the riot area, using the tools for public opinion research that I had learned at Harvard.

I waved a copy of a newly released Associated Press report on a survey-based study of the 1965 Watts riot in Los Angeles, two summers earlier. Sponsored by the Office of Economic Opportunity, it had just been released by faculty at the University of California. It contradicted what had become known as the "riffraff theory," that the rioters were the most economically deprived blacks. It also pointed to police brutality and exploitation by white merchants, as primary causes. My modest suggestion was that we do what the California professors had done, but with a difference. We were newspaper people, and it would not take us two years.

"How long, then?" asked Daniels.

"Give me three weeks," I said.

"Write me a memo."

I had emerged from my Nieman year at Harvard feeling pretty smart, but not smart enough to launch such a major project without help. I called Kent Jennings from my graduate student cohort at North Carolina, who had completed his PhD and joined the Institute for Social Research at the University of Michigan. He put me in touch with Nathan Caplan, a psychologist at the Institute, and Caplan in turn recruited John Robinson, who specialized in sampling. Caplan agreed to help write the questions and train the interviewers, and Robinson was willing to draw the probability sample. I negotiated fees for them at $100 a day.

Taking the shooting and fire event data that I had collected, I drew lines on the map of Detroit to define the riot area. It was actually two areas, not contiguous. Because young people were visible participants in the riot, I set 15 as the minimum age for inclusion in the sample. Robinson produced a beautiful, yet practical, sample design. Working from the city directory and giving each residential address an equal chance of being included, he specified that half of all the age-eligible people in each household would be interviewed. That made the sample self-weighting for household size.

This feat was accomplished by having the interviewer prelist the first names and ages of everyone 15 and older in the household on first contact. They were listed in order of age and numbered. If the home was an odd-numbered address, the odd-numbered residents would be interviewed, if was an even-numbered address, their even numbered cohabitants would get that honor.

Now we needed just two things: interviewers and money to pay them. The *Free Press* had not, of course, budgeted for such a contingency, but Frank Angelo, who had grown up in Detroit, was the resourceful managing editor, and he solved both problems on the same day.

He persuaded the Detroit Urban League to be the designated sponsor of the study, and he got Henry Ford II and other private donors to put up the money. They made tax-deductible contributions to the League, which paid the interviewers, and the *Free Press* "coordinated" the project. Angelo learned that a summer enrichment program for public school teachers had just broken up, and we recruited the interviewers from its roster of participants.

Caplan and I created the questionnaire in a couple of days and had its pages reproduced in house. I still have a picture in my head of the copy boys walking a circle around two abutted desks where the stacks of pages were waiting to be picked up. One loop by one person yielded one collated questionnaire.

We started training interviewers the next morning. The most important lesson: maintain an attitude of sympathetic neutrality. Don't show shock or surprise when someone admits being a rioter.

Many of our questionnaire items came from the Watts survey. Social scientists look favorably on such copying because it allows comparisons across time and populations while testing the validity and reliability of the questions. The hardest was the question used to identify riot participants. In framing it we tried to make rioting seem like a perfectly natural, wholesome thing to do. Modifying the California question somewhat, we asked, "Would you describe yourself as being very active, somewhat active, or slightly active in the disturbance?" Those who did not participate at all had to volunteer that fact.

Sixty-three percent said they were uninvolved, 25 percent refused to answer, and 11 percent admitted some degree of riot activity.

Completed interviews came in at an average rate of 70 a day, and, just two weeks after the Sunday night decision to proceed, we had a sample of 437, good enough for some fairly fine-grained analysis.

The University of Michigan used a new computer, the IBM 360, and that was a disadvantage. It was so new that advanced statistical software had not yet been written for it. But it did have an adequate crosstab program, called Filter Tau, which could run tables and perform chi-square tests. We hired Judith Goldberg, an ISR programmer, to write the code.

There had been two popular theories of the causes of the Watts and Detroit riots, and our survey contradicted them both. The riffraff theory held that the rioters were the most desperate residents at the bottom of the socio-economic scale. If that were true, low income and lack of education should predict riot participation. As in Watts, this theory had no predictive power in our study.

Another theory, advanced by a psychiatrist specializing

in violence, held that rioting was caused by the frustration felt by southern immigrants who had difficulty assimilating in the industrial north. If so, there should have been more participation among those who grew up in the south. There was actually less.

By elimination, that left a third theory that still looks pretty good today: relative deprivation. The phenomenon was the serendipitous discovery of Samuel A. Stouffer when he did morale studies for the Army in World War II. To his surprise, he found that morale was highest in units with the lowest promotion rates. Upon reflection and further investigation, he found that a low prospect for promotion was not much of a problem for men who saw their peers in the same situation. But in units with high promotion rates, every promotion created feelings of frustration among those who were left behind.[26] This theory was a good fit to Detroit's situation, because the city had good leadership in the 1960s, and its reputation for handling race relations was better than most. But every black person who got ahead was a visible reminder of defeat for those left behind.

The survey provided a corrective tool for the impressions left by TV coverage and its images of burning buildings, broken windows, and looting. There was no basic breakdown in respect for law and order. The vast majority of black citizens in the riot area, including the riot participants, thought of burning and looting as crimes. They had simply been caught up in the pressure of the moment. As the Watts rioter I had interviewed the year before had told me, they were "just going along with the program."

And it was not a random program. There was a striking parallel between the kinds of businesses burned and the kinds of businesses complained about in the survey.

The *Free Press* played the opening story in my series on page one under the headline "The Non-Rioters: A Hopeful Majority." And the lead was:

Despite the recent week of rioting, Detroit's Negro community is basically stable and committed to basic American values. The rioters were a small and deviant minority, protesting not only against society in general, but against prevailing Negro social standards.

———————————

Derick Daniels had a possible Pulitzer in mind, and when he supervised the layout of the pages, he took care to place the credit to the Detroit Urban League for sponsoring the survey in a remote location that could be withheld from the prize entry package. Then he went home. Frank Angelo, who had negotiated the deal, saw what Daniels had done, and moved the Urban League credit back to a prominent position. When Daniels saw the published version, he had, according to Kurt Luedtke, who witnessed the event, a rare temper tantrum. "I had never seen him so angry," Luedtke told me.

But the Pulitzer jury didn't mind. I was in San Francisco, covering the 1968 California presidential primary election, when the announcement came that the Pulitzer Prize for local general reporting had been awarded to the staff of the *Detroit Free Press*.

The commendation, a copy of which has hung on my wall for four decades, cited the staff

———————————

... for its coverage of the Detroit riots of 1967, recognizing both the brilliance of its detailed spot news staff work and its swift and accurate investigation into the underlying causes of the tragedy.

———————————

Later, Lee Hills told me that he had learned, from his sources on the committee, that the survey project had been a major factor in the award.

But the best part was the learning experience. Guided in the

265

application of my Harvard learning by the two Michigan faculty members, Caplan and Robinson, I was gaining confidence as a survey researcher. This had been a quality project, meeting scholarly standards. Professor Caplan and I had made a deal. I would get first use of the data for journalistic purposes, and then he could do whatever he wanted for academic publication. He reanalyzed the data, along with material from a study of the Newark riot, which happened earlier that same July, for the National Advisory Commission on Civil Disorders that President Johnson had appointed before the violence in Detroit was over. In its summary, the commission had a section on race relations and the media. It found that media performance was generally poor, but it called the *Free Press* riot coverage "a brilliant exception."

The most important accolade came in the form of peer recognition. All three of the major news magazines cited my survey story. In Ed Lahey's view, that was about as high as a Washington correspondent could go – to be quoted in *Newsweek*.

The catch was that I wasn't being recognized for anything I had done in Washington. But it didn't matter. Washington was a fine base for a reporter for a group of newspapers. With the Harvard-learned skill I had just demonstrated, I could be on call anytime a Knight newspaper had a situation that could not be handled by conventional means. Survey research was an ideal tool for the turbulent 1960s because media coverage of both the civil rights movement and the anti-Vietnam War movement suffered from the same problem. Journalists were drawn to the most outrageous and extreme spokespersons of those movements, and it was never clear who or how many they represented. Public opinion research, directed at specialized publics, could provide the answers.

We can't control the kind of luck we have, but we can control our response to it. Things are always changing, as the narrator in a now-forgotten newspaper novel said. When we don't like a change, we roll with its punch, and, when there is change we like, we ride it hell-for-leather for all it is worth. If my Nieman fellowship had been just one year earlier or one year later, I would not have been nearly as well positioned as I was in 1967.

Now it was time to find another target of opportunity. The year 1968 would prove to be full of them.

20. A year with too much news

At Knight Newspapers, we felt guilty about having waited until there was a riot before reporting on black attitudes and grievances in Detroit. Perhaps we could atone for that by doing such a study in a place that had not – so far – had a riot. I privately thought of it as a "pre-riot study."

The *Miami Herald* volunteered, and put some money in its budget for a survey. As the New Year began, I flew with Sue to Miami. The trip gave her a chance to reconnect with old friends while I worked out details of the new project with John McMullan and his managing editor, Larry Jinks, along with Landon Haynes, the director of Market Research. Haynes was experienced in survey research, and volunteered to recruit the interviewers and run the field operation. All I had to do was design the questionnaire, analyze the data, and write the story. In the elevator, I encountered reporter Bill Montalbano, and he was a little bit hostile.

"So you're here to cover race relations in Miami," he said. "Isn't that Juanita Greene's job?"

Greene was the Herald's well-respected urban affairs specialist, and race was indeed high among her interests. I assured Bill that there would be a role for her in the project.

For theoretical guidance, I relied on a new book by Gary Marx, *Protest and Prejudice*, which had developed a series of attitude scales to measure different dimensions of black attitudes toward the civil rights movement. In writing the interview schedule, I borrowed shamelessly from his questions.

When some of them were challenged at an editors' meeting, I tried to explain the value of replication in order to compare against an existing baseline. The questions would mean more to readers if we could compare their results with those of other black populations at other times. McMullan was more inclined toward originality.

"What Meyer is trying to say, John," said Larry Jinks, "is, 'this is the way we've always done it.'"

Everybody laughed. McMullan sighed.

"I can remember," he said, "when the only thing that Meyer knew more about than I did was what the School Board was doing."

The Gary Marx questions stayed.

This time, I was determined to do my own programming, so I called Doug Price at Harvard, and he agreed to arrange some computer time for me. In addition, I got help from two of his graduate students, Peter Natchez and Irwin Bupp.

We finished the fieldwork in late March, and the Herald data-processing department punched the cards. Clark Lambert, the department head, thumbed through my DATA-TEXT manual and was impressed.

"Somebody went to a lot of trouble to do this," he said.

But the Herald's computer was an IBM 360. Ironically, to use the most advanced software of the time, I had to borrow Harvard's out-of-date 7090. With a long box of punched IBM cards, hand-carried all the way, I flew to Boston.

The first step in data analysis is running frequencies on all the questionnaire items. You look at demographics first to see if they square with what you already know about the population being studied – an external test of validity. They didn't look right.

The sample was the right size, 530 cases. Landon Haynes had sent his interviewers back as many as nine times to get people not found at home on previous visits. The response rate was better than 80 percent. So my heart sank when I looked at the gender distribution. Our sample was two-thirds female!

Something was seriously wrong. Women slightly outnumber men in the adult population, but this was ridiculous. Sampling error could not account for a difference that size. I went to the library and tracked down the 1960 Census report and was both puzzled and relieved to see that it, too, reported the black population in Miami as two-thirds female.

The missing men had to be there, I reasoned, but the combined effects of racism, homelessness, and the welfare regulations made them invisible – to census takers and survey interviewers alike. For a family in 1968 to be eligible for the Aid to Families with Dependent Children program, there could be no adult male in the household. The men must surely be there – they were just hiding out.

Thus, the discrepancy that at first appeared to be a fatal flaw in the *Herald* survey turned out to be an opportunity. At my suggestion, Juanita Greene was put on the case, and she reported and wrote a beautiful sidebar: "The Invisible Population: 23,000 Males."

Here is her lead:

The census taker would have a hard time finding Franklin Baker "at home."

His domicile floats, as does Baker.

In the daytime he lives on street corners, sometimes sitting all day on a wooden crate.

At night he sleeps on top of the clothes dryers in an open front coin laundry if he can't afford the 75 cents for a bed in a flop house.

The census taker would have an even more difficult time finding Willie George, a younger man.

Willie has a home, a wife, children, and an on and off job. He doesn't hang around home in the daytime; and he doesn't

271

hang his clothes in the closet at anytime. Officially, Willie (not his real name) is a missing person, a father who has deserted. This enables his family to qualify for welfare.

Frank and Willie are members of the "lost ghetto population."

The man-in-the-house rule was invalidated by the Supreme Court later that year. In King v. Smith, the court ruled that such state regulations were contrary to the original purpose of the program, which had been established by the Social Security Act of 1935.

Meanwhile, our survey was good, so long as we limited our generalizations to the visible segment of the black population in Miami.

I followed Gary Marx's scheme to classify the different versions of black militancy: the conventional militants who endorsed Martin Luther King's strategy of nonviolent confrontation accounted for 25 percent. About 10 percent endorsed violent confrontation to some degree, and five percent identified themselves as black separatists. There was some overlap among these categories, so only about one out of three expressed any kind of militancy at all. But Miami's profile, when compared with cities studied by Marx, was more like Chicago's than other southern cities like Atlanta or Birmingham, where black militancy was more subdued. This was going to be a pretty good story.

I was poring over printout at the Sheraton-Commander hotel on the evening of March 31, when I heard shouting coming from Harvard Square. I went outside to see what was going on.

"Johnson's not going to run for re-election!" an excited student told me.

It was true. The President had been a candidate for renomination in the New Hampshire primary and won – but by an unexpectedly close margin. Thousands of college students, including some from Harvard, had campaigned against him, going door to door, on behalf of Eugene McCarthy, who opposed the war in Vietnam. This was going to be an interesting year.

When I had wrung as much information out of the data as I could in a reasonable time, I packed up the printout and the IBM cards and headed home to write a profile of Miami's blacks and their political attitudes. My basement office was a former physician's examining room with tile floor and solid walls, providing a quiet place to concentrate. This was turning into a good-news story. Miami blacks had high expectations and a good sense of making progress. And they supported Martin Luther King over his radical competitor for media attention, Malcom X, by 77 percent to 1 percent. I began feeding these details to Miami so that Juanita Greene and George Kennedy could start the legwork on sidebars to flesh out the statistical picture with real people and their stories.

By April 4, I was close to wrapping up the story, but at 6:01 that evening, everything changed. Martin Luther King was assassinated while standing on a motel balcony in Memphis.

I drove downtown the next morning. Fires and looting had broken out in a section east of 14th Street and north of H Street. A young black man whom I passed as I left the parking lot raised his fist and made a threatening gesture. I did what I could to help with the spot news of the day, then went back to my project.

The story was published as a series, starting on April 28 and ending May 2, along with the Greene and Kennedy sidebars. But I knew, well before then, that we needed to get back in the field. Already, a movement like King's 1963 March on Washington, but with a more somber theme, had begun. It was called the Poor People's Campaign, and participants began building a tent city on the National Mall.

The media were hungry for theories on what was happening to the civil rights movement, and they had no trouble finding them. All involved various shades of dire forecast.

"King was the last prince of nonviolence. Nonviolence is a dead philosophy," said Floyd McKissick, national director of the Congress of Racial Equality.

"The rebellions that have been occurring around these cities and this country is just light stuff to what is about to happen," warned Stokely Carmichael.

Even the moderate head of the Urban League, Whitney Young, warned that people like himself might turn "revolutionist."

And Dr. Lewis Killian, a sociologist at Florida State University, saw "a great probability" that advocates of violence would "become the dominant element in Negro leadership in the next few months."

These were testable propositions, because our Miami study, fielded from February 26 to March 25, provided a perfect baseline for a pretest-posttest research design of the sort I had learned about in Doug Price's class. While our survey design provided for confidentiality, it had not promised anonymity. The difference is that an anonymous survey leaves no traces that could be used to link a respondent to his or her views. A confidential survey preserves that record with a promise not to publicly identify anyone without permission.

All we had to do was to go back to Miami, interview the same people, merge the two databases, and find out what, if anything, had changed after King's death. Well, there was one other thing. We had to find the money to do it.

Getting the *Miami Herald* to budget for the original survey had been something of a coup for me, as was my success in getting the *Detroit Free Press* to budget for a one-year follow-up to the 1967 riot study. But budgeting, by definition, is done in advance. There wasn't any money for short-term, fast-response research.

I worried aloud about this problem while visiting one of my regular Washington sources. T. M. "Tommy" Tomlinson, was a psychologist from Wamego, Kan., and he oversaw evaluation studies in the Office of Economic Opportunity, one of President Johnson's Great Society programs. He had been helpful with ideas for the Miami survey, and he was intrigued by the chance to convert it into a panel (which is what the participants in a pre-test, post-test design are called). He talked it over with his boss, Robert A. Levine, an economist and OEO's assistant director for research, planning, and programming, who wanted to know, as badly as we did, how King's death would affect the civil rights movement. Levine said OEO would pay the field costs of the survey.

Wait a minute. I am a reporter, and OEO is one of my beats. And it wants to give me taxpayers' money to do a story?

This was not an ethical dilemma. It was clearly, transparently, obviously unethical. It was a violation of the journalist's rule to act independently. "Avoid conflicts of interest, real or perceived," says the code of the Society of Professional Journalists.

But I scarcely thought about it. The conflict could be cured by disclosure, I rationalized. And everybody – the government, the media, the public – needed the answer to the question that this project posed. OEO's only requirement would be that we place our data in a public archive for secondary analysis and that I write a formal report of the findings – not a journalistic report, but a scholarly one. I could do that.

The proposal sailed through the *Miami Herald* management. Hal Jurgensmeyer, the business manager, saw at once the opportunity offered by a posttest, and gave it his enthusiastic endorsement. Landon Haynes was happy to run the fieldwork again. The editors loved the idea. Nobody mentioned conflict of interest.

Anxious to save time and money, we drew a 50 percent subsample of the completed portion of the original sample. In the field from May 23 to July 17, Haynes managed a 70 percent response rate, giving us 186 good cases, and they matched the full sample on degrees of militancy within a fraction of a percentage point. Acting on a suggestion by Thomas Pettigrew,

I included a new sample of people who had not been interviewed before, to test for the possibility that the first interview had contaminated our sample and made its members atypical.

The results were encouraging. The sample was untainted. And the numbers advocating violence or separatism did not budge. But the proportion favoring King's nonviolent strategies had jumped from 24 percent to 31 percent.

To get some insight beyond the numbers, I flew to Miami and talked to some of the respondents myself. Part of the effect might have been due to the publication of my first survey report in the Herald. Several people mentioned those articles.

"I was surprised to see that many people thought the way I thought," said one youth.

And a 33-year-old housewife said, "I didn't know as many people thought things were as really in as bad a shape as what they was."

Later, I would learn that there is a theory to account for this, Elisabeth Noelle-Neumann's "spiral of silence." Developed in Germany, it holds that people will keep quiet about views that they believe are not widely shared, and this silence leads others to underestimate their prevalence.

I was still too green a statistician to know that there are statistical tests designed explicitly for panel studies. After I turned in my report to OEO, Bob Levine called to congratulate me, but also asked why I had not used any significance tests.

"Because it was a panel," I blustered. "We talked to the same people, so the differences have to be real."

"Fair enough," he said, and he let it go at that.

Hoping to verify that I had performed actual scholarship, I sent my OEO report to *Public Opinion Quarterly*. Editor W. Phillips Davison was planning a special section on the impact of various dramatic 1960s events on public opinion, so this report was made to order for that collection. In fact, he led the issue with my piece. The article was my first academic publication, and I loved the footnote that explained my qualification to write it: "Philip

Meyer is a correspondent in the Washington Bureau of Knight Newspapers, Inc." I hoped Jack Knight was as thrilled as I was. While the second Miami wave was still in the field, I went to California to cover the Democratic primary and attend my second meeting of AAPOR, this one in Santa Barbara. I started in San Francisco and that was where Dick Stewart's telegram found me after the Pulitzer Prizes were announced. My Nieman classmate from the *Boston Globe* had been kind enough to track down my location and send me a congratulatory telegram on the prize. Then, in a triumphal mood, I rented a Mustang convertible, put the top down, and drove down the coast to Santa Barbara. Paul Sheatsley, co-author of a leading textbook on survey research, gave the AAPOR presidential address. This meeting was being held jointly with the World Association for Public Opinion Research, and I began to get a sense of how universal the desire to understand public opinion really is.

Naturally, the current political situation was a common theme, and the most memorable comment came from Amitai Etzioni, the Columbia University sociologist. He was in the audience for a session on youthful political participation and the 18-year-old vote, which had been discussed but not yet enacted. (The 26th Amendment to the Constitution would become effective in 1971).

Etzioni stood up and made the point that voting is not the most important form of political participation, and he used youthful anti-war protests as an example.

"Think of all those college kids who rang doorbells for Eugene McCarthy – most of them weren't old enough to vote," he said. "But each one of them was more powerful, by that act, than any of their elders whose only participation was voting."

The Miami survey was still in the field when I returned home to start work on the year-after Detroit project. I was in bed in the dark with the radio on when the news came of Robert Kennedy's assassination. He had been campaigning in

California for the Democratic presidential nomination. And 1968 was not yet half over.

How the invitation was delivered, I don't remember. But there it was, on paper, addressed to me: the Kennedy family's personal invitation to attend Robert Kennedy's funeral at St. Patrick's Cathedral in New York City on June 8. So I did something quite rare for a newspaper reporter: I traveled at my own expense, catching the Eastern Shuttle to New York. At National Airport, I recognized two people waiting for the same flight: Sander Vanocur, the CBS correspondent, and Shirley MacLaine, the movie star. They had been mentioned as a couple in the gossip columns.

The Cathedral was packed, and the highlight, of course, was Edward M. Kennedy's eulogy. His brother, he said, should be "remembered simply as a good and decent man, who saw wrong and tried to right it, saw suffering and tried to heal it, saw war and tried to stop it."

Two weeks later, the Poor People's Campaign shut down, and rioting broke out on NW 14th Street in Washington. I had visited the tent city on the mall and kept some track of its progress, so I went out to see what was going on. There was glass breaking and looting, but not on the Detroit scale. Walter Fauntroy, the vice-chairman of the D.C. City Council was there, and he shouted when he spotted me in the middle of 14th Street.

"Get out," he said. "Your face is too white for this place."

But I was still there when the police came and started lobbing tear gas grenades to disperse the crowd. It was my first taste of the stuff. In addition to inducing tears, it gives you a painfully dry throat. I needed something to drink. Looking around, I spotted a drug store with a broken window and open door, so I ducked inside, and found it deserted. Slipping behind the soda fountain, I found a clean glass, and drew myself a Coca-Cola from the spigot. *I'm looting a Coke!*

My second experience with tear gas came in Chicago

two months later. As a political science major, I had always wanted to cover a national presidential nominating convention, and this was an exciting one because of the contest between Eugene McCarthy, the peace candidate, and Hubert Humphrey, President Johnson's choice. I carried binoculars, so that I could pick up details across the arena. The Knight newspapers had a huge convention bureau, which included Jack Knight himself. On the afternoon of Tuesday, August 27, our guys scored an exclusive interview with McCarthy in his Conrad Hilton suite. Knight was there along with *Miami Herald* editors Don Shoemaker and John McMullan and *Detroit Free Press* editor Mark Ethridge Jr. Present to write the story were Bob Boyd and Saul Friedman from the Washington bureau. It proved to be a big one. McCarthy effectively conceded the nomination to Humphrey, admitting that he did not have the delegates.

It caused a stir. Dick Harwood, who by then had left Louisville to report for the *Washington Post*, dropped by our enclosure with a worried look on his face. "Knight Newspapers is big on the tube right now" he said. We gave him our story, because the *Post* was a client of the *Chicago Daily News* wire, which our bureau still supplied. It carried a copyright which meant that Knight Newspapers would have to be credited. And we took pleasure when the *Washington Post* and the TV talking heads were forced to cite us.

After deadline, we wandered outside, where the police, on orders from Mayor Daley, were attacking anti-war demonstrators with clubs and tear gas. Now here was a story that television could do better than we could, and we left it to them, although toward the end of the week I wrote an analytic sidebar (known to cynical journalists as a "thumb-sucker") on whether the police behaved appropriately. My main source was John Spiegel from Brandeis University, whose views on riot causes I had challenged the year before. He was attending the convention as an observer, and thought the mayor and his cops had overreacted. City officials expressed zero remorse.

279

Sidebars were my specialty at this convention. I found Herbert Alexander, then one of two leading authorities on money in politics, also in Chicago as an observer and got his views on the two parties' prospects for fund raising. Republicans would have the easiest time of it, he predicted, although a peace candidate would have attracted small donors in enough volume to make the Democrats competitive.

And on Wednesday, after McCarthy's concession was on the newsstands, I wandered around listening to his young supporters. "The children's' crusade is over," I wrote, "and the tears shed in Chicago Wednesday by the young followers of Eugene McCarthy were not so much for him as for their own lost innocence."

I had to leave early to get the Detroit year-after riot survey launched, and so I checked out of the Pick-Congress Hotel and found a cab. On the way to the airport, I saw a crowd gathered in Grant Park and asked the driver to stop and wait while I went over to investigate. It was Senator McCarthy, making a farewell speech to his young supporters.

"I'll not compromise, I'm not departing from my commitment to you, nor are you departing from your commitment to me," he said. "And so we will go on in the same spirit . . .

"Let us go on from here to do the things we can do and not worry about the things we can't do."

I wrote down as much as I could in the eight-by-five-inch Paper King spiral notebook that I had carried throughout the convention. At the airport, I called the Knight convention bureau and dictated my notes to Barbara Stanton, our ace rewrite person from the *Detroit Free Press.* Then I finally let go of the convention story.

The year-after Detroit riot survey showed a seeming paradox. Grievances were higher than immediately after the riot, but the city's blacks were more optimistic. The lead to my report published in October 1968 shows how I resolved that.

Detroit Negroes are franker, more outspoken, and quicker to complain than they were a year ago.

Yet, when asked how things are going for them in general, they tend to report that things have improved since the riot.

A paradox? Not really. The new mood is one of black unity, pride, and a sense of newly discovered effectiveness. Blacks complain because they expect complaints to lead to action, and this is the sign of a people on the move.

Since the riot, said a black militant who lives near 12th Street, "The white man will stand up and take notice of you, when before he has not."

For this survey, I had more time to consult with mentors at both Harvard and Michigan. Thomas Pettigrew guided me to a tool invented by Hadley Cantril and Lloyd A. Free to make cross-cultural comparisons of a given public's sense of progress. It was called the "self-anchoring striving scale." It used an exhibit, a picture of a ladder with rungs numbered from 1 to 10.

"Here is a picture of a ladder," the interviewers said. "Suppose we say that the top of the ladder represents the best possible life for you, and the bottom represents the worst possible life for you. Where on the ladder do you feel you personally stand at the present time?"

Respondents were then asked where they stood the previous summer, just before the riot, where they were five years ago, and where they expected to be five years into the future. The average scores revealed a sense of progress.

Five years ago	4.2
Last summer	4.9
Now	5.7
Next five years	7.7

"The city has begun to get something to build on," said a *Free Press* editorial.

And so had I. The Harvard experience was by now more than a year in the past, and good things were still happening. When Sue had traveled to Miami with me for the launch of our so-called pre-riot survey the previous January, we stayed in Larry and Joan Jinks's guesthouse. It had a romantic setting by their swimming pool. Nine months later, soon after I was back from writing the new Detroit study for publication in October, our fourth daughter was born. And in that same month, *Newsweek* profiled me in its Press section as "a computer reporter."

One more important thing happened before the year was over. I had never gone back to cigarettes after leaving the Navy, but maintained a pipe-and-cigar habit, even after covering the 1964 Surgeon General's Report, which gave official gravitas to what was already known about the consequences of smoking and health. New Year's Day 1969 would fall on a Wednesday, and on Monday, Bob Boyd assigned me to draw on my experience as a medical writer and prepare a story that would help smokers decide whether to make a resolution to quit.

So I went to the National Institutes of Health library and searched the literature, looking for articles with gruesome details. I found one about nose and throat cancer, describing patients who needed parts of their faces cut away to save their lives. I wrote about that, smoking a Tiparillo as I did so. They were small, plastic-tipped cigars that had been popularized with the slogan, "Does a gentleman offer a lady a Tiparillo?" I took my last puff as I typed "30" at the bottom of the page, ground out the stub, turned the story in, and never smoked again.

I have often told this story with the explanation, "I am a very persuasive writer," but the fact is that I never got addicted to pipes and cigars. Cigarettes, if I had stayed with them, might have been another story. And I did give myself mental permission to take up cigars again should I ever reach the ripe old age of 70. But that year came and went, and I had no desire to have anything to do with tobacco. I had watched too many people suffering its consequences, including my mentor Ed Lahey.

21. "You're a sound man."

As 1969 dawned, the Detroit and Miami projects brought all kinds of interesting proposals my way. Thomas Pettigrew had told the Russell Sage Foundation about my work, and I received a friendly letter from President Orville G. Brim inviting me to visit him and his staff in New York and consider our possible common interests. AAPOR invited me to appear on a plenary panel with Burns Roper and Leo Bogart to discuss the links between polling and journalism. Harvard President Nathan Pusey invited me to join a committee chaired by Osborne Elliott, editor of *Newsweek*, to formally review the Nieman Fellowship program. When Lahey heard about that, he grinned and said, "You're a sound man, Meyer!" I took this to mean that I had been judged unlikely to do anything that would embarrass the university.

There was more. In the early months of 1969, I sold the game theory piece to *Playboy*. It was based, as I described in Chapter 18, on my lecture notes and readings from Thomas Schelling's course. My twist was using the theory to build strategies for chasing women. "In the direct interest of our readers," said an editor. Then I landed the assignment from *Esquire* to write the first popular explanation of Stanley Milgram's obedience studies.

And *Congressional Quarterly* offered me a job at a much larger salary than Knight Newspapers thought I was worth. There was a lot of quantitative analysis, including roll call votes, in CQ, and the editor thought that I could bring some fresh thinking and new methodology to its content. I took some time to seek advice and think this one over. Robert Sherrill, who had worked for CQ's publisher Nelson Poynter at his newspaper, the *St. Petersburg Times*, argued strongly against such a move. Although Poynter produced good publications, he was too unpredictable to be trustworthy, Sherrill insisted. But I got serious enough about the offer to tell my employer, and Knight Newspapers came up with a pretty good raise. I stayed. Congress was interesting, but there were so many more varied opportunities to explore by applying my Harvard-learned superpower to newspaper reporting.

It was in this period that I got serious about writing a book about the techniques I had been using. Donald Tacheron, a staff member at the American Political Science Association, had put the idea in my head. It could be a "seminal work" as a handbook for reporters interested in trying social science tools, he said, and it might even be marketed as a textbook for the small subset of journalism students who would be interested in such esoterica. So when Tom Pettigrew's intervention led to the Russell Sage Foundation invitation, I jumped at the chance.

It turned out to be a surprisingly easy sell. Housed on an upper floor of the New York General Building on Park Avenue, Russell Sage was an operating foundation, meaning that it did not give grants in the traditional sense, but commissioned works for hire. A textbook on social science methods for journalists was right up its alley, because President Orville G. Brim Jr. and his staff believed that computers were starting to revolutionize social science, bringing new power to its quantitative methods. Journalists would pay more attention to this important development if they could be made to see how these methods might be useful in their own work.

The staff was mostly eastern PhDs, weighted toward Yale. There was a black, two females, and one land-grant college graduate, although I did not think of them as tokens, that concept not yet having entered my consciousness in 1969. It was, I was told, like a university's sociology department, but without students, a place to think and talk and write. Brim outlined the requirements for getting their support.

I would need a letter justifying the need for the book that I proposed to write, an outline, a resume, and a budget. The budget should provide for spending two to three days a week at the foundation's Park Avenue suite where I would be given my own office and a part-time secretary. If the proposal were accepted, the foundation would get first publication rights to whatever I produced. It had its own publishing program, and the marketing of its output was subcontracted to an academic publisher, Basic Books. There would be no author royalties, although if the Foundation decided the work did not fit its publishing program, the rights would revert to me, and I would be free to find a publisher on my own – not such a bad outcome.

Brim even gave me a title for the project: "A Study of the Applications of Social and Behavioral Science Methodology to the Practice of Journalism." He emphasized the word "practice."

There was precedent for adding journalists to the rich mix of social scientists at the foundation. Alfred Balk, who would later become editor of *Columbia Journalism Review*, was there as a project director, working on an expose of the uneven application of local property taxes. It would eventually be published by the Foundation as *The Free List: Property Without Taxes*. And Alvin Toffler was coming aboard as a visiting scholar in anticipation of the 1970 publication of his and his wife's soon-to-be seminal work, *Future Shock*. He would use the time for exploratory research on their next book.

So I went home to Washington and whipped up a proposal as specified, then had it professionally typed by Linda Strompf, whose day job was secretary in the Knight bureau. Here are the nut graphs:

———————————————

I propose to survey the literature on social science methodology, interview social scientists and journalists, and draw on my own experience in synthesizing the two fields to gather material for, and write, a book.

This book, whose tentative outline is part of this proposal, would be addressed to the working journalist. It would attempt to show him how existing social science research methods can be applied to correct some of the shortcomings of traditional newspaper reporting methods. It would also enhance the reporter's ability to appreciate and report on the application of the social sciences to public policy.

Two secondary audiences would also be reached by this book: the editors and managers of the press, and the students and faculty of journalism schools. Today's thoughtful newspaper editors are aware of the failure of traditional journalistic methods to reach below the crisis manifestations of social change. They know, as James Reston has said, "Things don't have to 'happen' to be news. They can just be going on quietly." They do not know how to discover and describe systematically these "quiet" developments.

The budget was $39,964, which replaced my salary and provided for 48 Washington-New York round trips, plus three hours of IBM 7090 computer time for testing ideas and generating examples. When Knight Newspapers, wanting to show some support, offered to keep my fringe benefits in place, the budget was reduced by $1,500. My resume at that time included five articles in journalism professional journals, the one juried article in *Public Opinion Quarterly*, and the *Playboy* piece. Rather nicely balanced, I thought. I pledged to complete the manuscript in 12 months, starting July 15, 1969.

No further negotiation was needed. Staff and board approval for the proposal as submitted took only six weeks. I was about to take my second yearlong leave of absence from the Washington bureau in three years.

I went to visit Ed Lahey to talk about it. He was bedridden at home with emphysema, but cheerful and able to speak slowly. Breathing was a struggle. His wife Grace fixed me a drink as I set at his bedside.

"I'm a little scared," I said. "I've never written a book before."

"You'll do fine," he chuckled.

The Apollo 11 moon shot, carrying the first men to walk on the moon, was launched on July 16, at about the same time that Lahey's breathing became so labored that he had to be rushed to the hospital. I joined Grace and the doctor at his bedside.

"I've got to get some sleep," Ed told his physician, gasping for air. "Just give me something to let me sleep."

The doctor looked at us, and we stepped outside for a short conference.

"I think this will be the last episode," the doctor said.

Ed died peacefully in his sleep on July 17. He was 67.

On July 18, Mary Jo Kopechne died in a car that had been driven by Senator Edward M. Kennedy off the Chappaquidick Bridge on Martha's Vineyard in Massachusetts. The national media were all over the story. The day after Ed Lahey's funeral, an editor in Miami sensed a chance to get ahead on the Kennedy story. Eventually, somebody would go down the senator's back trail and reconstruct the narrative of what happened, but it was customary to wait a few days while the spot news repercussions settled down. Why not start working on the narrative right now?

So I flew to Boston and drove to Martha's Vineyard with Gene Miller on my heels. We visited the scene, interviewed everyone in sight, even talked a maid into letting us inspect the senator's room until the manager got wind of our presence and threw us out. The room was furnished with attractive antiques.

I viewed Neil Armstrong's first steps on the moon at 10:56 p.m. EDT July 21, 1969, on a black-and-white TV in my hotel room on Martha's Vineyard while reviewing my notes on the senator's tragic indiscretion. The news business could be like that – too many things happening at once.

Thanks mostly to Miller's dogged reporting and eye for detail, we were able to write the narrative and get it in the paper several days before the wire services and the national papers did.

And then the pace changed – from daily deadlines to just one, a year away. I started writing my first book – with offices at home in Washington and in a skyscraper in New York. The commuting wasn't so bad. I alternated between the Eastern Shuttle from Washington National to LaGuardia airport, and the brand new Metroliner which then had a good track and a two-and-a-half hour trip between Union Station in D.C. and Manhattan's Pennsylvania Station.

The time away from home was compensated by the four-day weekends, which I used for reading and reflecting more than writing. For convenient lodging in New York, I joined the Harvard Club, which was willing to admit people with only brief ties to the university. It was friendlier than a hotel, had a fireplace, a cat, and a well-stocked library. Like the National Press Club of that day, it did not admit women, and, also like the Press Club, it restricted female visitors to certain public areas of the club. But the pressure for fairer treatment was starting to build, and there was one embarrassing moment. I had a few Foundation staffers over for drinks, and Eleanor B. Sheldon, the eminent sociologist, wandered away from our group and started climbing the stairs toward the library. The staff yelled at her until she stopped and came down. I apologized, but she was pleased to have made a point.

Brim assigned David Goslin, a PhD sociologist not long out of Yale to be my overseer. His enthusiasm for the project was obvious, and he took my side in some of the inevitable academic arguments – all of which I enjoyed.

One was about the question of whether significance tests have any value for non-sample data. I claimed that they do, Eleanor Sheldon argued that they do not. This is one of those meaning-of-life questions for which the textbooks have no simple answer. A significance test compares an interesting difference with what would be expected by chance, and its most common application is in sample surveys. But I could imagine situations where you would want to make the comparison to chance even in cases where you have data for the whole population.

Consider a vote in the U.S. House of Representatives. The measure passes, but with a slightly higher level of support from Democrats than from Republicans. Is the party difference important? There is no scientific way to answer that question, but one way to evaluate it would be to find out often such a difference would occur if every member voted by flipping a coin. I would consider an improbable difference in those terms more important than one that could easily be explained by chance alone. Sheldon's argument was that the only purpose of such a comparison is to test for sampling error. My response, with which Goslin agreed, was that one could think of that vote as a sample of all possible House votes, past and future. The important thing was that all three of us enjoyed the argument. It reminded me of some of the beery conversations that I had with my graduate school peers in the Rathskellar at Chapel Hill.

Work on the manuscript proceeded steadily despite two distractions. Mike Maidenberg, nephew of Ben Maidenburg (they used different spellings of the family name), my editor in Akron, was interested in the student unrest of that period. It had begun with the Free Speech Movement at the University of California, Berkeley. The trouble started in October 1964 when an activist soliciting support for civil rights causes was arrested on campus. A spontaneous protest led to his charges being dropped. In December, a crowd of students, more than a thousand, went to Sproul Hall in protest of restrictions on political speech and activism on campus. The mass arrest that followed drew national attention and is considered the starting point for the wave of student activism that continued throughout the anti-war and civil rights movements of the 1960s and 1970s. An unintended consequence was a boost to Ronald Reagan's career. A campaign pledge to "clean up" Berkeley helped his successful campaign for governor in 1966.

Maidenberg wondered if that incident had a lasting effect on the students who participated or if they were outgrowing their youthful activism. We decided on a five-year follow-up mail survey of the arrestees. The names of the younger participants had been expunged from the public record but were preserved in newspaper accounts that we are able to retrieve. Crossing the newspaper list with the student directory and a Berkeley alumni list gave us their recent addresses, and, with two mailings, we managed a response rate of 50 percent – not what we had hoped, but good enough to keep the data and report it.

I used one of my long weekends at home to do the statistical analysis, and Mike provided the narrative. We concluded that the youthful rebels had, for the most part, retained their radicalism, at least in attitude, while job and family responsibilities limited their options for action. My numbers and Mike's follow-up interviews combined to make a seven-part series. It has since been widely cited in academic studies of student activism.[27]

The other distraction was jury duty. It kept me grounded in Washington for a month, and my civic contribution was minimal. In the D.C. district court system, a panel of citizens is called to sit in the courthouse and serve on cases as needed. Although summoned to a number of voir dire examinations I was rejected in every case but one. I had had too many biasing experiences. For example, I was rejected in a landlord-tenant dispute because I had been a landlord, albeit absentee, from 1962 to 1967 while we waited for the value of our Florida house to recover. I was excused from a criminal case because the public defender, Sally Temple, had gone to Topeka High School with my wife. I finally landed on an actual jury for – I am not making this up – a third-rate burglary in a case whose judge was John Sirica who would later gain fame as the tough D.C. judge who got the Watergate burglars to talk.

The Foundation staff was nervous at my forced absence, but I managed to continue progress on the manuscript working evenings and weekends.

In the spring of 1970, I was invited to attend the Foundation's annual retreat at the Sterling Forest Conference Center in upstate New York, along with the staff, the board, and other project directors and grantees. We gave progress reports on our projects. I don't remember what I said about mine, but two memorable things did happen then, one funny and one serious.

One of the trustees was Frederick Moesteller. I had not met him at Harvard, where he was the founding head of the Department of Statistics. But I knew some of his work including a path-breaking analysis of word patterns in the Federalist papers to identify the origin of those whose authorship, either Madison or Hamilton, was previously unknown. And I had watched some of his Continental Classroom lectures on public television in the early 1960s. Now I not only got to meet the man, I sat in a poker game with him!

He cleaned my clock. I might have done better, but one of the staff members, apparently too scared to go up against the master himself, kept looking over my shoulder and giving me distracting and unwanted advice. It was fun all the same.

We were still at the conference center on May 4, when the Ohio National Guard starting shooting anti-war-demonstrating students at Kent State University. Business was suspended for a while as we watched the TV reports, and I felt some serious regret about being away from a big story.

After the conference, Bert Brim sent a description of my project to Lloyd M. Morrisett, president of the John R. and

Mary Markle Foundation. "I believe he would be worth your talking to," he told Morrisett. I was unaware of this gesture at the time, but it planted a seed that would bloom more than a decade later.

In that spring, I had two career decisions to make. Bert Brim suggested that I would make a good staff member of the Foundation, handling public relations. My ability to interpret social science was just what it needed. "Besides, we like having you around," he said.

And Bob Levine, who had funded my second Miami study from the Office of Economic Opportunity, had yet another offer. He had left the government to run the New York City office of the RAND Corporation, and thought I was just the person to interpret its work for the public.

What made both of these proposals interesting was that Sue and I had already decided to leave the District of Columbia. Our oldest daughter had finished Shepherd Elementary School, and the middle school to which she would be assigned lay deep in the inner city. It wasn't race that worried us, we told ourselves, it was the social class climate of the school. Our justification came from the 1967 report of the U.S. Civil Rights Commission, *Racial Isolation in the Public Schools*, which had cited social science evidence that providing racial balance in schools would have a direct benefit on educational achievement. Its reasoning would soon lead to busing to establish that balance. Eugene Patterson, who had served on my Nieman selection committee, was a member of that commission, and I had reported on its work.

But we couldn't wait for the racial balance of Paul Junior High School to change, so we decided to move to the suburbs and live in Robert E. Simon's idealistically planned town of Reston, Va., an early example of what is now called New Urbanism. Either of the New York jobs would have paid for the cost of moving out of D.C., but I had little interest in changing course while my present career trajectory was going so well. So I stuck with Knight Newspapers. Writing the book about precision journalism wouldn't be enough. To convince the world that it was a good idea, I would have to continue to be a practitioner, as well as an advocate of precision journalism, and set the best examples I could.

22. Precision Journalism

As I did the last rewrites and the final organization of my manuscript, it took a slightly different form than first intended. My original outline had 17 chapters. It quickly shrank to 12 through consolidation. For example, I had proposed to open with a chapter on "The Journalistic Tradition," followed by one on "The Scientific Tradition." The latter was a direct quote from my Chapel Hill seminar with Alexander Heard, and I hoped to recycle some of that material. But I quickly realized that the opening chapter needed to be a theoretical justification for synthesizing the two traditions, a contrast of journalism's timeliness with the accountability of science. That realization gave me the lead:

"Sometimes we get things wrong."

The outline called for a section on the use of social science by policy makers, with chapters on two Johnson era programs, the War on Poverty and assistance to early childhood education, Operation Head Start. I dropped those to keep the book from getting too long, but wrote, as intended, chapters on public polls, political campaign polls, and a sanitized version of my *Playboy* article on game theory. (As first submitted, the article included several personal anecdotes involving my wife. At the *Playboy* editor's direction, I concealed her identity, referring to her only as a female companion, to make the anecdotes seem more risqué. For the *Precision Journalism* version, I put Sue back in the story.)

And I had planned to include a couple of case histories on

exemplary projects, but I decided that the supply of possible cases was too thin, and that they could wait for a future edition.

It took me two drafts to get the preface right. The first draft was too long, had too much self-centered "Look, Ma, I wrote a book!" in it. At the urgent suggestion of a Russell Sage staff member, I cut it back by two thirds and included just the important part of the book's history. Later, after settling on the title, I inserted a brief nod to Everette Dennis for supplying it.

That inspiration had come in the spring of 1970 on a trip to K-State to talk about my work. Dennis was on the journalism faculty then, and he asked me what I would call the book.

"Well," I said, "the working title is *The Application of Social and Behavioral Science Research Methods to the Practice of Journalism*."

"Oh," said Dennis. "I call that *Precision Journalism*."

Bingo.

As a professional communicator, I knew that something new is easier to sell if its name can fit on a bumper sticker. So that became the title.

My Russell Sage office was a comfortable place to work. It had a view of the East River and Queens and came supplied with a standard-size manual typewriter. *Precision Journalism* was the only book that I would write with a manual typewriter. I finished the manuscript on time and under budget. In August, I asked Brim to hold the unused funds, some $3,000, for travel to handle the mechanical details of getting the book into print, including proofing, indexing, and design consultation. He agreed. On September 1, I went back to work in the Washington Bureau.

A long silence followed.

Dave Goslin had taken leave, so I couldn't ask him what was happening. Late in October, Brim advised me that his friend Paul Lancaster, the front-page editor of the *Wall Street Journal*, would evaluate the manuscript for the Foundation. "A fine choice," I said. My contract with the Foundation had called for a decision on publication within two months of receiving the manuscript, and that time was almost up, but I did not feel in a position to raise the issue. More time went by.

The letter from Brim finally came in late April 1971.

I write to say that following my own personal and careful reading of your manuscript, and getting the opinions of other persons I asked to read it, I have decided that Russell Sage Foundation is not the appropriate publisher for your book. Although the book did not turn out the way I expected it to, it is nevertheless interesting to read from other perspectives, and I guess that a commercial publisher might take it on. If so, that would be good news all around.

If this does not work out, then I would be glad to work with you to see if the book could be re-oriented to make it appropriate it for Russell Sage Foundation publication.

I sincerely hope that this decision will not affect our personal relationship as well as any possible future joint activities.

Creativity involves melding knowledge from different areas into something new. One way to get creative is to acquire some expert knowledge in seemingly unrelated fields and find a way to combine them. The problem becomes that the people who are asked to evaluate a product of this melding are likely to be expert in only one of the merged fields. That is what happened to precision journalism.

Paul Lancaster had tried his best to be generous, but he could find no frame for it. "For whom are you publishing it?" he asked.

Obviously, the book is not intended for social scientists; everything in it must be elementary to them. Seemingly, it's aimed at working reporters and lower-level editors – the guys who would be carrying out surveys – because it so quickly plunges into the nuts and bolts of sampling, polling, and the like. But I strongly doubt that a reporter or editor would feel competent in handling many of the procedures described even after the closest of readings.

―――――――――――――――

Lancaster was particularly bothered by my description of the IBM counter-sorter.

"Surely," he said, "most of the people who would read this book would hire people to run their counter-sorters."

I had fallen between the two stools of journalism and social science, just what Bob Boyd had warned me about when I first discussed the possibility of the book in the Washington Bureau. It was as though precision journalism's failure to fit neatly into a pre-existing frame prevented it from existing. I was too far outside the box.

Being quite unready to accept that judgment, I boldly started sending the manuscript out to publishers, one at a time. Meanwhile, opportunities to apply precision journalism kept turning up.

One was the huge anti-war demonstration in Washington D.C. that began on May 1, 1971. Thousands of protestors camped out in West Potomac Park with the avowed goal of stopping the government. When they proved to be too many for Park Police and D.C. police, the Nixon administration sent in paratroopers and the National Guard. Finally, on May 3, the streets were swept and 7,000 arrested. Detainees were held on the fenced practice field of the Washington Redskins, in a courtyard of the D.C. jail, and at the Washington Coliseum.

Most were eventually released after paying, and forfeiting, $10 collateral. The media focused on the most extreme spokespersons, those who said things like, "The government won't stop the war, so we're going to stop the government."

But I wondered what the demonstrators were really like, and I figured out a way. By collecting data from arrest records in a systematic manner, I could get a purposeful sample of people who happened to be from cities where the Knights had newspapers. Staff from those papers then interviewed and photographed a selection of them, and they turned out to be surprisingly ordinary. Working with Steve Seplow of the *Philadelphia Inquirer*, I assembled an argument that these demonstrators, instead of being the deviant yippies perceived by the Nixon administration, were for the most part quite ordinary citizens, people with whom the average newspaper reader could identify. The project was illustrated with photos and profiles of typical participants.

When that story was done, my attention turned again to the search for a publisher for *Precision Journalism.*

My first choice was Basic Books, which had a good working relationship with the Foundation. I sent it to Bill Gum, an editor who often attended the end-of-week sherry hours. He decided it would be "a hard market for Basic Books to get at."

Next was Praeger Publishers of New York, which had a good track record in the social sciences. "Your manuscript is lively and informative, but, as I feared, it's too specialized in its appeal for us to take on," said Gladys S. Topkis. "We don't normally reach schools of journalism, and it's simply not economically sound for us to promote a single book in an area."

Doubleday had the same objection.

Another New York publisher, The Free Press, now an imprint of Simon and Schuster, proposed recasting the book for a general audience at the junior college level. That would, of course, have made it a totally different book.

Next, I tried Harvard University Press, whose editor for the social sciences, Max Hall, had been on my Nieman selection committee. "Our difficulty," he said, "is that we just can't see a big enough market for your book. The case worries me because you have tackled such an important task in such a conscientious manner." He suggested that I try a university press at a place with a good journalism school.

It so happened that I had a contact at a university with a good press and a good journalism school. Indiana had invited me to Bloomington for a public lecture on the topic, and Dean Richard Gray put me in touch with John Gallman, the energetic editor of Indiana University Press. By now it was October 1971, and David Goslin was back from his leave of absence. He started lobbying the Russell Sage Foundation for a reconsideration of its rejection. To help build a case, he asked Columbia's W. Phillips Davison for advice. Davison's view, sent in late winter, 1972, was the obverse of the Wall Street Journal editor's, and he addressed his comments directly to me with a copy to the Foundation:

For selfish reasons, I wish that the manuscript had already been published, and that I could have a copy on my bookshelf right now. You have included a lot of examples I can use, and there are several chapters that I would assign as required reading in at least two courses.

But, as you would be the first to point out, I am a sample of one. How far can I be extrapolated to a larger audience? Unfortunately, my representativeness is probably poor. There are not many social scientists interested in the interface between social science and journalism.

The next question is whether there are many journalists or journalism teachers who would find such a book useful. My feeling is that a great many of them should read it, but I'm doubtful how many actually would ..."

Davison had some suggestions for revisions that would make it more marketable. Instead of telling journalists how to act like social scientists, he said, I should put the emphasis on real social scientists and "what *they* do." This approach would maintain the natural divide between social scientists and journalists while still enlightening the latter.

It was the between-the-stools problem again. But at this point, I had a good conversation going with John Gallman of Indiana, and, with Richard Gray backing him, he called me at the Knight Bureau and said he was ready to take a chance on the manuscript. By March 14, 1972, three years after my initial proposal to the Russell Sage Foundation, I had a publishing contract.

The production process, as was normal for the letterpress technology of the time, took a year, and *Precision Journalism* was finally shipped in the spring of 1973. Its acceptance at journalism schools turned out to be surprisingly easy. In hindsight, the reason is clear enough. Journalism education had a historic conflict between its theoretical and practical sides, the "Green Eyeshades" who taught on the basis of their experience at practicing journalism and the "Chi Squares" who did quantitative analysis on the process and effects of mass communication. Here was a book that bridged that gap and that both sides could appreciate. Reviews, in both the trade and academic journals, were pretty good.

Some came from unexpected places. A reviewer for *Antioch Review* called it "an ebullient introduction to the statistics of social surveys."

On the other hand, William Stockton wrote in *Nieman Reports* that, while journalism should adopt more social science methods, "personally, I'll always root for a journalism that borrows more from the novelist than the social scientist."

But Dennis J. Chase, in *The Quill*, said, "If this book doesn't replace most of the current university journalism texts, then students might as well play hooky."

Unfortunately, he had to add:

"In fact, however, Meyer is too far ahead of us. His case rests on association of news and truth that does not

exist in the newsroom. News is only accidentally true ..."
The bitterest rejection came from a professor at Loyola
University Department of Communications who wrote a letter
addressed to "Complaint Dept." at Indiana University Press.
His opinion of the book was straightforward.

"It is junk," he said. "The book is NOT clear. It is NOT
easily read."

But it met the important test, that of the marketplace. The
book went through four editions and was still in print in 2012.

Throughout this three-year process of getting the book into
print, news that cried out for social science tools kept happening.
Both of the 1972 presidential nominating conventions were held
in Miami Beach, and I was assigned to help cover both of them.
The Democrats went first, meeting in July, but my work there
was interrupted by the unexpected death of my mother-in-law,
Helen Peppard Quail, of a heart condition. I met Sue and the
girls at the Kansas City airport, and we went on to Topeka
to make final arrangements and begin closing the house on
Canterbury Lane. We stayed up late and were among the few
Americans to hear George McGovern's pre-dawn acceptance
speech (at 3 a.m. Miami time) with its promise to end the war in
Vietnam. We watched it on a small black-and-white television
set in the Quail house.

For the Republican convention in August 1972, I got the
company to pay for a mail survey of the delegates. The issue
was not for whom they would vote, the nomination of Richard
M. Nixon being a foregone conclusion, but where they stood on
the issues that might turn up in the Republican platform. We
were also interested in knowing how representative they were
of the population at large.

This idea turned out to be better than I had anticipated
because, in contrast to the disorganized Democrats, the
Republicans had carefully scripted their convention to avoid
surprises and to maximize its theatrical appeal. The physical
layout was designed expressly for television. The podium was

angled forward and set high for the best camera angle, so high that it was invisible to the delegates in the first six rows. They had to watch the proceedings on TV monitors placed in front of them.

My assignment was to cover the media covering the convention, and that got me a pass to the TV studios where I had the pleasure of watching John Chancellor, stumped for something fresh to report, reading from my delegate survey in that morning's *Miami Herald*. There were some anti-war demonstrators, and one of them crushed a raw egg on the back of my suit while I was going through the police line in front of the convention center. The networks, still stung by criticism of their focus on violence in Chicago four years earlier, averted their gaze.

One of my Nieman classmates, Ken Clawson, had gone to work for the Nixon campaign, and I interviewed him about their strategic planning. He was pretty pleased with himself.

"An incumbent president has so much more control," he said. "McGovern is tromping across corn fields because that is what you have to do in his situation. We don't." That was also the summer that two young investigative reporters at the *Philadelphia Inquirer*, Don Barlett and James Steele, approached me for advice. They wanted to test the fairness of the criminal justice system in Philadelphia by doing content analysis of court records. A smart reporter and former Nieman fellow, Clarence Jones, had done something like that for the *Miami Herald* with help from a COBOL programmer on the paper's production staff.

But crosstabs with COBOL proved cumbersome, so Jones ended up doing most of the analysis on a counter-sorter. His goal of uncovering corruption in the system was not met, but it did show a surprisingly high proportion of youth crime, and it revealed that most criminal arrests never resulted in prison time. And the database that he built was so much better than anything the county had, that the sheriff asked for, and received from the *Herald*, a custom report on arrests by certain deputies who were under investigation.

I was able to provide Barlett and Steele with better technology, and together we designed a coding system that recorded various details of each crime, demographics of the arrestee, and the outcome, including, in case of conviction, the length of sentence. Then we designed a sample based on time units.

For the analysis, we bought time at $75 an hour on an IBM 7090 mainframe at a service bureau in Kensington, Md. I made a deal with Barlett and Steele. I would teach them how to do crosstabs with Harvard DATA-TEXT, and they would learn it well enough to do their next computer project on their own. They agreed.

The crosstabs told an interesting story. The district attorney had complained that lenient judges were returning too many criminals to the streets. The data indicated that DA-instigated plea bargains were more to blame. Moreover, there was systematic inequity. Crimes with black victims resulted in greater leniency than those against whites. Crimes committed at a place of business received tougher sentences than those committed in homes.

The evidence of unfairness in the system was strong, but it did not hurt the DA's long-term career prospects. His name was Arlen Specter, and he was elected U.S. senator from Pennsylvania eight years later.

Barlett and Steele went on to an outstanding career in investigative reporting, specializing in paper trails that could be documented without the need for anonymous sources. But they did not become DATA-TEXT programmers as I had hoped. They postponed using computers on their own until personal computers, with their friendlier software, were available. Their criminal justice series was nominated for a Pulitzer Prize, but it was shot down, Barlett told me later, by a juror who insisted that using a computer to analyze the public records gave them an unfair advantage. Working with me had put them too far out of the box. Indeed, it would be another 15 years before an investigation using computer analysis would win a Pulitzer: Bill Dedman's "The Color of Money" on racial discrimination in mortgage lending in Atlanta, using Lotus 1-2-3, on a personal computer.

Despite the slow start, *Precision Journalism* was giving me both visibility and unexpected benefits. Journalism faculties started to approach me about the possibility of joining them. One nibble came from Indiana, where I had given that pre-publication lecture about my work. Another was from my alma mater, Kansas State, which was in the market for a department head. These were attractive overtures, because, ever since I left the education beat in Miami, the thought of switching to an academic post at some point in my career had been on my mind. But I was reluctant to make a move while things were going so well in my practitioner role.

One unexpected benefit was an invitation to participate in a 1973 seminar on "The Future of Reporting" at the Aspen Institute in Colorado. First we drove out to Kansas with the four daughters, dropped the younger two off with my parents in Manhattan, and then headed for the Rockies. This was the year of the Arab oil embargo, and we had made a poor choice of automobiles, a 1973 Mercury Colony Park station wagon that burned a gallon of fuel every 13 miles on the highway, every eight miles in town. The comfort of its ride was offset by the anxiety it generated. Gasoline was so scarce that we never knew when to expect an open service station, and prudence required us to make frequent stops to top off the tank.

But Aspen was well worth the trip. Sue and the girls went sightseeing in the mountains while I attended meetings. At the first meeting, we were still in the milling-around stage, when a tall, energetic man bounded into the room, asking loudly, "Where's Phil Meyer?" I shyly raised my hand.

He turned out to be Fred W. Friendly, Edward R. Murrow's

producer, and he wanted to congratulate me on *Precision Journalism*, particularly the theoretical justification in the opening chapter. As an example of evidence-based journalism, I had cited Murrow's broadcasts on Senator Joseph McCarthy as a significant departure from the traditional journalistic distortion of objectivity into a simple-minded tendency to take whatever public officials say at face value. Friendly appreciated that.

I loved the Aspen Institute, and hoped to be invited again, but it was not to be except for a lesser conference, many years later, at its Wye River facility in Maryland.

We had been back in Reston only a few days when an emergency call came from my mother. Bige, just past his 77th birthday, had suffered a stroke. I flew back to Kansas, visited him in the hospital, and tried to help my mother adjust to the possibility of living alone. My dad had some aphasia, but he could make himself understood, and, with a nurse's help, he could walk up and down the hallway outside his room. It looked like he might recover.

Instead, his brain just started slowly shutting down. It was like sitting at the top of the hill at Marlatt Park, northwest of Manhattan, late at night and watching the city lights wink out one by one. Eventually, he was transferred to a nursing home, where I saw him again the following summer. By then he had neither mobility nor speech. I squeezed his hand, and said, "So long, old soldier." He died a few months later, and we buried him in the family plot at Reiter Cemetery in Washington County, midway between the Meyer and Morrison farms. My mother, supported by strong neighborhood and church connections, managed the house herself for a few years, and then moved to an apartment. At least my dad had lived long enough to see my first book published.

That year, another publishing opportunity came in an unexpected telephone call from an editor at McGraw-Hill, a major publisher of college textbooks. He and his team had identified a rising young political scientist at Indiana, David Olson, whom they wanted to write a text for the introductory course in American government. The best-selling book for that market had been co-authored by a journalist, David Wise, and a professor, Milton Cummings. It had a catchy title, *The Irony of Democracy*. Olson, whom I had met while covering a political science meeting, had given them my name as a possible co-author.

When the McGraw-Hill recruiters discovered that I had a successful journalism book in print, their interest increased. But what clinched the deal was my history at Chapel Hill. I had taught the exact course for which this project would be designed. They offered a contract that included an advance against royalties large enough to replace my salary for a year. All I needed was another leave of absence from Knight Newspapers.

I had received two such leaves, 1966-1967 for Harvard, and 1969-1970 for *Precision Journalism*. Would the company let me take time off in 1973-1974 as well? The person to make that decision was Derick Daniels, who by now was back in Miami, this time as vice-president for news of Knight Newspapers. He approved. Maybe, he said, I would make so much money on this project that I could afford to stay in the newspaper business. It was certainly possible, the market for that particular course being so large.

We were well settled in Reston by then, in a house that was a Mediterranean version of midcentury modern. In a cluster of glass-and-stucco townhouses, it was nearly all glass on the north and south sides, and had a charming interior courtyard. Although the house was built to the east and west lot lines, the cluster had been cleverly configured so that no home's living-space walls touched those of its neighbors' living spaces. Gardens, patios, and garages separated them.

We were on a hillside, and there were two basement rooms with sliding glass doors at ground level in the back, opening to a wooded area. The smaller of the two made an ideal place to sit, think, and write another book. Olson outlined the chapters, his graduate students rounded up and copied the relevant literature, and we were off and running.

The downside, it turned out, was missing out on the Watergate story – a series of events that threatened to revise the American system of government even as we wrote about it. On October 20, 1973, I was sorely tempted to abandon the writing and drive down to the office in the National Press Building and lend a hand at covering what is remembered now as the Saturday Night Massacre. President Nixon fired two attorneys general in order to engineer the removal of the special prosecutor, Archibald Cox, who was investigating White House involvement in the Watergate burglary. But I had a deadline, and I stayed on task. The book was published in 1975 under the title *To Keep the Republic*, based on something Benjamin Franklin told an onlooker when he emerged from the constitutional convention of 1787. Asked what kind of a government he and his peers had designed, he replied, "A republic – if you can keep it." It wasn't a blockbuster, but it did well enough to pay back my advance and make McGraw-Hill want to do a second edition based on careful study of market reaction to the first. The second time around, I was able to do my share of the work using weekends and vacation time. But there was stiffer competition in 1978, and the second edition was less successful than the first. The publisher decided to let it go at that.

Meanwhile, the variety of assignments I got in the Washington bureau keep getting better. In the 1976 election campaign between Jerry Ford and Jimmy Carter, I designed my own national pre-election poll using a random-digit telephone sample obligingly provided by my AAPOR friend from CBS, Warren Mitofsky. Knight Newspapers had merged with Ridder Publications in 1974 to create a company with 32 daily newspapers. With corporate approval, I broke the sample into geographic segments and assigned a portion to each paper.

Their reporters did the interviews, and then I merged the results in Washington.

One of the major themes of that campaign was Jimmy Carter's religiosity. He talked about his religion a lot, and reporters assumed that it was helping his cause. But the Gallup Poll released some counter-intuitive data. It announced that religion was not helping Carter, because churchgoers were no more likely to support him than non-attenders. By then I had enough experience in data analysis to recognize the possibility of a confounding variable, and, with data of my own, I could look for one. In hindsight, it was rather obvious. Carter was different enough from the traditional politician to have a lot of appeal for young voters. And young people tend to be less religious. That would mask the religion effect.

So all I had to do was replicate Gallup's simple two-way cross tabulation within each of several categories of age. With age thus held constant, churchgoers were revealed to be strongly and significantly more for Carter. Religion really was working for him.

I wrote that story. It was an exclusive. No other reporter in Washington knew what I knew. In fact, not many understood it.

After it went out on the wire, I overheard a bit of conversation between two of my colleagues. It was in the men's room, and I was out of sight in a stall.

"Did you see Meyer's story on Carter and religion?" one of them asked.

"Yeah," said the other. "Meyer is getting pretty academic."

They had a point there. I had a chance to get academic again on election night.

ABC let me watch the returns at its New York headquarters where Louis Harris was providing early projections based on sample precincts where the vote count had been completed. I looked at the Harris data as it rolled in and noticed that in every case, the vote was smaller than it had been in 1972.

In preparing for election night, I had examined recent history and found that America was experiencing a long-term decline in voter participation. If 1976 turnout was less than 1972, it had to be the lowest in a generation.

Journalistically, turnout is more important than you might think because for Tuesday afternoon papers and bulldog editions of Wednesday morning papers, turnout is the only election story there is. Wire service reporters talk to precinct workers to ask for their evaluations of turnout, and they get casual impressions, which are often wrong. The worker will mentally compare the lines outside the polling place with those in the previous election two years before, which was not a presidential election. Or, perhaps the worker is just unconsciously inflating his or her self-importance.

This is an example of what I now call hunter-gatherer journalism as opposed to evidence-based journalism. Early in the evening, I wrote a story with a lead that proclaimed the lowest presidential election turnout in a generation.

Soon after I had filed it, I got an irritable phone call from Bob Boyd. "The wires are saying it's a huge turnout," he said. "Where are you getting this 'lowest in a generation' thing?"

"I have data," I said. "The wires don't."

Boyd trusted me, and the story ran. *Columbia Journalism Review*, in its post-election assessment of news coverage, included an article asking, "What became of that 'heavy vote?'" It was illustrated with headlines from a number of large and prestigious newspapers all proclaiming a "huge" or "heavy" turnout. Then it gave the contradictory facts and one more illustration: the headline from my story in the *Miami Herald*: "Voter Turnout Appears Lowest In Generation."

Sweet.

Getting academic wasn't the only thing that was happening to me. I was also getting commercial. The folks on the sixth floor of the *Miami Herald* building, where company headquarters was located, started to wonder if my new skills might have some business-side value. If I was so good at finding hidden facts and trends, their thinking went, why couldn't I help them figure out how to stop the decline in newspaper readership?

So I accepted a few marketing research assignments. The first was for the *Detroit Free Press* in the fall of 1971. Leo Bogart had perfected his "read-yesterday" method of estimating average daily readership in 1968 and obtained a satisfying national figure of 80 percent of adults. But the next measure was smaller, and the 80 percent figure was never reached again. Editors were worried about reader trust as a possible factor, and so I worked with the marketing research department in Detroit to see how the *Free Press* and its rival the *Detroit News* were doing on that dimension. A series of questions on credibility was asked, including whether newspapers, "in presenting the news dealing with social and political issues," generally dealt fairly with all sides or tended to favor one side of an issue. A 52-41 majority felt that the Detroit papers were fair.

But, as with most survey research, the interesting part was in the crosstabs. Spiro Agnew was vice president, and had accused the media of "elitism," losing touch with the public. I asked about newspaper treatment of a number of specific groups, and then factor-analyzed the list to simplify the descriptors to three categories. I was showing off here. Only a few academics and market researchers used factor analysis in 1971, but the Harvard software made it easy. One category represented the counterculture of that day, another covered civil and political authorities, and there was a third category that I labeled "plain folks." It included veterans, senior citizens, working people, and consumers.

The "plain folks" factor was a strong predictor of whether or not citizens trusted their newspapers. If they thought people in those categories were being treated badly, their trust in newspapers was also low. Perceived treatment of authorities or the counterculture had no effect. That was potentially useful guidance for editors.

After I had reported to the Knight editors, I redrafted my piece as an academic article and submitted it to *Journalism Quarterly*. Publishing in a juried journal, I told my bosses, would give my research credibility, and they accepted that rationale. I did not mention my other motivation: to build an academic hole card. If I should ever decide to switch to a university career, a record of academic publication would make it easier. By this time, I had landed two pieces in *Public Opinion Quarterly*. Getting the Detroit credibility study published turned out to be surprisingly easy. *Journalism Quarterly* took me up on it and used the academic version of my report in its Spring 1973 issue.[28]

One of my better projects helped Gene Roberts develop his suburban strategy for the *Philadelphia Inquirer's* mortal combat with the *Philadelphia Bulletin*. As a morning paper, the *Inquirer* could make deliveries in the quiet pre-dawn hours, and that made it better positioned to grow in the suburbs. I worked out a regression equation that compared the paper's household penetration in minor civil divisions – a Census classification – with what could be expected from the effects of various population demographics, including income, population density, percent younger families, and suburban paper penetration. There were 11 variables in all, and they explained 63 percent of the variance in *Inquirer* penetration.

By mapping the residuals – the difference between what the equation predicted and what each MCD actually had – I could show editors and circulation people alike where the opportunities were. It made the neighborhoods with unrealized potential seem to cry out for attention.

Soon these assignments, plus computer-based news projects became frequent enough that I was spending a great deal of time traveling to cheap computer service bureaus. I needed better access to computing power, and I found it in a service bureau with an IBM 360 not far from my house in Reston, Va. David Armor and his colleagues had finally produced the 360 version of DATA-TEXT, and that gave me a wider range of choice among suppliers of computer time. But I found that I could ensure even more choices by switching to SPSS, because it was already installed in many service bureaus. Soon I was spending so much time in Reston that it seemed reasonable to move my office out there, too, and the company agreed.

The American Newspaper Publishers Association (ANPA) had built a beautiful headquarters in the industrial park area of Reston and it had an unused office that it was willing to rent to one of its members. Even better, I was now considered important enough to have an assistant. After working with a few temporary interns from different graduate schools, I hired a permanent assistant, Louise McReynolds, daughter of my old professor, who had degrees from Southern Methodist and Indiana University and just happened to drop by in search of career advice. She was brilliant, like her father, and quickly learned SPSS.

My relationship with my ANPA landlords was cordial, but there was a cultural barrier. When a story broke over a weekend, and I needed access to my office, I had trouble getting someone to open the building. The ANPA staff kept regular business hours and did not understand why I wanted to work on a weekend.

"I work for a newspaper company," I explained.

They got it, and weekend access was easier after that, but the organization soon discovered that it needed my office for its own projects, and I was politely evicted. I found another office, a sublet from an educational software company, in what was then Reston's lone high-rise office building. It had a fine view of the sun setting over the Blue Ridge, and I continued to have the luxury of living and working in the same walkable community. But it was not to last.

What I was doing was clearly a corporate function, and the

corporation needed closer oversight of my varied activities – and faster access to my wisdom. Jim Batten, who had succeeded Derick Daniels as vice president for news, invited me to Miami so that he could began the process of talking me into moving there. I would be director of a new staff division, news and circulation research, and get a nice raise. Jim mentioned several vice presidents who had been division directors before ascending to the level of corporate officer. I was already part of the management-by-objective system, a formal method of establishing annual goals and being rewarded with bonuses attenuated by the degree to which the goals were met. These would get bigger. So eager was I to accept the reposting that I agreed to it without consulting my family. I regretted it after Sue later told me that the children wept when she put down the phone and gave them the news that we were leaving Reston.

Knight Ridder engaged a professional relocation service to assist with our move, and its services relieved us of the burden of selling our house. The appraisal price was agreeable to us, and we sold it to the relocation service. Much later, we learned that we had avoided an expensive problem by that decision. Our title was defective. The builder had carelessly placed our house on top of a sewer easement, and the lawyer who represented us at closing had dismissed that exception in the title insurance as a mere technicality. It would eventually cost my employer $20,000 in legal fees to make the house marketable.

23. Executive suite

After two house-hunting expeditions, we found a pleasant place with some architectural significance in Coral Gables, one of the nation's first fully planned communities. It was a one-story, art deco home built in 1940 with a design by Upton C. Ewing, a nationally known architect and religious historian. It had a separate guesthouse behind the garage that I could use for an office while I finished the second edition of *Precision Journalism.* We were walking distance from the library and the Coral Gables Youth Center, and a 20-minute drive to the *Miami Herald* building on the bay. And at the end of that drive was my first executive perquisite: a dedicated parking space under the building, sheltered from the South Florida sun.

As further evidence of my new status, I had a half-time secretary in addition to the full-time research assistant, Louise McReynolds, who preceded me to Miami.

Although corporate headquarters on the sixth floor was only one floor away from the newsroom, the culture was totally different. It was a command-and-control hierarchy whose precision I began to appreciate on my first day. I had scarcely sat down at the desk in my windowless office when a representative from human resources came in with a tape measure. He carefully took the dimensions of the desk to make certain that it was the specified size for my rank. The CEO, Alvah Chapman, was a Citadel graduate and Army Air Corps veteran of World War II. As a squadron leader, he had piloted a B-17 Flying Fortress for 37 missions in Europe, a task that demands, as I knew from my unheroic flying experience, strict attention to detail.

It was about this time that Sue received an unexpected phone call from Jean Batten, wife of my boss. Jean advised us to join the First United Methodist Church of Coral Gables and attend the Sunday school classes taught by Chapman. She didn't say why, just that it was "very important."

I took this as very good news. Jim Batten was using this back channel to help my career, because it wasn't the sort of thing he could tell me directly. He was showing me a path to the Inner Ring. Evidently, the interaction in Sunday school helped Chapman evaluate his headquarters people, and the results of those interactions had something to do with who became part of the circle that really mattered. We were Episcopalians, but it wouldn't be that big a stretch – John Wesley had been an Anglican before he founded the Methodist church – and I had attended a Methodist Sunday school back in Washington, Kan., before my parents found out about the Episcopal Church. It would be a trivial compromise to our sense of who we were.

But where would it stop? I remembered what C. S. Lewis, himself an Anglican, had said about the desire for that Inner Ring.

Unless you take measures to prevent it, this desire is going to be one of the chief motives of your life, from the first day on which you enter your profession until the day when you are too old to care. ...

And then, if you are drawn in, next week it will be something a little further from the rules, and next year something further still, but all in the jolliest, friendliest spirit. It may end in a crash, a scandal, and penal servitude; it may end in millions, a peerage and giving the prizes at your old school. But you will be a scoundrel.

No, this would not be a hard decision. We would stay Episcopalians.

In an effort to figure out where I stood, I asked Byron Harless, our vice-president for human resources, to run me through the psychological testing program one more time. I wanted a report with all my scores.

"We don't do reports," Harless said. "But we will be happy to administer the tests and then discuss the results with you."

So I took the tests and then sat down with one of Byron's sidekicks, Ivan Jones, another psychologist.

"You knocked the top off the intelligence test," he said.

But there were darker findings.

"You have low energy."

Really? How do you tell that from a psychological test? Was my daily three-mile run sapping too much of my strength? Or maybe I should have been doing six miles. There's always ten percent that don't get the word.

Later, I figured it out. At lunch in the *Miami Herald* cafeteria, where Harless and I had gone because neither of us had time that day for the Executive Dining Room, he asked about my interest in playing squash.

"No," I said. "Running is enough for me. I don't like exercise activities where you need special equipment, show up at a special place, and have to coordinate your schedule with somebody else."

He frowned.

"That says something important about you."

Obviously, it was not good. Perhaps I had missed yet another opportunity to enter an Inner Ring.

The other part of Ivan's evaluation that I remember was his observation that I didn't relish conflict.

"You push back if you're pushed," he said. "But you won't start a fight. If there's conflict, you just walk away."

Uh-oh. I had heard this one before. And now it was a

judgment that had found its way into a little folder that was going to follow me around for the rest of my career!

As a reward for making the move, the company let me accept an invitation from the International Association for Mass Communication Research to speak on the topic of precision journalism at its annual meeting, which happened that year to be in Warsaw. What made it especially interesting was that Poland was still a Soviet-dominated Communist nation. The invitation was made at the initiative of Richard Cole and Donald Shaw of the journalism school at Chapel Hill. Knight Ridder paid the travel costs.

It was a strange experience. In Poland, every interaction with any level of service, from the visa checkers at the airport to the hotel registration desk, felt like being processed by the Fairfax County, Va., auto license agency: cold, impersonal, bureaucratic. The one exception was the doorman at the hotel. I had no small bills and nothing with which to tip him but a couple of American quarters. He was so happy to receive U.S. coins that he grinned and saluted. It turned out that Polish money was losing value every day, and there was a busy black market in dollars. Walking the streets, people who thought I looked American kept asking, "Change money?" And they offered far better terms than the official rate. Not wanting to see the inside of a Polish jail, I nervously declined.

At the scholarly meetings, the issues of cultural imperialism and "the new world order" kept coming up. One speaker, who was especially vigorous at denouncing the former, was embarrassed when someone invited his attention to the bottle of Coca Cola from which he sipped while at the lectern. It was an indicator of cultural imperialism.

One brief scary moment came after dinner with some students. It was a foggy night, and they were politely escorting me back to the hotel. We were crossing a wide street when suddenly a tall soldier in a large coat loomed out of the fog.

His arm was thrust out, palm forward. We obeyed the gesture and stopped.

Uh-oh, I thought. *For all I know, these students are carrying some kind of contraband, and we're all going to jail.*

One of the students advanced to consult with the soldier. She nodded and returned.

"We have to go back," she said. "And cross between the lines."

But the city was beautiful, especially the Old Town. Like most of Warsaw, this historic district had been totally destroyed toward the end of World War II, but the design specifications had been safely preserved. And so the district was rebuilt, in the same spirit as our Williamsburg, Va. There was an underlying strength here that would survive the Soviet influence.

Back in Miami, I started to learn how to see newspapers from a business-side perspective. A briefing by Hal Jurgensmeyer sounded refreshingly intellectual. Hal was by now the main vice-president for the business side but had been slowed down by a stroke and needed a cane. But his mind was sharp, and he had formed a business-side view of the coming challenge from new technology. We weren't going to make the mistake that the railroad companies had made, he said. When railroads noticed trucks and airplanes starting to compete with them for the movement of people and goods, they failed to see the threat because they were focused on the railroad business. If they had defined their business as transportation, they might have been more aggressive about adapting to the new technology.

Knight Ridder did not want to fall into that trap. Our company understood, he said, that the newspaper alone did not define our business. We were primarily in the "influence business." We produced two kinds of influence: societal influence, which was not for sale, and commercial influence, which we sold in the form of advertising. I loved this theoretical framework because it provided an economic justification for excellence on the news-editorial side of the business.

It was Jurgensmeyer who introduced me to Norman Morrison, a vice president with a doctorate in electrical engineering and the company's new-technology guru. Morrison had a vision for a new platform for selling influence, and he explained it to me.

Knight Ridder was planning a computer-based electronic information utility. Information, including news and advertising from the Miami Herald, would be stored in a central computer and made accessible to customers through a home terminal being designed by our new partner in this enterprise, AT&T, whose telephone service monopoly was on the verge of being broken up by the U.S. Department of Justice. Newspapers and phone companies were equally threatened by new technology.

As an information carrier, the 1970s telephone wire was a narrow pipe. And the AT&T system used the customers' existing home television sets for its display terminals. The computer would be a fairly large – by the standards of the late 1970s – VAX mainframe. There would be graphics as well as text, Morrison said, but they would be crude. I tried to visualize it.

"Will the resolution be enough," I asked, "so that if a human figure is shown in silhouette, you can tell whether it is male or female?"

Morrison stopped to think. "Yes," he finally said.

The project's name was Bowsprit, symbolizing the leading edge of progress. Eventually it would be called Viewtron, and the entity building and operating it would be Viewdata Corporation of America. I would be its director of market research and have the collateral duty of supervising the writing of the user's manual. That was a great assignment because it gave me access to all aspects of the creative process. If the designers should overlook something, I would know about it because the omission would leave a hole in the user's manual.

In this period, I had to cope with two cultural clashes, the one between news and business sides, and the much worse one between the newspaper and telephone businesses. For the phone company, the anxiety was aggravated by its impending breakup. It would have to become an entrepreneurial company instead of a regulated monopoly.

I knew a little bit about its culture from my Navy reserve training in telecommunications. It was intensely focused on improving service. Providing more and charging for it was its growth strategy. As one AT&T engineer was reported to have explained, it looked forward to a future where every person would be issued a telephone number at birth. And everyone would carry a portable picture phone. Whenever you dialed your friend's number, you would see his picture and hear his voice. It would be so reliable that if you did not see his picture and hear his voice, you would know that your friend was dead.

So the telephone company was quite ready to embrace new technology. It was not so ready to sell it against competition. Within the company there was tension between the new marketing experts, led by a smart young University of Virginia business school graduate, John Kelsey, and the old AT&T management. The marketing folks liked to refer to the latter as "pole climbers." It was Kelsey who introduced us to the concept of "positioning," which is marketing jargon for finding the right placement for your product in the mind of the potential customer.

For products that are essentially the same, e.g. laundry detergent, positioning helps a manufacturer target a product to a specified demographic. I had read a Harvard case study written on the problem, and it used laundry detergent as an example. One brand of detergent can go after working families worried about ring around the collar while another, with pretty much the same product, attracts families with young children who want their clothes to come out soft and fluffy. Positioning is in the mind of the consumer.

Viewtron was so different from other information media, that it would surely position itself, or so we news folks thought.

But we liked Kelsey's concept of finding "leading edge consumers" and targeting them. As director of market research, I had to figure out a way to identify and recruit such consumers for our first focus groups.

In a hierarchical organization where there is constant competition for the limited routes upward, there are a lot of sharp elbows. I discovered something else that was more of a surprise. Getting your way was more important than being right. The ability to get things done your way earned you respect, and if your way proved to be wrong, you could use your accumulated respect to repair the damage. In one painful conflict with the marketing research people on the AT&T side, we disagreed on who should get a research contract. I had good connections with smart suppliers through AAPOR, but my AT&T counterpart wanted to be the one to make the decision. Instead of fighting for my choice, and under some pressure from my bosses, I gave in. The phone guy's choice turned out to be a disaster, but it didn't hurt his career. He still won because he was the one who got his way. Reflecting on it later, I realized that being right does no good if you don't push hard enough to get the right thing done, and I should not have backed down. Perhaps I should have taken a management course – or been born with a bit more hostility in my nature. Sometimes it pays to stir the pot just to show who owns the spoon.

We worried constantly about the need to maintain good relationships with the "foreign" corporation (foreign to Knight Ridder, not to the U.S.). A good deal of diplomacy was required, and our different cultures complicated that. One of my manual writers had a personality conflict with counterparts in "the other company," as we called it, and had to go.

When our experimental subjects were equipped with Viewtron terminals, and they began to interact through a bulletin board service that we provided, one of them posted some criticism of AT&T. The project manager for the phone company insisted that the post be taken down with such unyielding vehemence that Norman Morrison walked him across the street to a meeting with Jim Batten. Jim explained the First Amendment to him.

There was also conflict on the newspaper side of my job. While still attached to the Washington Bureau, I had joined the Newspaper Research Council, an association of newspaper market research managers. They met twice a year and greatly enjoyed their meetings, but their technical skills varied considerably, and there was not a lot of innovation. Much of the talk was about comparing and managing research suppliers – who, like academics, were barred from the meetings. Newspaper marketing was still a new and undeveloped skill. I clashed with one of the leaders over the simple issue of developing a continuous measure of newspaper readership, such as number of days read per week, or total amount of time spent with the newspaper.

The justly admired "read yesterday" measure was binary: a respondent either had read yesterday or had not. If you are looking for attitudinal and demographic predictors to readership, you can get more statistical power with a continuous measure, such as frequency of reading. Such a measure permits scatterplots and correlations. These guys didn't want to hear about it, and they planted some spurious feedback at headquarters.

Jim Batten dropped by my office to inquire. "They say the software you are using is ten years old," he said.

"Sure is," I said. "That's what makes SPSS so good. They keep improving it and issuing new versions that make it better. And, trust me, nothing tops this year's edition."

Of course, the underdevelopment of marketing research in the newspaper business contained a benefit for me; the situation provided many opportunities to demonstrate creativity. One of my more lasting contributions was a decision model for evaluating the second paper in those markets where Knight Ridder owned both the morning and afternoon papers. Around the USA, newspaper companies were killing their second papers in reaction to the continuing decline in household penetration.

My model borrowed from two Harvard courses, Doug Price's quantitative methods and John Lintner's managerial economics. I based it on chi-square to compare the duplication of two papers in a single market to the duplication that would be expected from chance alone. And then, with some help from *Miami Herald* accountants, I worked out an equation for estimating the marginal cost of the second paper.

Producing two newspapers in the same plant costs less than twice as much as producing just one because the same physical facilities can be used. But the second paper adds variable costs because it needs ink and paper in direct proportion to its circulation. My model compared the marginal cost of the second paper to its marginal contribution to net household penetration.

One market stood out from all the rest: Philadelphia. The afternoon *News* had fairly low duplication with the morning *Inquirer*. It added 52 percent to the combination's net audience while increasing costs by only 21 percent, clearly a winner. Three decades have gone by as I write this, and Philadelphia still has its second paper. I choose to believe that I had something to do with that.[29]

One of the best things I did for the company in market research, starting while I was still in Reston, was develop a daily feature for kids.

It had been Jim Batten's idea. His own children kept asking why there was nothing for them in the paper. And our readership studies showed that the decline was mostly in the younger age groups. We had a newspaper-in-the-classroom program to introduce school children to newspaper reading, but no content directed specifically at them.

I did some reporting and found several creative organizations in New York with experience in providing content to children. And I persuaded three of them to develop, on speculation, a prototype for a daily feature that would fill half a standard newspaper page, then 16 inches wide, divided into eight two-inch columns.

I tested their prototypes on school children in the Northern Virginia area.

The winner was one that Batten's kids liked, The Dynamite Kids Page, modeled by Scholastic Publications after their *Dynamite Magazine:* lots of humor, odd characters, and tips about playing jokes on adults. The *Akron Beacon Journal* provided the test market. My before-and-after studies showed it a rousing success. There was even a positive effect on families, because it brought adults and kids together to talk about things in the paper. At last! We had a feature with evidence-based potential for slowing or reversing the slide in readership. And I had something to do with validating it.

Knight Ridder dropped it.

The reason: the national advertising staff could not sell enough child-directed advertising to pay for the newsprint consumed by the page. The company had hoped to go after the same advertisers that used Saturday morning television, except, I hoped, for the purveyors of junk food and dangerous toys. No luck. The business side, I was learning, had an abysmally short planning horizon.

This short-term attitude was aggravated by the management-by-objective (MBO) system. We executives negotiated yearly lists of goals with our bosses, with point values to weight them for relative importance. Then we specified the evaluation criteria so that we had an objective means of determining whether the goal had been reached. At the end of the year we were rewarded with cash bonuses that were determined partly by our success in meeting the objectives and partly by the company's financial performance against the previous year's baseline. In my pay grade, these rewards could amount to as much as 15 to 20 percent of annual salary.

You can see the problem. Newspaper financial results are

quite sensitive to economic conditions that are beyond any individual's power to control. And, in good years and bad, the MBO system forced our attention on the minutiae of year-to-year comparisons and away from the distant, soaring horizon.

The short-horizon bias has, of course, been a problem with American business generally, not just the newspaper business. But it made the job less interesting. It also made me kind of sneaky.

When, at each year's end, I had an idea for an original newspaper research strategy, I would describe the project and build it into my MBO. Then, both as a goal and as an evaluation standard, I would propose publishing the results at an academic meeting or in an academic journal. Peer review, I argued, was the best test of research merit. I labeled this publication goal "upgrading the profession." I added three articles to my academic portfolio in that fashion, although by the third year, Jim wouldn't let me put it in my MBO.

"We'll let the profession take care of itself this year," he said.

I wondered if he suspected something.

The worst conflict in my time with Viewtron was over the design of the initial consumer evaluation. We had a test version up and running and a goodly number of subjects participating, and it was time to design an interview schedule that would let them tell us what they thought of it.

My superiors all wanted softball questions. I wanted questions that would produce variance.

Variance is critical in research. If you want to know what kind of people will buy something and what likes or dislikes will affect their decision, you need to ask them about it in a way that will produce different answers from different kinds of people. Sometimes this means loading the question to produce at least a few negative evaluations. If everyone gives the same answer, there is nothing to correlate it with. We were looking for covariance, right? And you can't have covariance without variance.

I tried to explain.

"It's like trying to measure oven temperature with a freezer thermometer."

That turned out to be a bad choice of analogy, because it was pretty much what they wanted to do: use questions that would yield a uniformly positive, top-of-the-scale response. Now I got it. The only groups we were marketing to were the boards of Knight Ridder and AT&T. We needed a glowing report to convince them to maintain the investment to keep the Viewtron trial going. Nobody wanted to take a chance with real research.

It is possible to be too careful. I was reminded of this fact one more time. One of the most interesting projects in my time at headquarters was development of a multi-market TV advertising campaign to promote the value of newspapers. We invited several agencies to make creative pitches, and the winner was a boutique spin-off from one of the large national agencies.

Its ideas were edgy and interesting. The proposed theme was, "Take the paper. It will take you where you want to go." One preliminary spot showed a fisherman at a dock, starting to wrap his catch in a newspaper but pausing to read it instead. Another depicted an African-American woman extolling the value of the newspaper to her young son. But those never made the cut. Too many company executives were asked for critiques, and they took all the juice out. The fish spot had to go because most Knight Ridder cities were not near the ocean. The mother-child scene was dropped because most readers were not minorities … and so on. The final products were bland, and when they were finally aired, they had no visible impact on newspaper subscription sales.

But I maintained my usefulness by keeping my precision journalism side active, chiefly by assigning assistants to train

Miami Herald reporters in SPSS analysis. The most interesting project was an analysis of criminal cases in Monroe County, where Key West is located. It yielded some useful information for potential felons: if you committed a crime in Monroe County in those days, you would do better to make it drug related. Yes, drug-related crimes were dealt with more leniently than similar crimes without a drug connection. Cocaine traffic from Latin America was, at that time, a main economic driver for Monroe County.

It appeared to have an effect in Dade County, as well. Housing prices in Coral Gables mysteriously and dramatically started to rise. Where was all the money coming from? It might have been drug money. Our art deco house started to look like an amazing and undeserved windfall.

My relationships with the people in the newsroom were pretty good, and I got invited to their parties. *Herald* reporters felt comfortable seeking me out on the sixth floor in search of advice. On one such occasion, the problem involved corporate policy. Fixing it seemed easy enough, and when Jim Batten happened by, I asked him about it, in the reporter's presence. Big mistake.

Jim gave an ambiguous answer, and later, in private, chided me for asking the question when the reporter was there to see his reaction.

After I thought about this response, it made perfect sense. Reporters talk to each other. The story of Batten's reaction would spread across the city room, getting more exaggerated with each iteration. Guys at the top had to be careful.

They had to be extremely careful. I realized then that a high-ranking administrator must always wear a mask. He represents so many constituencies, both above and below, that it would be dangerous to reveal too much about his inner attitudes. To do so would paint himself into a corner. Years later, I would be reminded of this constraint by Eli Rubenstein, an academic colleague, when I was offered a major administrative post at a university.

"You get so used to wearing the mask," he said, "that you blend into it. You lose your identity. You can no longer tell which is you and which is the mask."

In the third week of January 1980, the School of Journalism (as it was then called) at the University of North Carolina at Chapel Hill hosted a conference, "Public Opinion Polls and the News," for professional journalists. I was invited to talk about one of my current tasks, finding ways to use polls to sell newspapers. Most of the meeting was on a weekend, so I didn't have trouble getting away. I sent a copy of my resume up to Chapel Hill at the request of the event's publicist.

Between sessions at the Carolina Inn, Dean Richard Cole mentioned that he had been pleasantly surprised to see on the resume that I was a Carolina alumnus with an advanced degree, my MA in political science.

Would I ever be interested in coming back as a faculty member? The question was relevant, he said, because Vermont Royster, who had left the *Wall Street Journal* in 1971 to be the first and only Kenan professor in the school, was getting ready to retire.

I told him that I had often considered a teaching career, and I hoped to keep the option open for the future. Right now, corporate headquarters felt like the place where I belonged. But the thought lingered.

William Rand Kenan Jr. had been a chemistry major at Carolina, graduating in 1894. With his professor, James Venable, he discovered a method of making acetylene gas out of calcium carbide. His sister, Mary Lily Kenan, married Henry Flagler, the founder of the Florida East Coast Railroad. Flagler and Kenan combined their business activities, and Kenan was able to devote his later years to philanthropy, much of it benefitting his alma mater.

The professorships bearing his name were established with

his bequest in 1965, and the university used them in a strategic way, to attract new talent to the university. A Kenan professor received the basic university salary for a full professor plus an increment from the Kenan endowment, plus an annual stipend for research and travel. One could authorize one's own travel!

A university, like a corporation, is a hierarchy. Academic politics can be as bitter as in a corporation. But, with an endowed professorship as my entry-level job, I would be starting at the top – and with tenure.

The best part would be the freedom. I remembered a psychological experiment where I was a subject while in the Navy. We were stationed in a room with high-fidelity speakers blasting the sound of an airplane engine at us while we solved problems in mathematics. Another group was in the same situation, but with one difference: its room had a red button that anyone could push to stop the noise. That group did better on the problems even though no one ever pushed the button. Just the knowledge that you are in control can make all the difference.

Then there was the financial incentive. As my friend Nelson Polsby, the political scientist, put it, I could use that freedom to do some trading for my own account. Stanley Milgram had told me that a rule of thumb for a professor's daily consulting fee was one percent of his or her nine-month salary. Sue and I had two more kids to put through college.

Back in Miami, I attended a lunch on an unrelated topic with several University of Miami professors. One of them asked a colleague about a mutual acquaintance. "Oh," said the other, "He went up to Chapel Hill to be a Kenan professor." The awe in his voice caught my attention.

And so the seed was planted. By summer of 1980, after commissioning yet another readership study, I realized that the real purpose of my research at Knight Ridder was less to test bold new ideas than to provide cover and emotional support for editors when they made decisions that departed from the routine. Rather than exploring innovative ways of serving our readers, I was focused on finding cost-free ways of tweaking content. All of the questions that I was trying to answer were trivial, the industry in which I worked was conservative and careful – too careful, given the risky future that technology was bringing. Although the Viewtron experiment showed promise, it was a struggle to mold its market research into a configuration that would yield useful knowledge. We were too constrained by commitment to the traditional newspaper business model.

I recalled the words of my old teacher. A professor investigates whatever aspect of the world interests him.

Going into my office and closing the door, I called Richard Cole in Chapel Hill.

"Let's continue the conversation," I said.

24. The rest of the story

The Morrison farmhouse, ca 1961

The Meyer and the Morrison farms are gone now, absorbed into the kinds of scaled-up operations that modern corporate agriculture demands. My mother died in Chapel Hill in 1990. After we took her back to Kansas and placed her next to my father in Reiter Cemetery, we went to her birthplace, the old Morrison farm, for a last look. The house was vacant, awaiting someone's bulldozer. My brother's family and mine stood on the front porch, and we looked south across the flat fields at the far-away silhouettes of the grain elevator and the water tower in Linn. There was something eternal about the prairie.

Lester "Pap" Meyer and farmhouse, 1961

When asked which of my two careers I enjoyed the most, I have a ready answer. For a person under 50, journalism is the best job in the world. Once I reached 50, I realized that academe, at least for me, would be better. The Carolina appointment proved to be a good fit. I enjoyed each of a professor's three missions, teaching, research, and service. They were like a journalist's, but at a different pace, and the choice of how to blend them was mine.

The research funding came easily, primed first by an unsolicited grant from the Markle Foundation through ASNE, which wanted a study of the editor-publisher relationship in making ethical decisions. The Kenan stipend and, later, a larger one from the Knight Foundation, provided seed money for more research. I wrote some more books. Interacting with students was invigorating. Summers were available for travel, consulting, writing and service. I advanced on the AAPOR ladder, served as its president in 1989-1990 and then led its sister organization, the World Association for Public Opinion Research, in 1993 and 1994. I developed a long-term consulting relationship with *USA Today* and am still a member of its Board of Contributors.

The travel demands of academe are more measured than those in journalism, and there is greater breathing space between the deadlines. Sue traveled with me, and we took side trips to track down her roots in Northern Ireland and mine in Switzerland, locating distant cousins in both places. We found unexpected adventures. We got mugged in Madrid, sang Karaoke in Taipei, and got arrested in Ljubljana for inadvertently passing a counterfeit tolar. We cruised overnight from Stockholm to Tallinn aboard the Estonia just one year before a storm sent that ship and more than 800 passengers to the bottom of the Baltic Sea. I found other service and research missions in Buenos Aires, Caracas, Copenhagen, Edinburgh, Dublin, Geneva, Johannesburg, Montreaux, Paris, Rio de Janiero, Santiago, and Sydney. The Asia Foundation engaged me to teach Philippine journalists about the uses of public opinion research, and I took time off to look for the grave of my mother's war-hero brother, Ernest R. Morrison. I found it in the hushed beauty of the American cemetery in Manila.

My students have done well and made their own contributions to society and to the profession. One became president of the National Press Club, and another rose to the top at the Society of Professional Journalists. A third is CEO of a national market research operation. Some remember hearing me read C. S. Lewis on the Inner Ring at the end of the semester.

Today I hope to teach my grandchildren about his warning. It ends with a statement of hope. Break the quest for the Inner Ring, he said, and a surprising result will follow.

If in your working hours you make the work your end, you will presently find yourself all unawares inside the only circle in your profession that really matters. You will be one of the sound craftsmen, and other sound craftsmen will know it.

Such a circle is not an Inner Ring. Neither secrecy nor exclusiveness brought its members together. What drew them was their craft and their friendship. Such friendship, said Lewis, "causes perhaps half of all the happiness in the world, and no Inner Ringer can ever have it."

In 2007, Sue and I moved our empty nest to a New Urbanism development with interesting architecture on the south side of Chapel Hill. It is two miles from the Carolina campus, and near the highway where we saw the fox upon our first arrival in 1956. When we use that road, we sometimes think of Edna St. Vincent Millay and the red brush of remembered joy.

Endnotes

1. Frank A. Meyer, *"Pictures on Memory's Wall,"* in *Kansas Memories,* edited by Mayme Meyer Totta 1998. Privately published.
2. Robert H. Ferrell, *Collapse at the Meuse Argonne: the Failure of the Missouri-Kansas Division* (Columbia, University of Missouri Press, 2004).
3. This quote is attributed to Argentine journalist Jose Narosky.
4. Reiter Cemetery and the Meyer farmhouse (as a tiny rectangle) can be found on the 1968 U.S. Geological Survey 7.5 minute series map for the Palmer Quadrangle in the SW quarter of Section 2. The Morrison house is on the map for the Linn Quadrangle, in the NW quarter of Section 16, just north of the unnamed creek.
5. To supplement my memory of Chick Boyes and his shows, I have relied on Landis K. Magnuson, *Circle Stock Theater: Touring American Small Towns, 1900-1960.* (Jefferson, N.C.: McFarland & Company, 1995).
6. *Historical Statistics of the United States, Colonial Times to 1970,* (Department of Commerce, 1975) 783.
7. C. S. Lewis, *The Weight of Glory and Other Addresses* (Riverside: Macmillan, 1980) 93.

8. Stausberg, Matthias F., *Der Ruf: a Newspaper for German Prisoners of War in the United States (1945-1946)* (M.A. Thesis, University of North Carolina at Chapel Hill, 1996).

9. Reported in K-State's yearbook, *The Royal Purple 1949,* 142.

10. "The Younger Generation," *Time* (Nov. 5, 1951) 46-52.

11. "Essay—The Silent Generation Revisited," *Time* (June 29, 1970).

12. James A. Carey, *Kansas State University: the Quest for Identity,* (Lawrence: The Regents Press of Kansas, 1977).

13. "Huntsman, what quarry," *Harper's Magazine,* November 1938

14. NLRB v Jones & Laughlin Steel Corp (301 U.S. 1, 1937).

15. U.S. Commission on Civil Rights Report, 1961, part IV.

16. Prentice-Hall Journalism Series, 1964

17. Miami Herald Publishing Co., Personnel Action Report No. 2044, Nov. 7, 1961

18. Caplan includes the story of Neighbors Inc. in *Farther Along: A Civil Rights Memoir* (Baton Rouge: LSU Press, 1999).

19. Margery T. Ware, Neighbors Inc. Executive Director, in her report to the seventh annual meeting (1965).

20. A brief history of the Nieman program is in the first chapter of Louis M. Lyons, *Reporting the News,* (Cambridge: The Belknap Press of Harvard University Press) 1965.

21. This is one of the "odd-ball measures" suggested by Donald Campbell and colleagues in *Unobtrusive Measures: Nonreactive Research in the Social Sciences,* (New York: Rand McNally 1966).

22. *Nieman Reports*, June 1967

23. "Playing for the Upper Hand," *Playboy,* April 1969.

24. "If Hitler Asked You to Electrocute a Stranger, Would You? Probably." *Esquire*, February 1970.

25. Bernice Kert, *The Hemingway Women* (New York: W. W. Norton, 1983) 355-364.

26. Samuel Stouffer, *The American Soldier* (Princeton: Princeton University Press, 1949).

27. For example, Alberta J. Nassi and Stephen I. Abramowitz, "Transition or transformation? Personal and political development of former Berkeley Free Speech Movement activists." *Journal of Youth and Adolescence,* Vol. 8, No. 1, 21-35.

28. "Elitism and Newspaper Believability," *Journalism Quarterly*, Spring 1973, pp. 31-36.

29. For details, see my *The Newspaper Survival Book: An Editor's Guide to Marketing Research* (Bloomington: Indiana University Press, 1985) 126-132.

Index

C

Campbell, Orville 169
Canterbury Club 69, 102
Cantril, Hadley 281
Caplan, Marvin 219
Caplan, Nathan 261, 266
Capp, Al 189, 255
Capper, Arthur 92, 170
Carey, James C. 114
Carmichael, Stokely 274
Carnegie Library 35
Carney, Ron 148
Carson, Marc 157
Carter, Jimmy 310
Carter, Roy 164
Chancellor, John 305
Chapel of the Cross 103
Chapman, Alvah 317
Charlotte Observer 163, 173, 207, 223
Chase, Dennis J. 303
Chicago Daily News 173, 208, 216, 218, 279
Chick Boyes Players 31
Clarke, Edwin Leavitt 72
Clawson, Ken 305
Clay Center Dispatch 47, 81
Cleaveland, Fred 169
Cleavinger, Ann 69
Cole, Albert 121
Cole, Richard 320, 331
Collins, LeRoy 191
Colt, John 151
Columbia Journalism Review 287, 312
Colvin, Bill 120, 160, 175
Conant, James Bryant 70, 242
Concordia, Kan. 39
Congressional fellowship 205, 207, 209
Congress of Racial Equality 274

Copple, Neale 205
Corps of Engineers 96
Cotten, Joseph 151
Cox, Archibald 310
Cozine, Earl 26, 38
Cozine, Eileen 38
Cozine, Ralph 34, 60, 120
Cummings, Milton 309

D

Dade County School Board 178
  desegregation strategy 185
Daniels, Derick 182, 188, 260, 265, 309, 316
DATA-TEXT 244, 246, 247, 256, 270, 306, 315
David, Kenneth 95
Davison, W. Phillips 276, 302
DeBerard, Phil 201
Dedman, Bill 307
Dennis, Everett 298
Denver Post 172
Deshler Rustler 26
Detroit Free Press 171, 173, 174, 207, 230, 260, 265, 274, 279, 280, 313
Detroit News 313
Detroit Urban League 262, 265
Diamond School 21
DiSalle, Mike 212
Divilbiss, James 101
Dugan's Barbershop 69, 71
Dukes of Dixieland 143
Durland, M. A. 107, 108, 109, 110, 204
Dust Bowl 18, 30
Dynamite Kids Page 327

E

Edgerton, Kan. 42, 43, 44, 47, 212
Editor & Publisher 150

other Kansas City deaths 233
Lambert, Clark 270
Lancaster, Paul 298
Landon, Alf 93
Lashbrook, Ralph 110
Lausche, Frank 210, 227
Law, Loren and Pauline 82
Layman, Earl 112, 242
Lederer, William J. 253
Levine, Robert A. 275, 276, 294
Lewis, C. S. 48, 67, 318, 337, 339
Lewis, Fulton Jr. 71, 76, 221
Lintner, John V. 249, 326
Lipset, Seymour Martin 239, 256
Lobaugh, Carrie 4
Lyons, Louis 243

M

MacArthur, Douglas 50
MacDougall, Curtis 180
Mack, George 99
MacLaine, Shirley 278
Maidenberg, Mike 291
Maidenburg, Ben 210, 235, 291
Mailen, Thelma 99
management-by-objective (MBO) 327
Marshall, Porter 40, 45
Marshall, Ward 39, 40
Martin Luther King 273
Marx, Gary 269
McCain, James A. 79, 80, 110, 111, 112, 113, 114, 115
McCarthy, Eugene 273, 277, 279, 280
McDaniel, Pat 47
McFadden, Ann 149
McGovern, George 304
McGraw-Hill 310
McKeel, Sam 173
McKissick, Floyd 274
McKnight, C. A. 173

McMullan, John 177, 180, 181, 211, 214, 217, 222, 269, 279
McReynolds, John W. 76, 77, 84, 106, 113, 156, 162, 164, 175, 244, 250
McReynolds, Louise 315, 317
Medical World News 202
Medlin, C. J. 101
Meitler, Anna 28, 29, 30, 39
Menninger, Karl 157
Merten, Abbie 115
Meyer, Elmer E. 7, 11, 19, 21, 26, 61, 308
Meyer, Frank 2, 17, 42
Meyer, Fred 21
Meyer, Gladys 65
Meyer, Heinrich viii
Meyer, Hilda Morrison
  as teacher 20
  death of 335
  Howard's return 57
  letter from Ernie 50
  married, 1928 22
  watches tornado 27
  wedding anniversary 42
Meyer, Jacob viii, 1, 2, 4, 7, 19, 20, 22
Meyer, John 36, 52, 114
Meyer, Kimberli 114
Meyer, Lester 5, 19, 22, 38, 215
Meyer, Mamie 7, 19, 20, 21, 26, 36, 38, 60
Meyer, Matilda 1, 4, 7, 21, 22
Meyer, Philip
  born 25
  covering Detroit riot 260
  finding Swiss roots 337
  first solo flight 136
  getting academic 311
  hired by Miami Herald 174
  hired in Topeka, 1954 153

Neutra, Richard 103, 105, 112
New Orleans 143
Newspaper Research Council 325
Newton, Sherman S. 47
Nichols, Dick 85, 86
Nieman Reports 235, 248
Noelle-Neumann, Elisabeth 276
Norfolk Virginian-Pilot 149

O

Obenland, Frank 82
Office of Economic Opportunity 275
Olson, David 309
Orchard Villa Elementary School 184, 186
Orwell, George 197

P

Patrie, Ellra 30
Patterson, Eugene 238, 294
Pearson, Charles 160
Peats Creek 2, 20
Penniman, Howard R. 205
Pensacola
    Battalion X 147
    formation flying 140
    pre-flight school 123
Perkins, Blanche 50
Pershing, John J. 12
Pettigrew, Thomas 256, 275, 281, 285–286
Philadelphia Bulletin 314
Philadelphia Inquirer 301, 305, 314
Phillips, Bill 200
Pick, Lewis A. 96
Pillsbury Crossing 85
Playboy 297
Plessey v. Ferguson 93
Pocono, USS 147

Polsby, Nelson 332
Pool, Ithiel 246
Poor People's Campaign 273, 278
Powers, Isabel 71
Poynter, Nelson 286
Precision Journalism 298, 303
Price, H. D. 256, 270, 326
Public Opinion Quarterly 276, 288, 314
Pulitzer Prize 251, 265, 277, 306
Purdue, S. I. 161

Q

Quail, Frank A. 154
Quail, Frank M. 154
Quail, Helen Peppard 154, 162, 304
Quail, Sue. *See* Meyer, Sue Quail
Quayle, Oliver 256

R

Rand, Ayn 89, 103
Raynolds, Ruth 49
Reagan, Ronald 292
Reddick, DeWitt 205
Reed, Jim 91, 92, 93, 153, 163
Reiter 20, 308, 335, 339
relative deprivation theory 264
Reno, Henry 189
Research Triangle Park 223, 224
Rhodes, James 212
Richard Cole 333
Richmond News Leader 177
riffraff theory of rioting 261, 263
Riley, Robert 102
Robinson, Harold 88
Robinson, James L. 93, 96, 154, 171
Robinson, James P. 191
Robinson, John 261

349

Robson, Charles B. 164
Roosevelt, Eleanor 201
Roosevelt Hotel 143
Roper, Burns W. 256
Royster, Vermont 242, 331
Rubenstein, Eli 330
Rusk, Dean 216
Russell Sage Foundation 285, 286,
    299, 302, 303

S

Sageser, Floyd 83, 111
Samuelson, Merrill 76
Sanford, Terry 223
Sargent, Dwight E. 238, 241, 243,
    248, 255
Saturday Night Massacre 310
Saufley field 145
Schelling, Thomas 250, 285
Schiavone, Jim 201
Schindler, Rudolf 103, 112, 114
Schwilling, Lyle 91, 101, 103, 110
Seaton, Faye 120
Seplow, Steve 301
Shaw, Donald 320
Shaw, Joy Reese 178
Sheatsley, Paul 277
Sheldon, Eleanor B. 290
Shepherd Park 219, 220, 221
Shepherd v. Maxwell 124
Sheppeard, Lee 61, 65, 102, 183
Sherrill, Robert 286
Shoemaker, Don 190, 279
Shuster, Alvin 241
Silent Generation 80, 101, 102,
    103, 107, 174, 340
Simon, Robert E. 294
Sirica, John 293
Sisk, Jack 134, 147
Sizemore, Vern 51
Smith, Maurice K. 111

Smith, Merriam 223
SNJ 134, 135, 140, 142
Snodgrass, Wayne 40, 47, 49
Society of Professional Journalists
    189, 275, 337
Spavin, John T. 148
Specter, Arlen 306
Spiegel, John 279
SPSS 315, 325, 330
Stanton, Barbara 280
Stauffer, Oscar 170
Steele, James 305
Stewart, Dick 277
St. Louis Post Dispatch 93
St. Mihiel 12, 13
Stockton, William 303
Stone, Chuck 220
Stoner, J. B. 188
Stouffer, Samuel A. 264
St. Petersburg Times 202, 286
Strawberry Township 2, 6, 7
Strompf, Linda 287
Struve, Herald 26
Superman 37
swimming 127

T

Tacheron, Donald 286
Tebow, Eric 99
Temple, Sally 293
Thomson, Jim 244
Thoreau, Henry David 189, 192
Time magazine 172
Toffler, Alvin 287
Tomlinson, T. M. 274
Topeka Daily Capital 55, 91, 100,
    120
    Kansas Day editor 86
Topeka State Journal 92, 161, 170
Topkis, Gladys S. 301
tornado (July 4, 1932) 27

Townsend, Newton 92
Trahan, Paul 231
Truman, President Harry S. 82
Tuttle Creek Dam 96, 121, 154,
    157, 162, 171
Tyler, John 200

U

University Daily Kansan 102, 161
University of Nebraska 26, 116,
    205
Unternaehrer, Anton vii
USA Today 337

V

Valentine, Harry 81
Van Natta, Constance 93, 153
Vanocur, Sander 215, 278
Viewtron 322, 323, 324, 328, 329,
    333

W

Wagner Labor Relations Act 169,
    208
Wall Street Journal 298
Walther, John 178
Washington County 1, 5, 6, 20,
    22, 27, 38, 39, 46, 308
Washington Post 172, 216, 218,
    220, 221, 279
Watergate 310
Weisbender Marillyn 112
Weller, George 251
Wesley, John 318
White, William H. 173
Whiting Field 133
Wilson, Don 59, 121
Wise, David 309
Wolfe, Thomas 127, 147

Wolfe, Tom 120, 138
Woo, William F. 241
World Association for Public
    Opinion Research 277, 336
Wright, Frank Lloyd 103, 113,
    114
Wylie, Philip 89, 196

Y

Young, Stephen 214
Young, Whitney 274

CPSIA information can be obtained at www.ICGtesting.com
Printed in the USA
BVOW011402040412

286856BV00005B/19/P